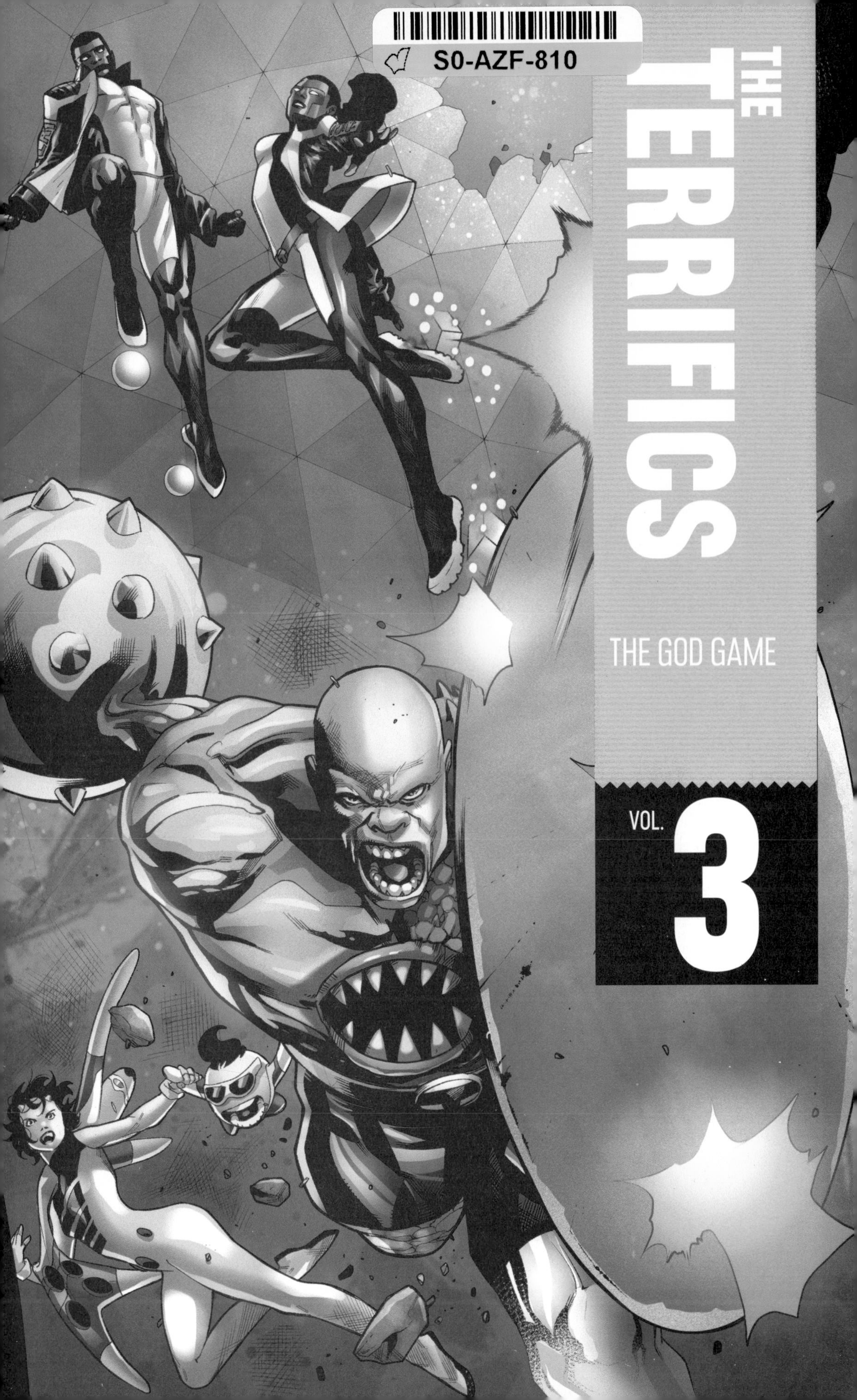
THE
TERRIFICS
THE GOD GAME
VOL. 3

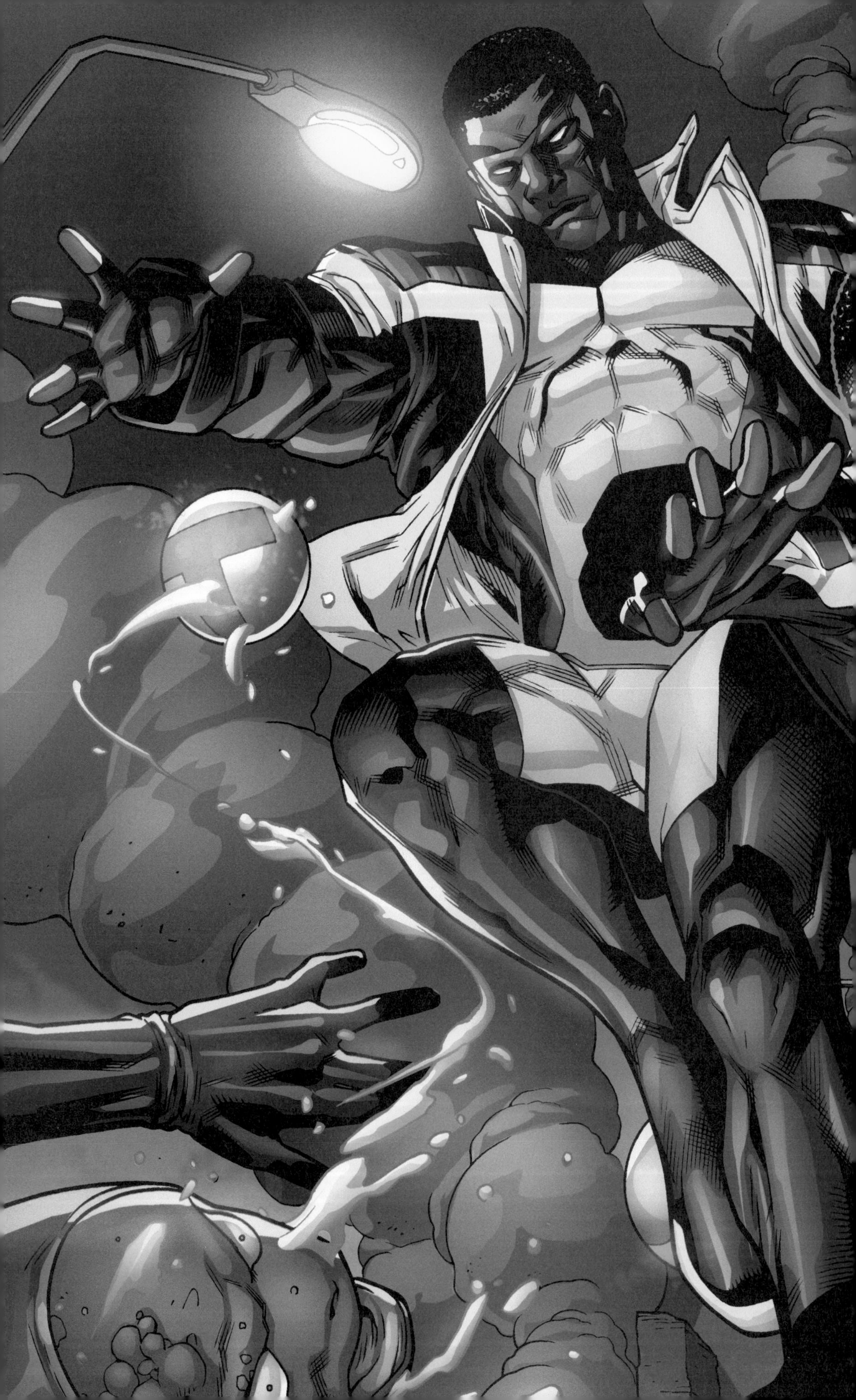

THE
TERRIFICS
THE GOD GAME

artists

STEPHEN SEGOVIA
JOE BENNETT \ EVAN "DOC" SHANER
JOSE LUIS \ DEXTER VINES
RAY McCARTHY \ MATT SANTORELLI
SCOTT HANNA \ RICHARD FRIEND
JORDI TARRAGONA

writers

GENE LUEN YANG
MARK RUSSELL \ JAMES ASMUS

colorists

PROTOBUNKER \ HI-FI
NATHAN FAIRBAIRN

letterer

TOM NAPOLITANO

collection cover artist

EVAN "DOC" SHANER

TOM STRONG created by **ALAN MOORE** and **CHRIS SPROUSE**

VOL.
3

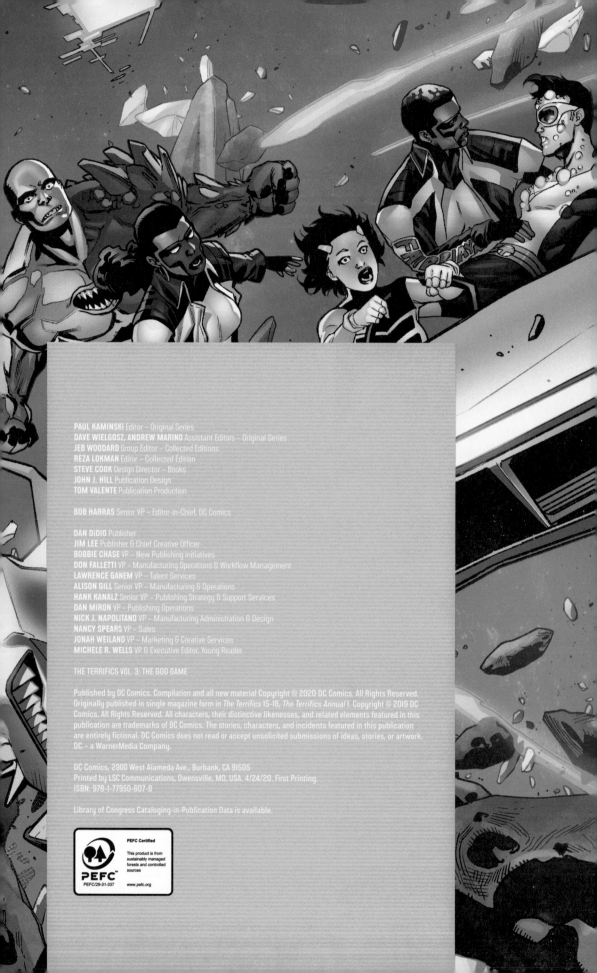

PAUL KAMINSKI Editor – Original Series
DAVE WIELGOSZ, ANDREW MARINO Assistant Editors – Original Series
JEB WOODARD Group Editor – Collected Editions
REZA LOKMAN Editor – Collected Edition
STEVE COOK Design Director – Books
JOHN J. HILL Publication Design
TOM VALENTE Publication Production

BOB HARRAS Senior VP – Editor-in-Chief, DC Comics

DAN DiDIO Publisher
JIM LEE Publisher & Chief Creative Officer
BOBBIE CHASE VP – New Publishing Initiatives
DON FALLETTI VP – Manufacturing Operations & Workflow Management
LAWRENCE GANEM VP – Talent Services
ALISON GILL Senior VP – Manufacturing & Operations
HANK KANALZ Senior VP – Publishing Strategy & Support Services
DAN MIRON VP – Publishing Operations
NICK J. NAPOLITANO VP – Manufacturing Administration & Design
NANCY SPEARS VP – Sales
JONAH WEILAND VP – Marketing & Creative Services
MICHELE R. WELLS VP & Executive Editor, Young Reader

THE TERRIFICS VOL. 3: THE GOD GAME

DC Comics, 2900 West Alameda Ave., Burbank, CA 91505
Printed by LSC Communications, Owensville, MO, USA. 4/24/20. First Printing.
ISBN: 978-1-77950-607-8

Library of Congress Cataloging-in-Publication Data is available.

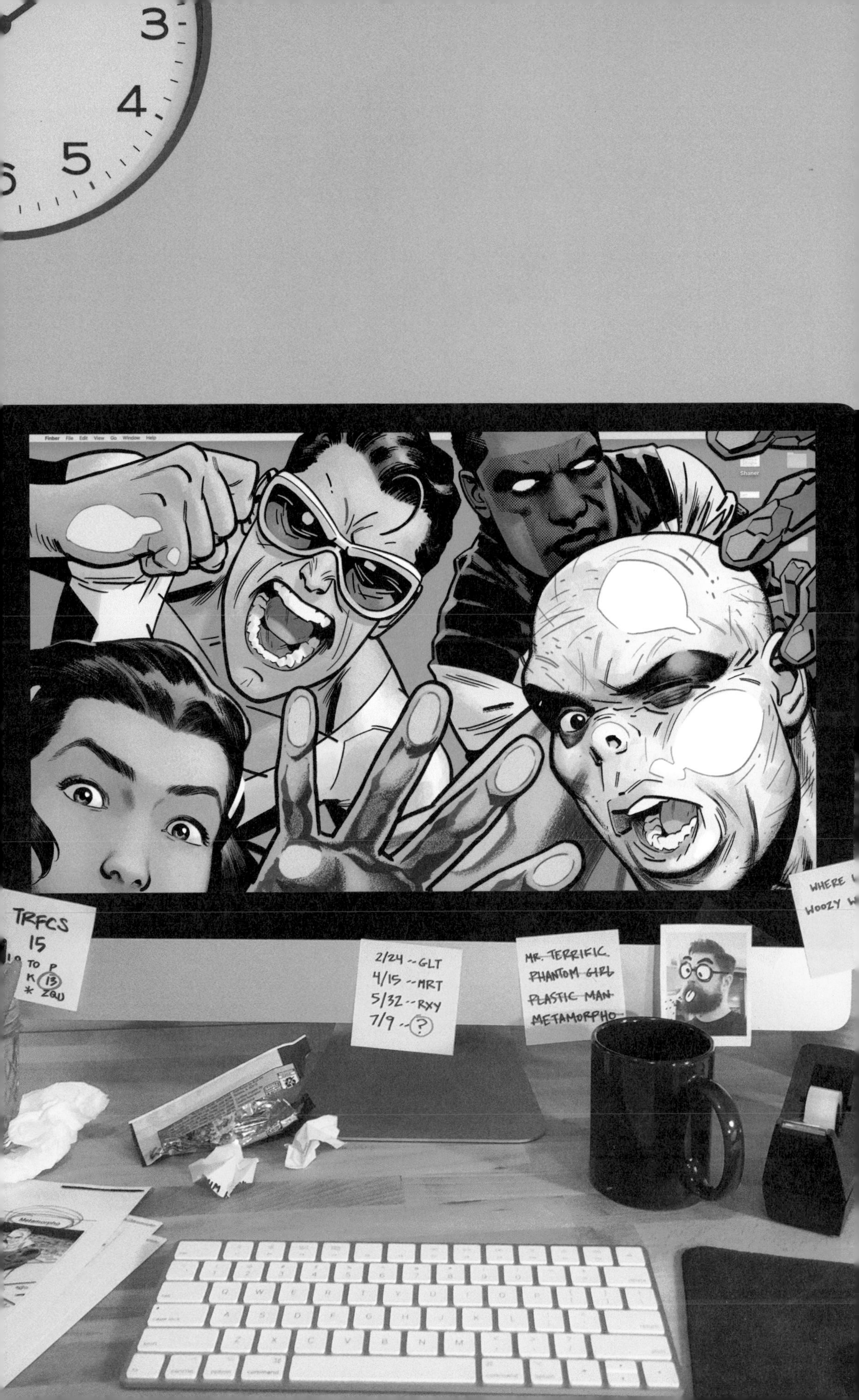
TRFCS
15
TO P
K 13
* ZQU
2/24 -- GLT
4/15 -- MRT
5/32 -- RXY
7/9 -- ?
MR. TERRIFIC
PHANTOM GIRL
PLASTIC MAN
METAMORPHO
WHERE
WOOZY

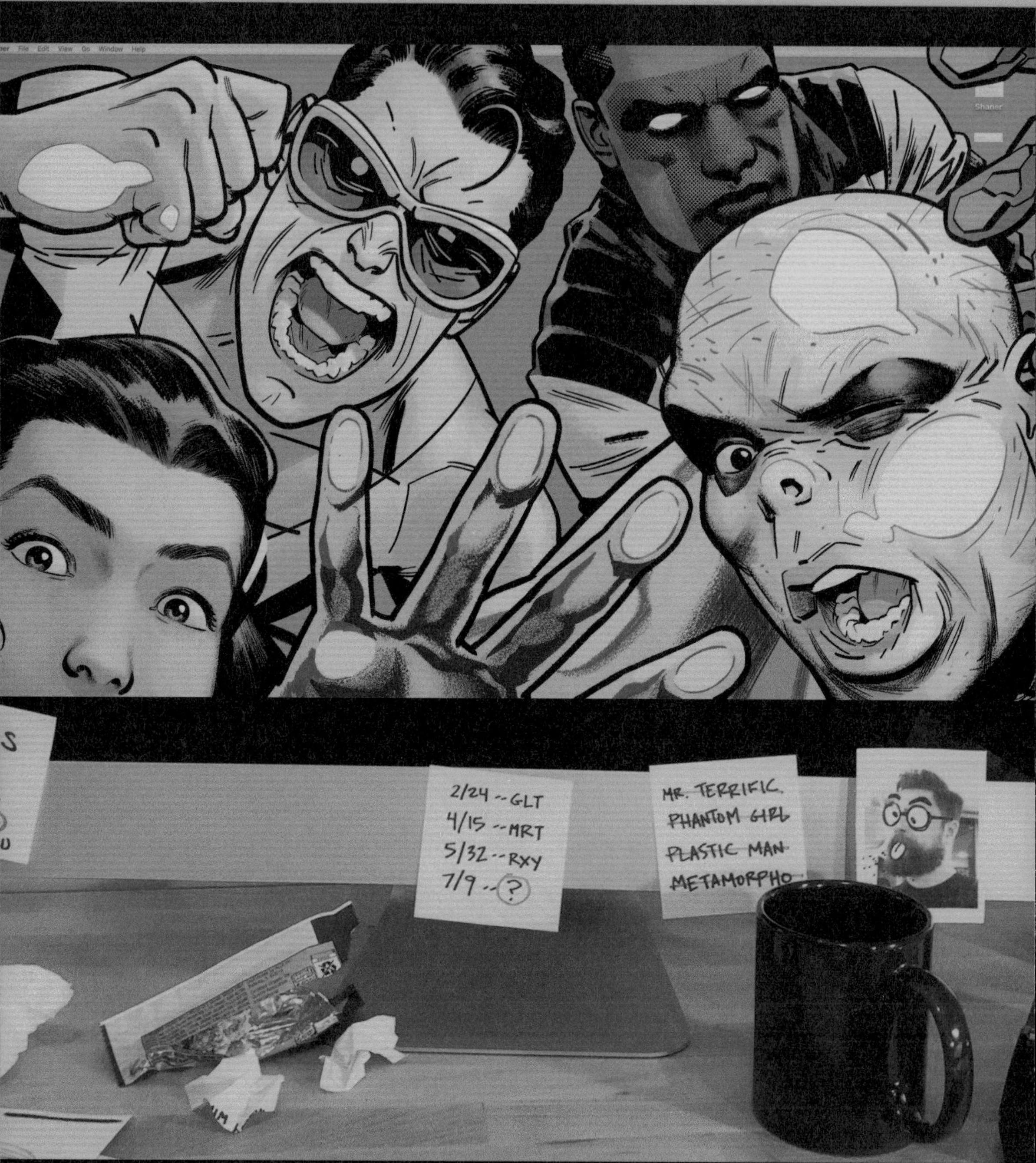
File Edit View Go Window Help
Shaner
2/24 -- GLT
4/15 -- MRT
5/32 -- RXY
7/9 -- ?
MR. TERRIFIC
PHANTOM GIRL
PLASTIC MAN
METAMORPHO

THE TERRIFICS
#15

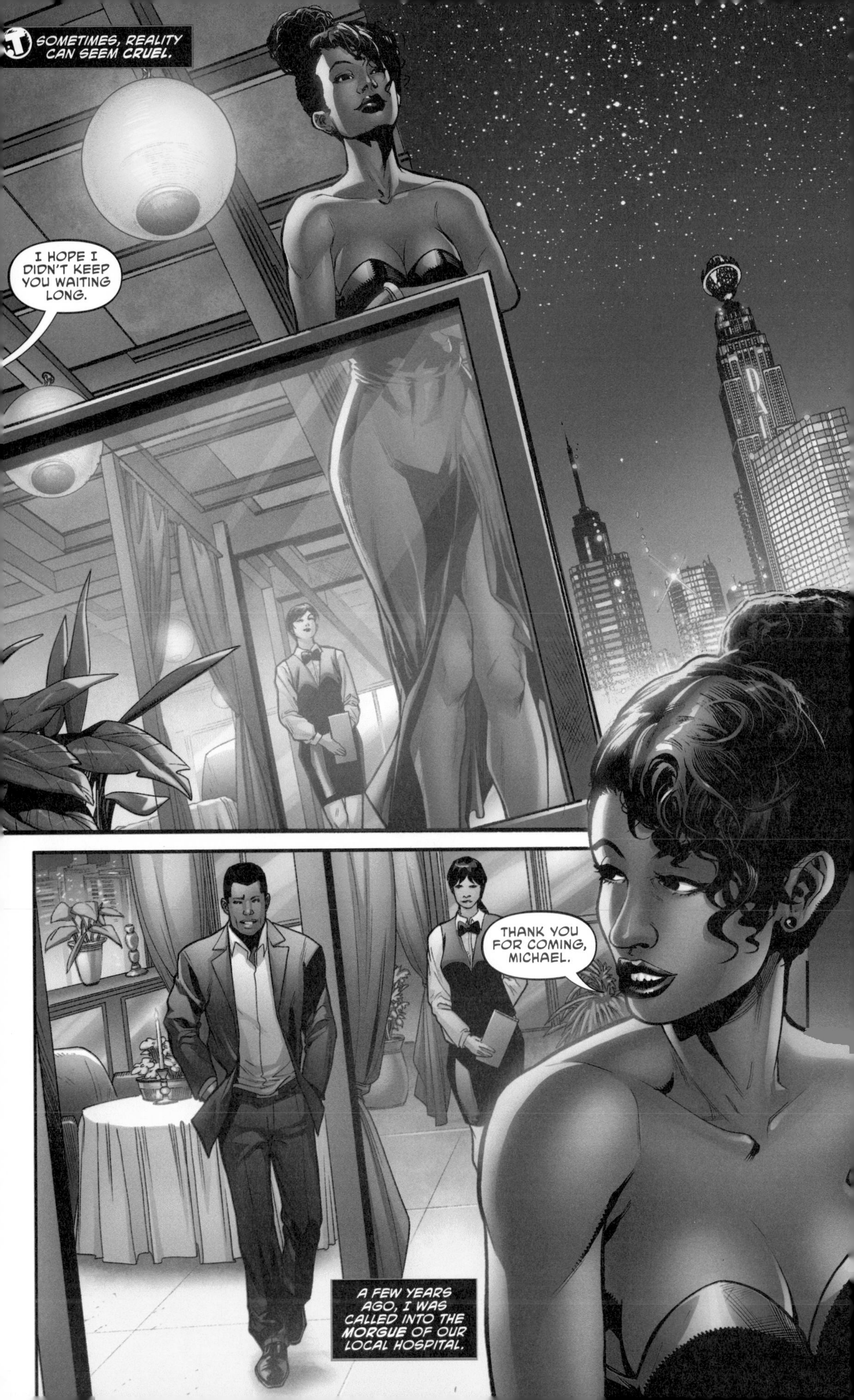
SOMETIMES, REALITY CAN SEEM CRUEL.
I HOPE I DIDN'T KEEP YOU WAITING LONG.
THANK YOU FOR COMING, MICHAEL.
A FEW YEARS AGO, I WAS CALLED INTO THE MORGUE OF OUR LOCAL HOSPITAL.

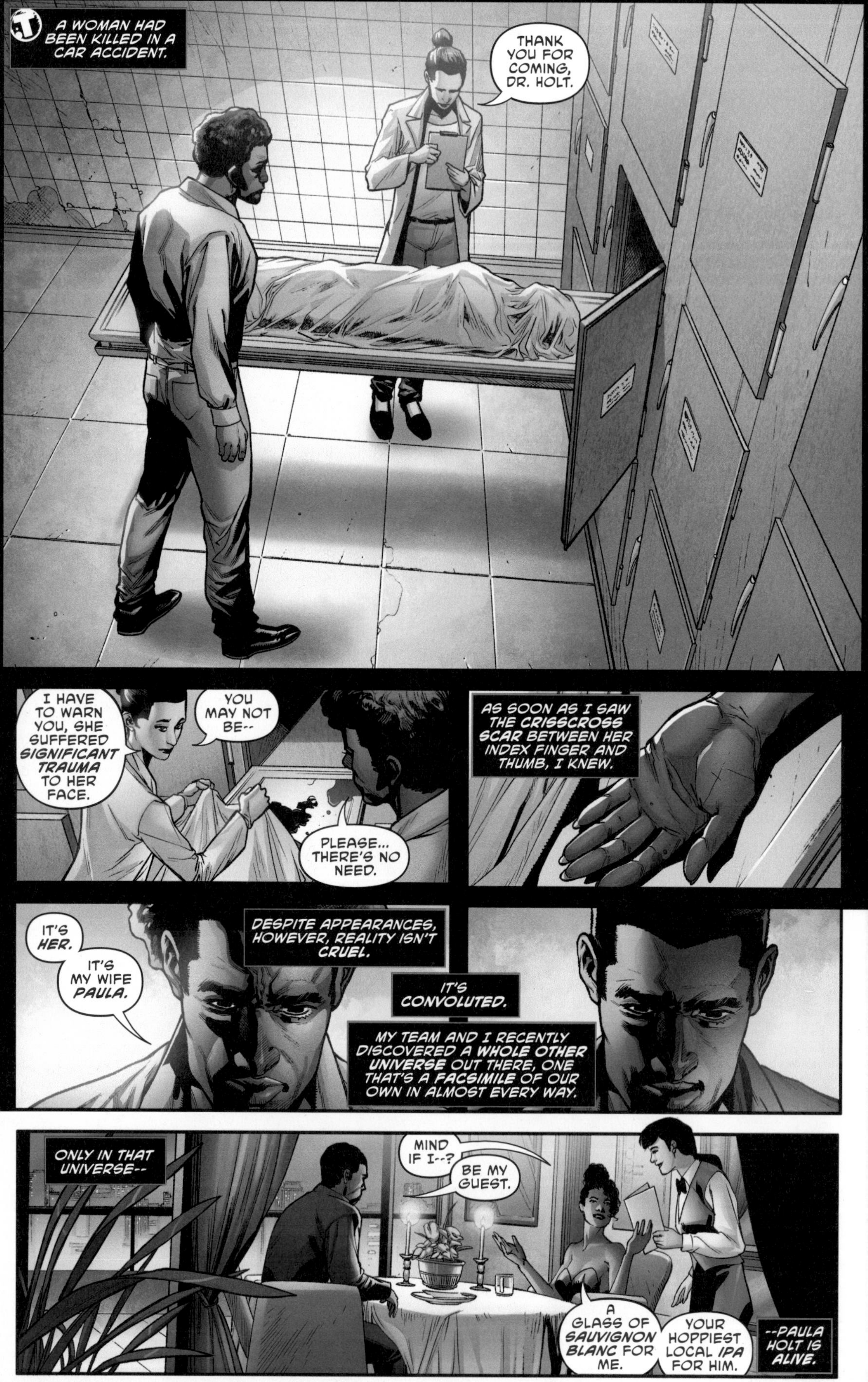
A WOMAN HAD BEEN KILLED IN A CAR ACCIDENT.
THANK YOU FOR COMING, DR. HOLT.
I HAVE TO WARN YOU, SHE SUFFERED SIGNIFICANT TRAUMA TO HER FACE.
YOU MAY NOT BE--
PLEASE... THERE'S NO NEED.
AS SOON AS I SAW THE CRISSCROSS SCAR BETWEEN HER INDEX FINGER AND THUMB, I KNEW.
IT'S HER.
IT'S MY WIFE PAULA.
DESPITE APPEARANCES, HOWEVER, REALITY ISN'T CRUEL.
IT'S CONVOLUTED.
MY TEAM AND I RECENTLY DISCOVERED A WHOLE OTHER UNIVERSE OUT THERE, ONE THAT'S A FACSIMILE OF OUR OWN IN ALMOST EVERY WAY.
ONLY IN THAT UNIVERSE--
MIND IF I--?
BE MY GUEST.
A GLASS OF SAUVIGNON BLANC FOR ME.
YOUR HOPPIEST LOCAL IPA FOR HIM.
--PAULA HOLT IS ALIVE.

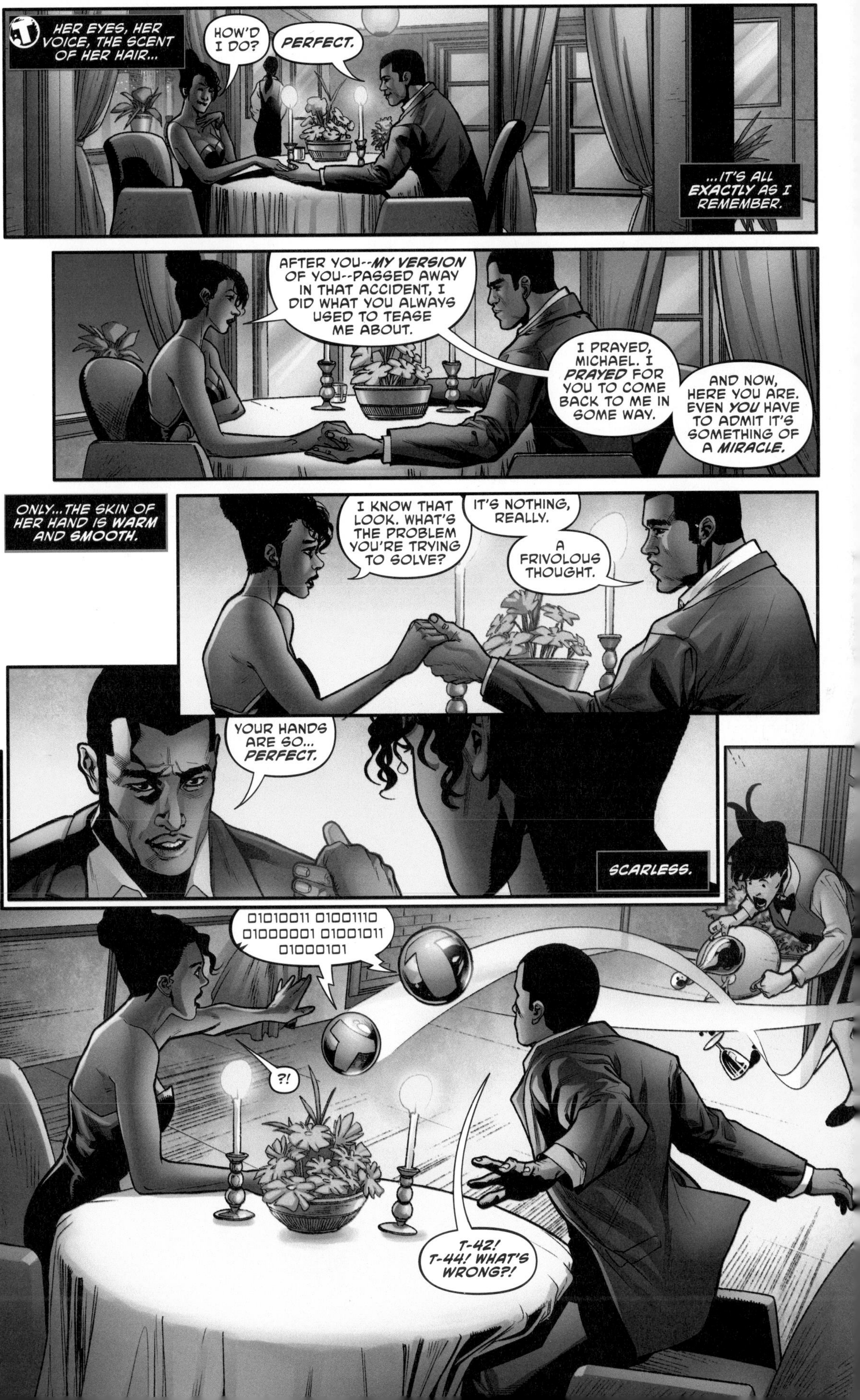
HER EYES, HER VOICE, THE SCENT OF HER HAIR...
HOW'D I DO?
PERFECT.
...IT'S ALL EXACTLY AS I REMEMBER.
AFTER YOU--MY VERSION OF YOU--PASSED AWAY IN THAT ACCIDENT, I DID WHAT YOU ALWAYS USED TO TEASE ME ABOUT.
I PRAYED, MICHAEL. I PRAYED FOR YOU TO COME BACK TO ME IN SOME WAY.
AND NOW, HERE YOU ARE. EVEN YOU HAVE TO ADMIT IT'S SOMETHING OF A MIRACLE.
ONLY...THE SKIN OF HER HAND IS WARM AND SMOOTH.
I KNOW THAT LOOK. WHAT'S THE PROBLEM YOU'RE TRYING TO SOLVE?
IT'S NOTHING, REALLY.
A FRIVOLOUS THOUGHT.
YOUR HANDS ARE SO... PERFECT.
SCARLESS.
01010011 01001110 01000001 01001011 01000101
?!
T-42! T-44! WHAT'S WRONG?!

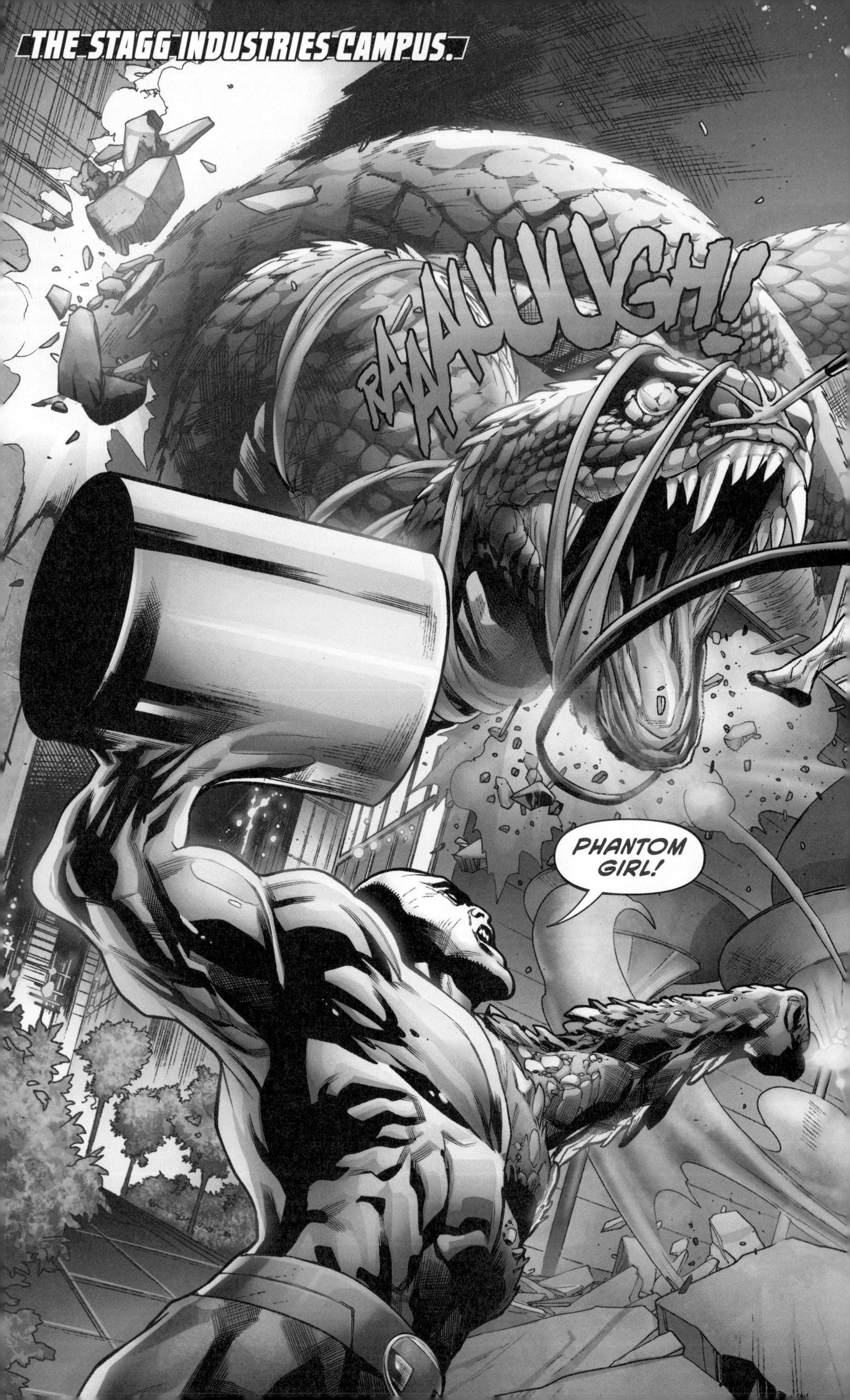
THE STAGG INDUSTRIES CAMPUS.
RAAAUUUGH!
PHANTOM GIRL!

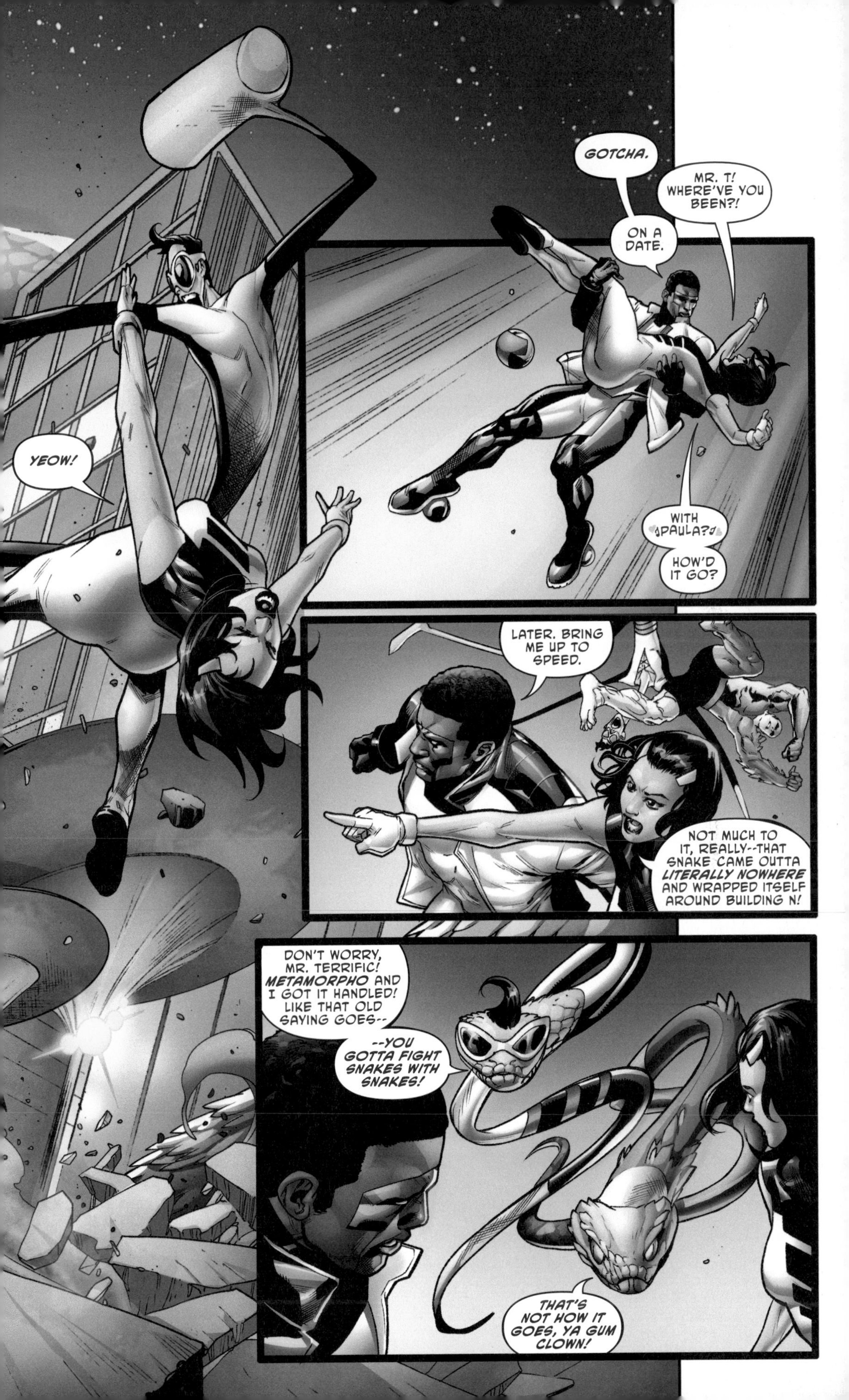
YEOW!
GOTCHA.
MR. T! WHERE'VE YOU BEEN?!
ON A DATE.
WITH ♪PAULA?♪
HOW'D IT GO?
LATER. BRING ME UP TO SPEED.
NOT MUCH TO IT, REALLY--THAT SNAKE CAME OUTTA *LITERALLY NOWHERE* AND WRAPPED ITSELF AROUND BUILDING N!
DON'T WORRY, MR. TERRIFIC! *METAMORPHO* AND I GOT IT HANDLED! LIKE THAT OLD SAYING GOES--
--YOU GOTTA FIGHT SNAKES WITH SNAKES!
THAT'S NOT HOW IT GOES, YA GUM CLOWN!

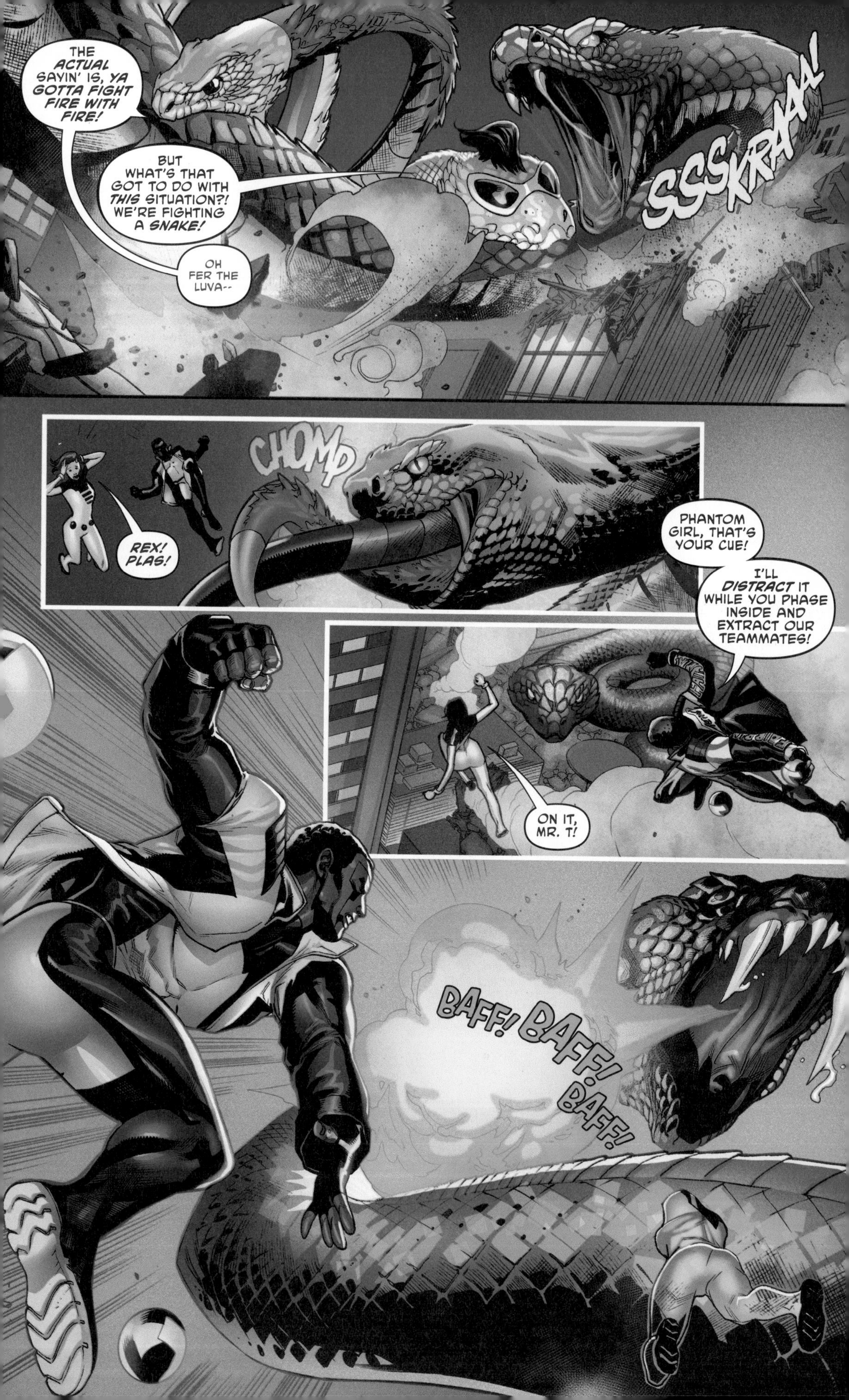
THE ACTUAL SAYIN' IS, YA GOTTA FIGHT FIRE WITH FIRE!
BUT WHAT'S THAT GOT TO DO WITH THIS SITUATION?! WE'RE FIGHTING A SNAKE!
OH FER THE LUVA--
SSSKRAAA!
CHOMP
REX! PLAS!
PHANTOM GIRL, THAT'S YOUR CUE!
I'LL DISTRACT IT WHILE YOU PHASE INSIDE AND EXTRACT OUR TEAMMATES!
ON IT, MR. T!
BAFF! BAFF! BAFF!

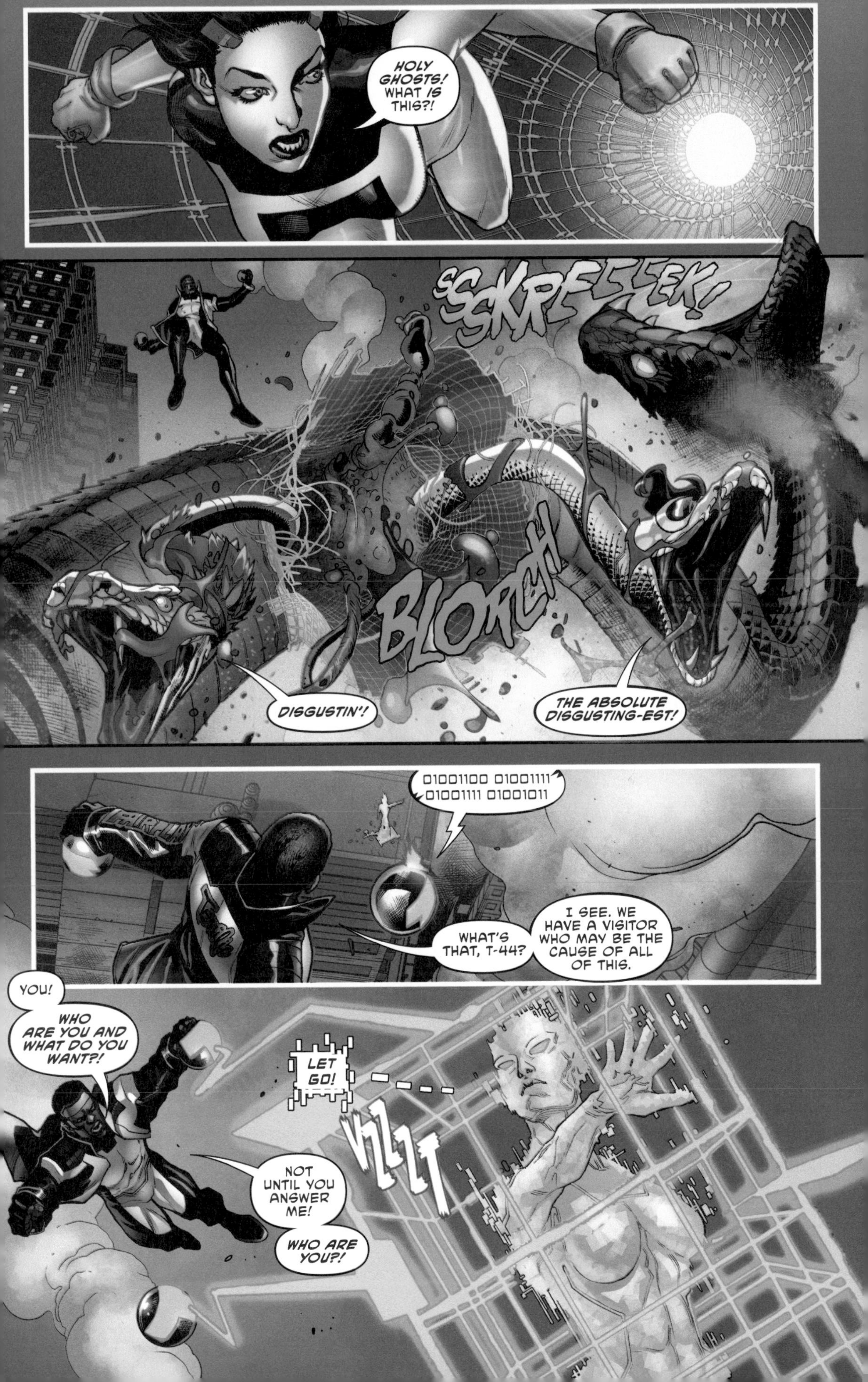
HOLY GHOSTS! WHAT IS THIS?!
SSSKREEEEK!
BLORCH
DISGUSTIN'!
THE ABSOLUTE DISGUSTING-EST!
01001100 01001111 01001111 01001011
WHAT'S THAT, T-44?
I SEE. WE HAVE A VISITOR WHO MAY BE THE CAUSE OF ALL OF THIS.
YOU!
WHO ARE YOU AND WHAT DO YOU WANT?!
LET GO!
VZZZT
NOT UNTIL YOU ANSWER ME!
WHO ARE YOU?!

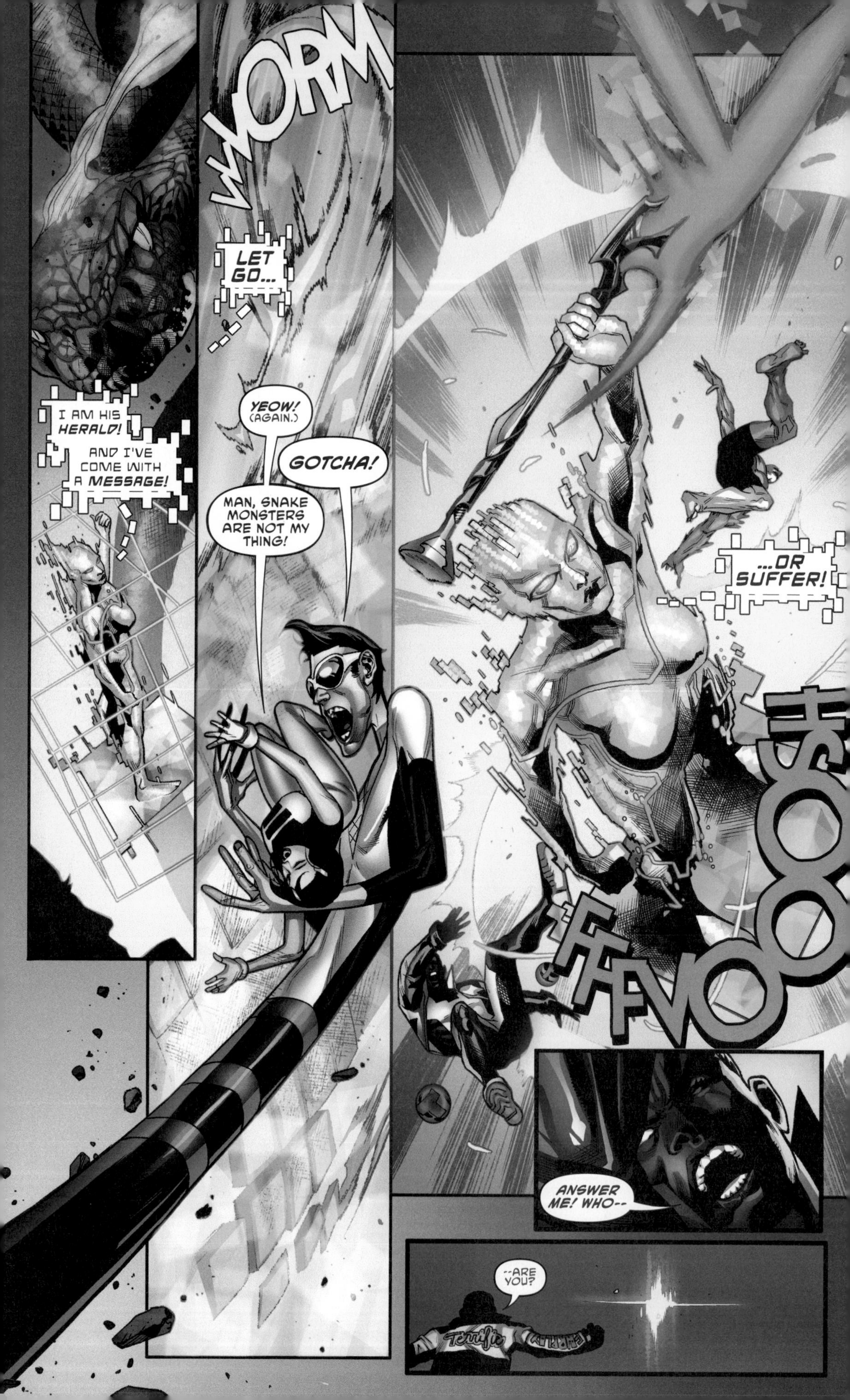
I AM HIS HERALD!
AND I'VE COME WITH A MESSAGE!
WWORM
LET GO...
YEOW! (AGAIN.)
GOTCHA!
MAN, SNAKE MONSTERS ARE NOT MY THING!
...OR SUFFER!
ANSWER ME! WHO--
--ARE YOU?

IT WAS THE *WEIRDEST* THING, MR. T!

INSIDE THAT SNAKE MONSTER WAS LITERALLY *NOTHING!*

NO BLOOD, NO GUTS, NO MACHINERY, EVEN!

BUT THAT DOESN'T MAKE SENSE! REX AND I WERE *COVERED* IN ITS BLOOD AND GUTS!

WHEN YOU PHASED IN, LINNYA, IT WAS OCCUPIED WITH PLASTIC MAN, METAMORPHO AND ME. PLUS, YOU WERE *INTANGIBLE.*

IT MUST'VE GENERATED ITS OWN DETAILS ON THE FLY, AS IT DEEMED NECESSARY. *FASCINATING.*

I WONDER IF THE SAME WAS TRUE OF THE *SILVER WOMAN.*

HOW MUCH YOU WANNA BET *HE* HAD SOMETHING TO DO WITH IT?

YOU LET THIS HAPPEN *TODAY* OF ALL DAYS?!

I DIDN'T *LET* IT HAPPEN, SIR. IT JUST *DID.*

STAGG! WE NEED TO TALK! LAST NIGHT, NEAR BUILDING N--

NOT NOW, HOLT!

WE'RE ABOUT TO RUN OUR MOST IMPORTANT *PRODUCT DEMONSTRATION* OF THE DECADE, AND THE PLUMBING ACROSS THE ENTIRE CAMPUS HAS GONE *HAYWIRE!*

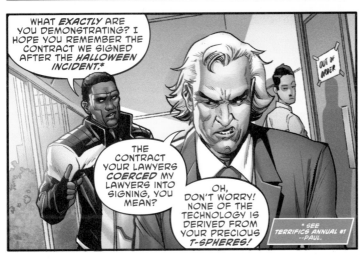

WHAT *EXACTLY* ARE YOU DEMONSTRATING? I HOPE YOU REMEMBER THE CONTRACT WE SIGNED AFTER THE *HALLOWEEN INCIDENT.**

THE CONTRACT YOUR LAWYERS *COERCED* MY LAWYERS INTO SIGNING, YOU MEAN?

OH, DON'T WORRY! NONE OF THE TECHNOLOGY IS DERIVED FROM YOUR PRECIOUS *T-SPHERES!*

* SEE *TERRIFICS ANNUAL #1* --PAUL.

OUT OF ORDER

BECAUSE IF IT WERE, OWNERSHIP OF *TERRIFICTECH* WOULD REVERT BACK TO ME.

YES, *WHATEVER!* NOW, IF YOU'LL EXCUSE ME!

GOOD TO KNOW STAGG IS LIKE THAT ON EVERY WORLD.

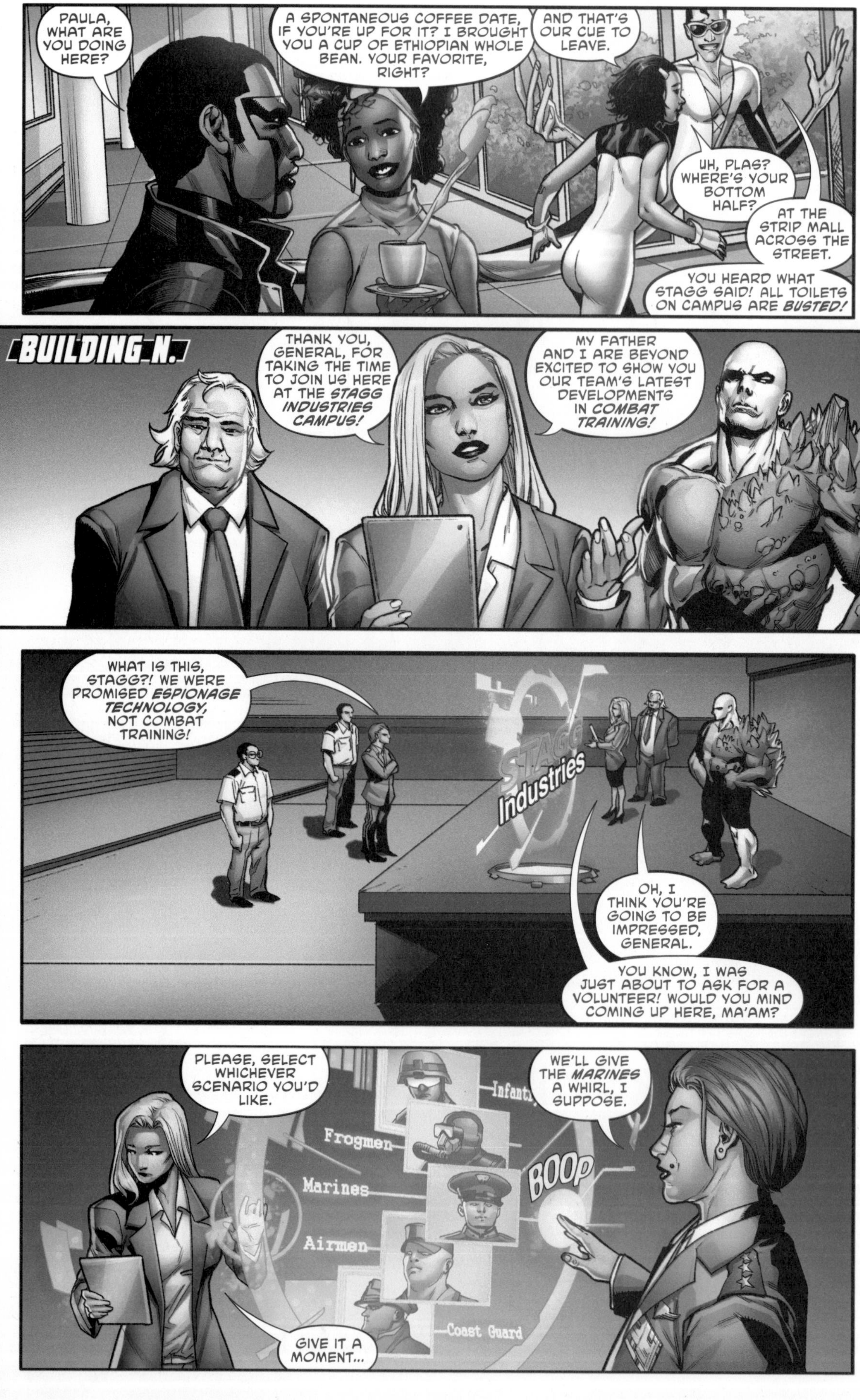
PAULA, WHAT ARE YOU DOING HERE?
A SPONTANEOUS COFFEE DATE, IF YOU'RE UP FOR IT? I BROUGHT YOU A CUP OF ETHIOPIAN WHOLE BEAN. YOUR FAVORITE, RIGHT?
AND THAT'S OUR CUE TO LEAVE.
UH, PLAS? WHERE'S YOUR BOTTOM HALF?
AT THE STRIP MALL ACROSS THE STREET.
YOU HEARD WHAT STAGG SAID! ALL TOILETS ON CAMPUS ARE BUSTED!
BUILDING N.
THANK YOU, GENERAL, FOR TAKING THE TIME TO JOIN US HERE AT THE STAGG INDUSTRIES CAMPUS!
MY FATHER AND I ARE BEYOND EXCITED TO SHOW YOU OUR TEAM'S LATEST DEVELOPMENTS IN COMBAT TRAINING!
WHAT IS THIS, STAGG?! WE WERE PROMISED ESPIONAGE TECHNOLOGY, NOT COMBAT TRAINING!
STAGG Industries
OH, I THINK YOU'RE GOING TO BE IMPRESSED, GENERAL.
YOU KNOW, I WAS JUST ABOUT TO ASK FOR A VOLUNTEER! WOULD YOU MIND COMING UP HERE, MA'AM?
PLEASE, SELECT WHICHEVER SCENARIO YOU'D LIKE.
WE'LL GIVE THE MARINES A WHIRL, I SUPPOSE.
Infantry
Frogmen
Marines
Airmen
Coast Guard
BOOP
GIVE IT A MOMENT...

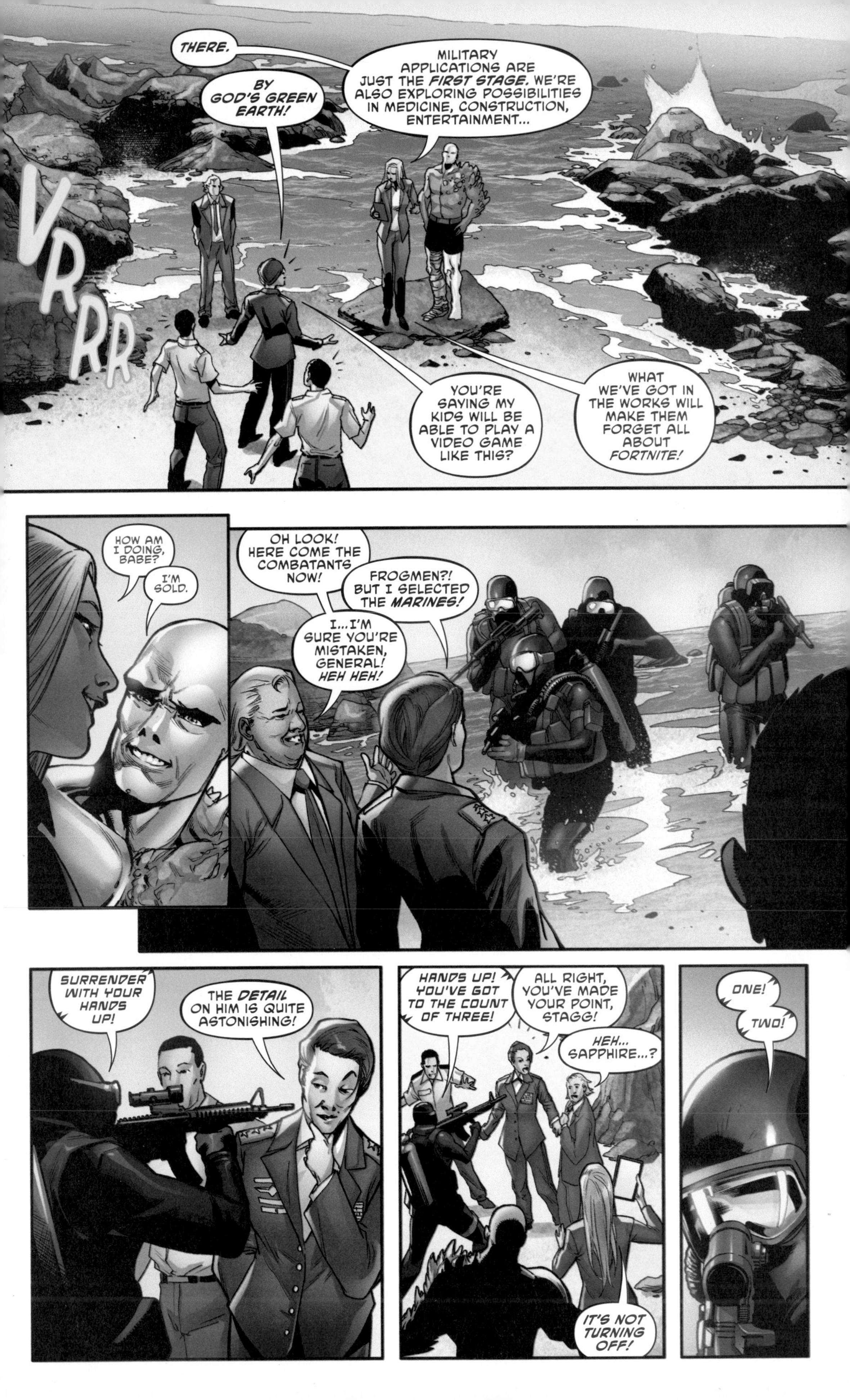
VRRR
THERE.
BY GOD'S GREEN EARTH!
MILITARY APPLICATIONS ARE JUST THE FIRST STAGE. WE'RE ALSO EXPLORING POSSIBILITIES IN MEDICINE, CONSTRUCTION, ENTERTAINMENT...
YOU'RE SAYING MY KIDS WILL BE ABLE TO PLAY A VIDEO GAME LIKE THIS?
WHAT WE'VE GOT IN THE WORKS WILL MAKE THEM FORGET ALL ABOUT FORTNITE!
HOW AM I DOING, BABE?
I'M SOLD.
OH LOOK! HERE COME THE COMBATANTS NOW!
FROGMEN?! BUT I SELECTED THE MARINES!
I...I'M SURE YOU'RE MISTAKEN, GENERAL! HEH HEH!
SURRENDER WITH YOUR HANDS UP!
THE DETAIL ON HIM IS QUITE ASTONISHING!
HANDS UP! YOU'VE GOT TO THE COUNT OF THREE!
ALL RIGHT, YOU'VE MADE YOUR POINT, STAGG!
HEH... SAPPHIRE...?
IT'S NOT TURNING OFF!
ONE!
TWO!

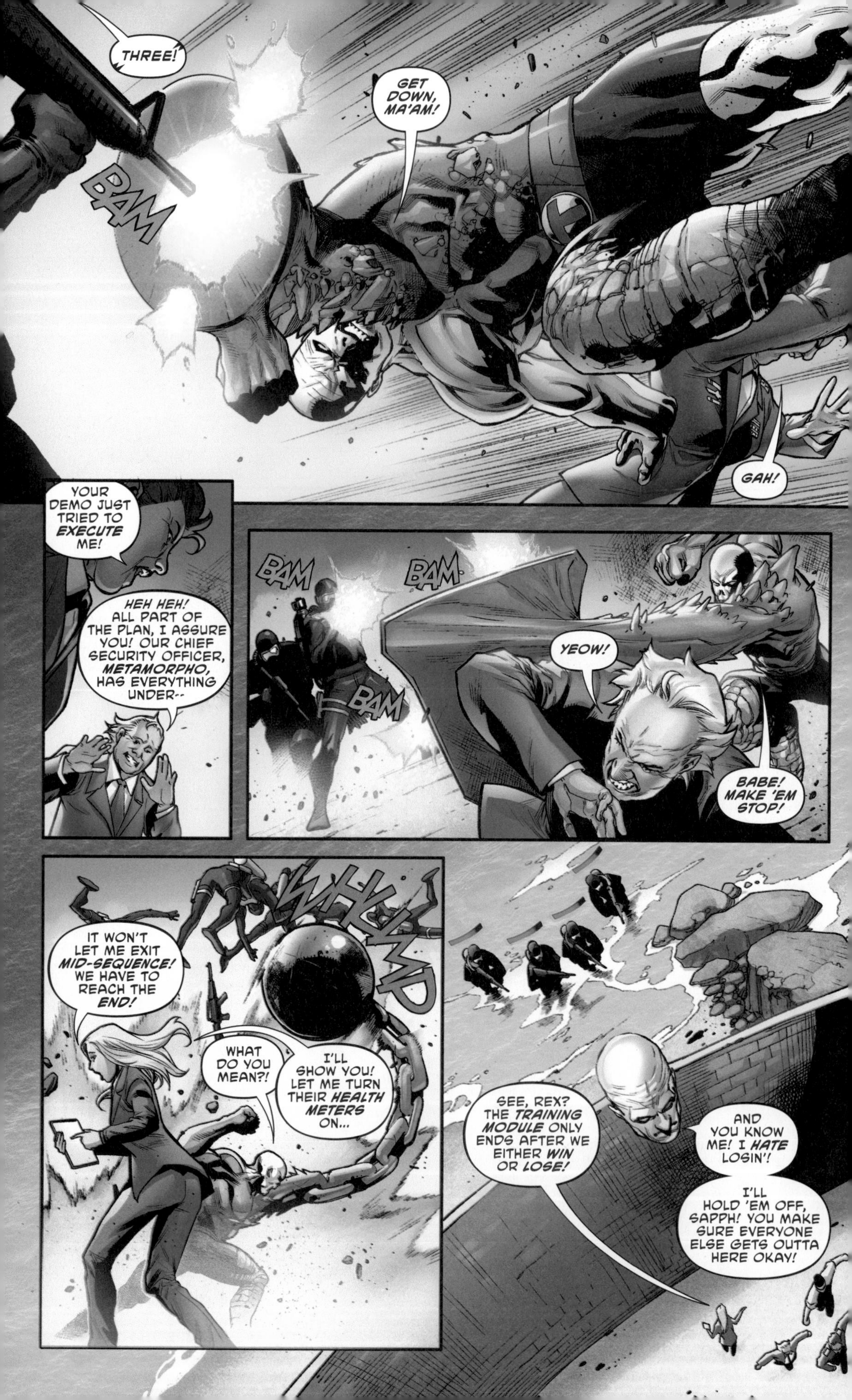
THREE!
GET DOWN, MA'AM!
BAM
GAH!
YOUR DEMO JUST TRIED TO *EXECUTE* ME!
HEH HEH! ALL PART OF THE PLAN, I ASSURE YOU! OUR CHIEF SECURITY OFFICER, *METAMORPHO*, HAS EVERYTHING UNDER--
BAM
BAM
BAM
YEOW!
BABE! MAKE 'EM STOP!
WHKMP
IT WON'T LET ME EXIT *MID-SEQUENCE!* WE HAVE TO REACH THE *END!*
WHAT DO YOU MEAN?!
I'LL SHOW YOU! LET ME TURN THEIR *HEALTH METERS* ON...
SEE, REX? THE *TRAINING MODULE* ONLY ENDS AFTER WE EITHER *WIN* OR *LOSE!*
AND YOU KNOW ME! I *HATE* LOSIN'!
I'LL HOLD 'EM OFF, SAPPH! YOU MAKE SURE EVERYONE ELSE GETS OUTTA HERE OKAY!

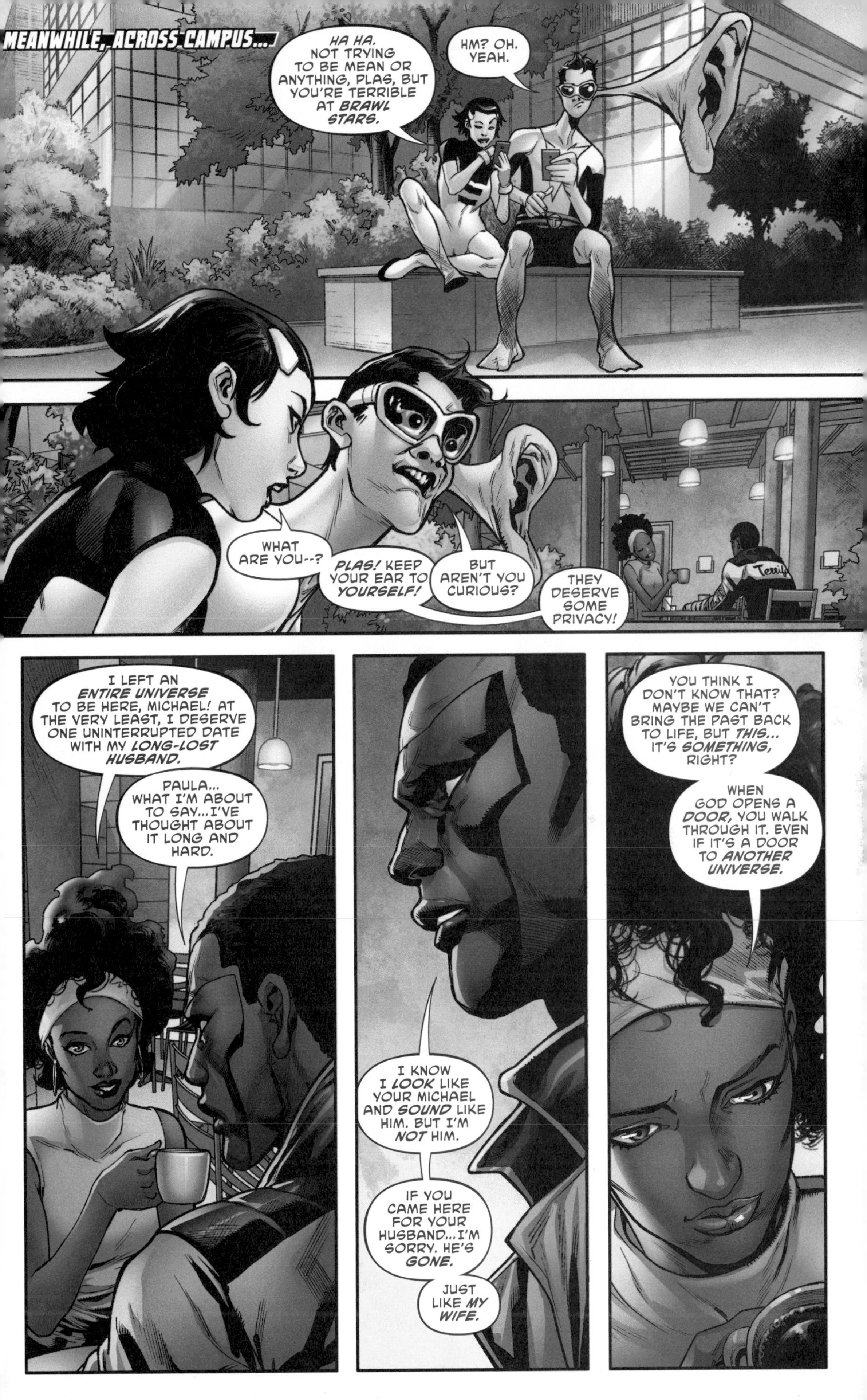
MEANWHILE, ACROSS CAMPUS...
HA HA. NOT TRYING TO BE MEAN OR ANYTHING, PLAS, BUT YOU'RE TERRIBLE AT BRAWL STARS.
HM? OH. YEAH.
WHAT ARE YOU--?
PLAS! KEEP YOUR EAR TO YOURSELF!
BUT AREN'T YOU CURIOUS?
THEY DESERVE SOME PRIVACY!
I LEFT AN ENTIRE UNIVERSE TO BE HERE, MICHAEL! AT THE VERY LEAST, I DESERVE ONE UNINTERRUPTED DATE WITH MY LONG-LOST HUSBAND.
PAULA... WHAT I'M ABOUT TO SAY...I'VE THOUGHT ABOUT IT LONG AND HARD.
I KNOW I LOOK LIKE YOUR MICHAEL AND SOUND LIKE HIM. BUT I'M NOT HIM.
IF YOU CAME HERE FOR YOUR HUSBAND...I'M SORRY. HE'S GONE.
JUST LIKE MY WIFE.
YOU THINK I DON'T KNOW THAT? MAYBE WE CAN'T BRING THE PAST BACK TO LIFE, BUT THIS... IT'S SOMETHING, RIGHT?
WHEN GOD OPENS A DOOR, YOU WALK THROUGH IT. EVEN IF IT'S A DOOR TO ANOTHER UNIVERSE.

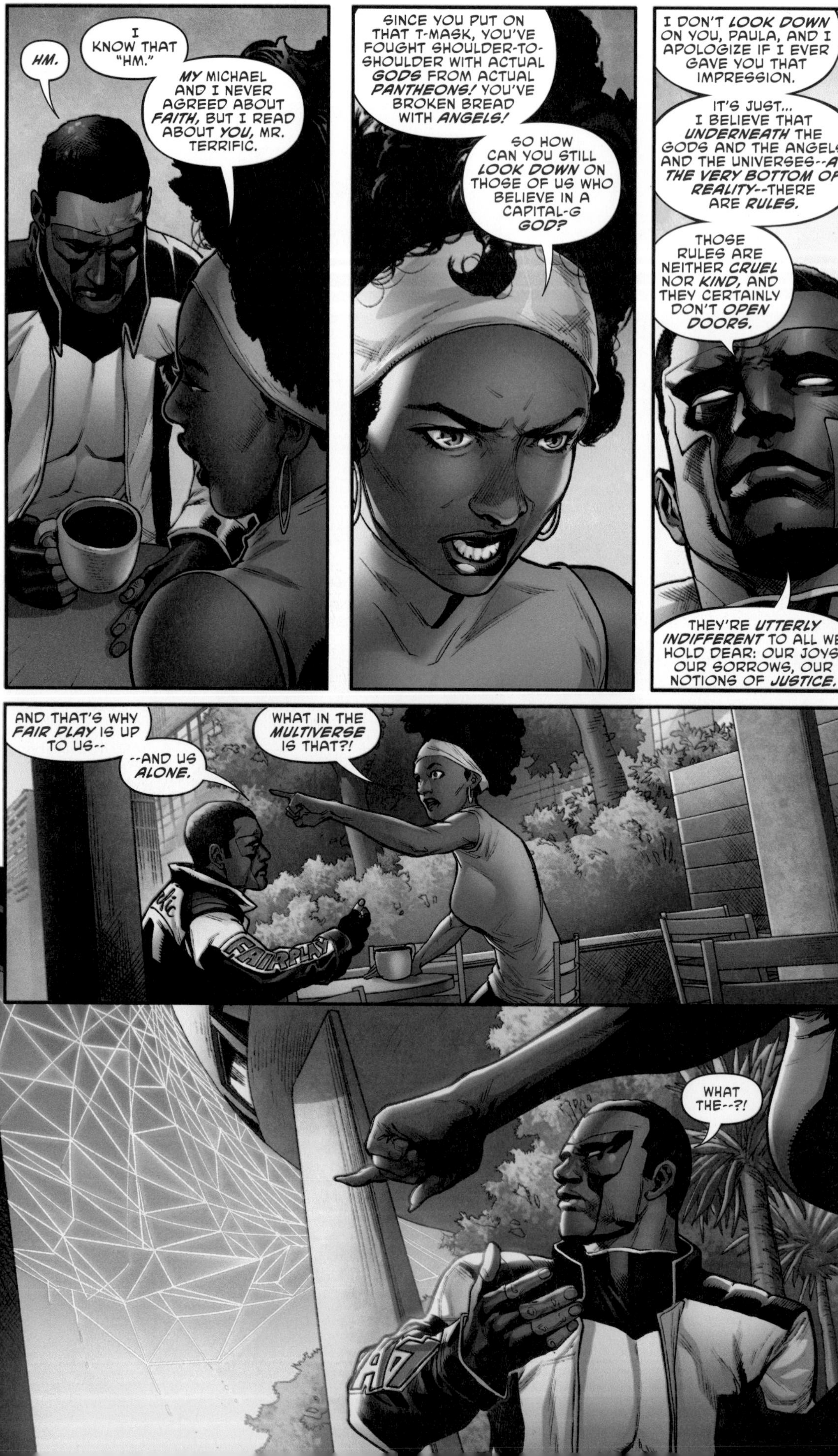
HM.
I KNOW THAT "HM."
MY MICHAEL AND I NEVER AGREED ABOUT FAITH, BUT I READ ABOUT YOU, MR. TERRIFIC.
SINCE YOU PUT ON THAT T-MASK, YOU'VE FOUGHT SHOULDER-TO-SHOULDER WITH ACTUAL GODS FROM ACTUAL PANTHEONS! YOU'VE BROKEN BREAD WITH ANGELS!
SO HOW CAN YOU STILL LOOK DOWN ON THOSE OF US WHO BELIEVE IN A CAPITAL-G GOD?
I DON'T LOOK DOWN ON YOU, PAULA, AND I APOLOGIZE IF I EVER GAVE YOU THAT IMPRESSION.
IT'S JUST... I BELIEVE THAT UNDERNEATH THE GODS AND THE ANGELS AND THE UNIVERSES--AT THE VERY BOTTOM OF REALITY--THERE ARE RULES.
THOSE RULES ARE NEITHER CRUEL NOR KIND, AND THEY CERTAINLY DON'T OPEN DOORS.
THEY'RE UTTERLY INDIFFERENT TO ALL WE HOLD DEAR: OUR JOYS, OUR SORROWS, OUR NOTIONS OF JUSTICE.
AND THAT'S WHY FAIR PLAY IS UP TO US--
--AND US ALONE.
WHAT IN THE MULTIVERSE IS THAT?!
FAIR PLAY
WHAT THE--?!

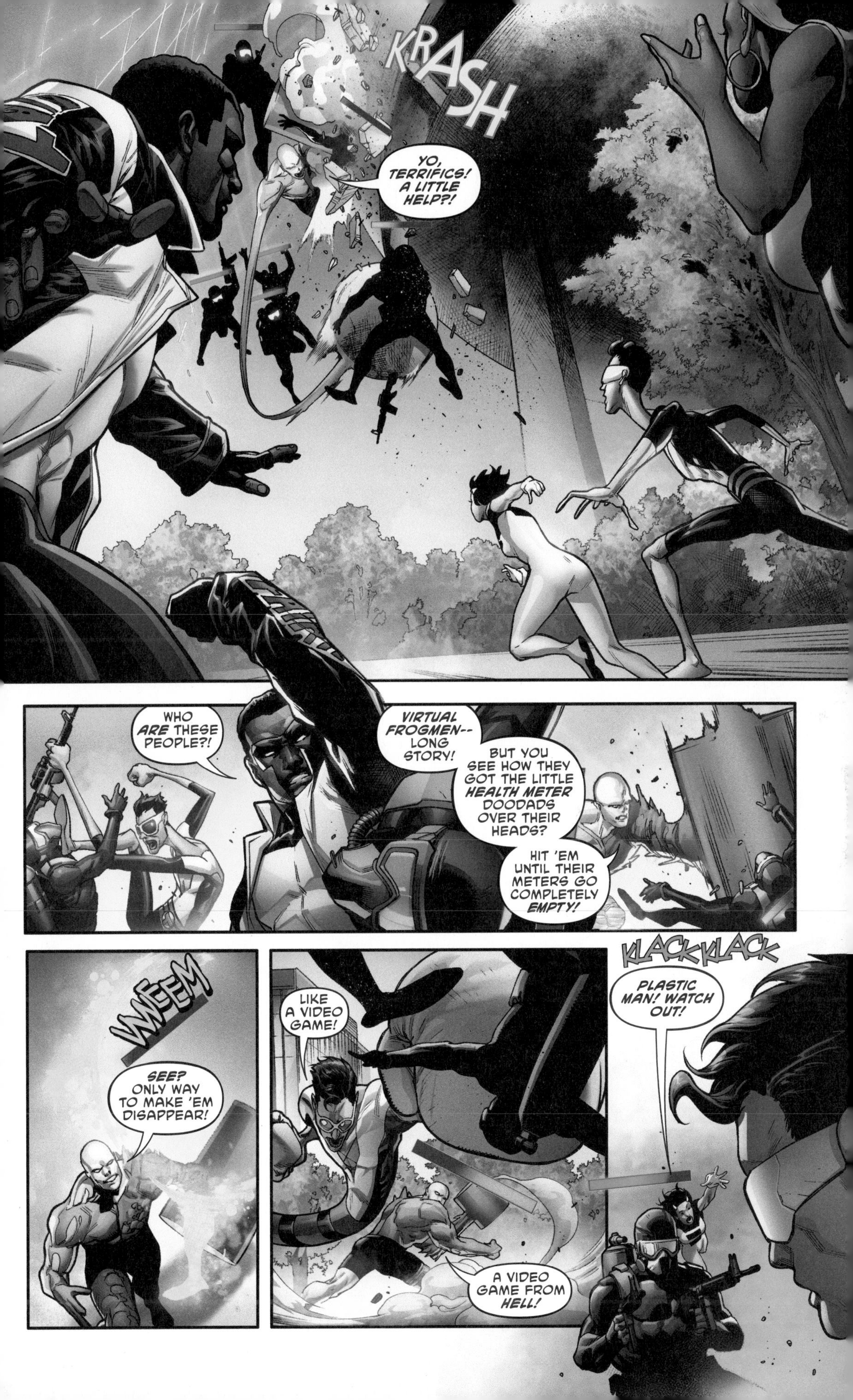
KRASH
YO, TERRIFICS! A LITTLE HELP?!
WHO ARE THESE PEOPLE?!
VIRTUAL FROGMEN-- LONG STORY!
BUT YOU SEE HOW THEY GOT THE LITTLE HEALTH METER DOODADS OVER THEIR HEADS?
HIT 'EM UNTIL THEIR METERS GO COMPLETELY EMPTY!
WEEEM
SEE? ONLY WAY TO MAKE 'EM DISAPPEAR!
LIKE A VIDEO GAME!
A VIDEO GAME FROM HELL!
KLACK KLACK
PLASTIC MAN! WATCH OUT!

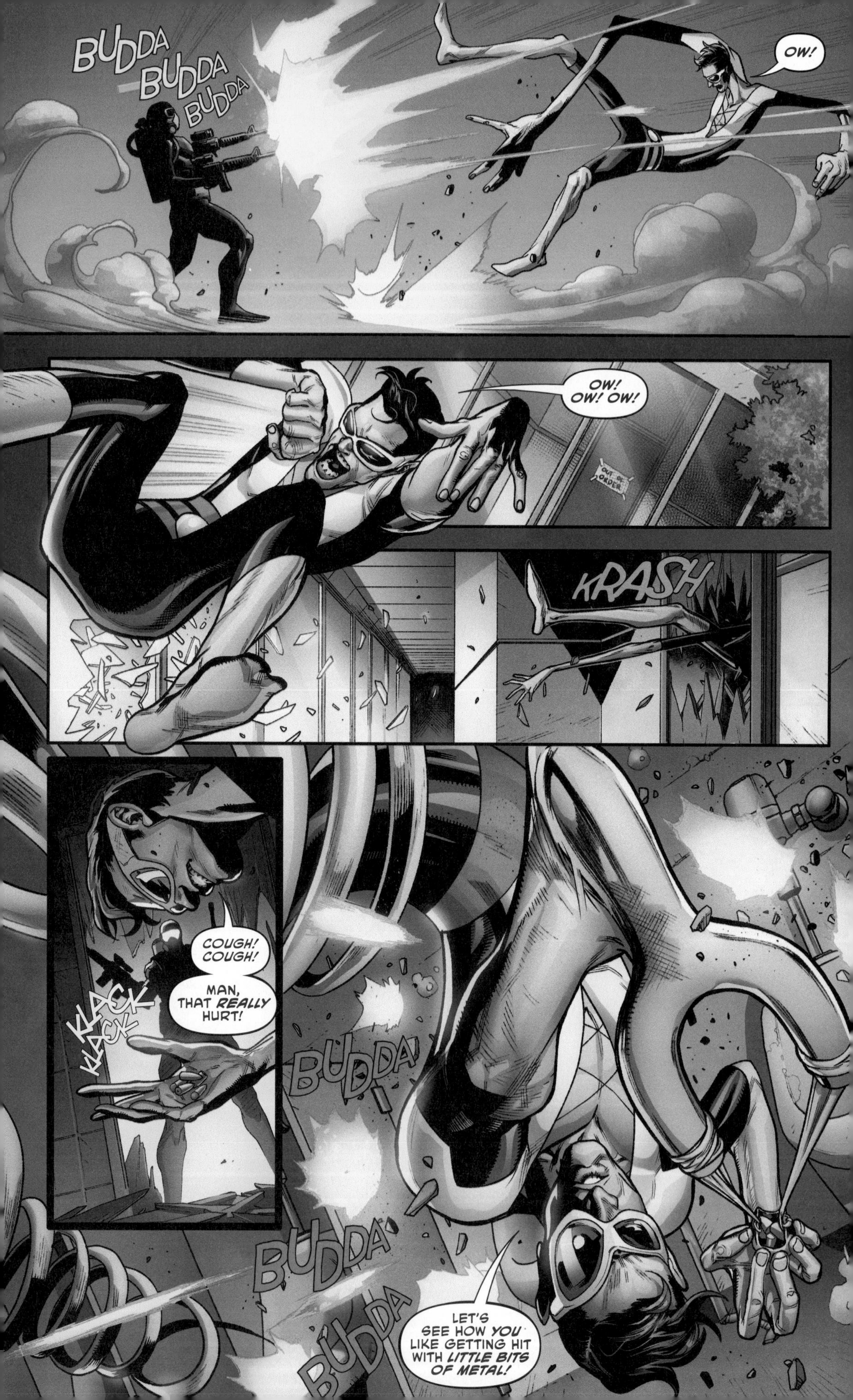
BUDDA BUDDA BUDDA
OW!
OW! OW! OW!
OUT OF ORDER
KRASH
COUGH! COUGH!
MAN, THAT REALLY HURT!
KLACK KLACK
BUDDA
BUDDA BUDDA
LET'S SEE HOW YOU LIKE GETTING HIT WITH LITTLE BITS OF METAL!

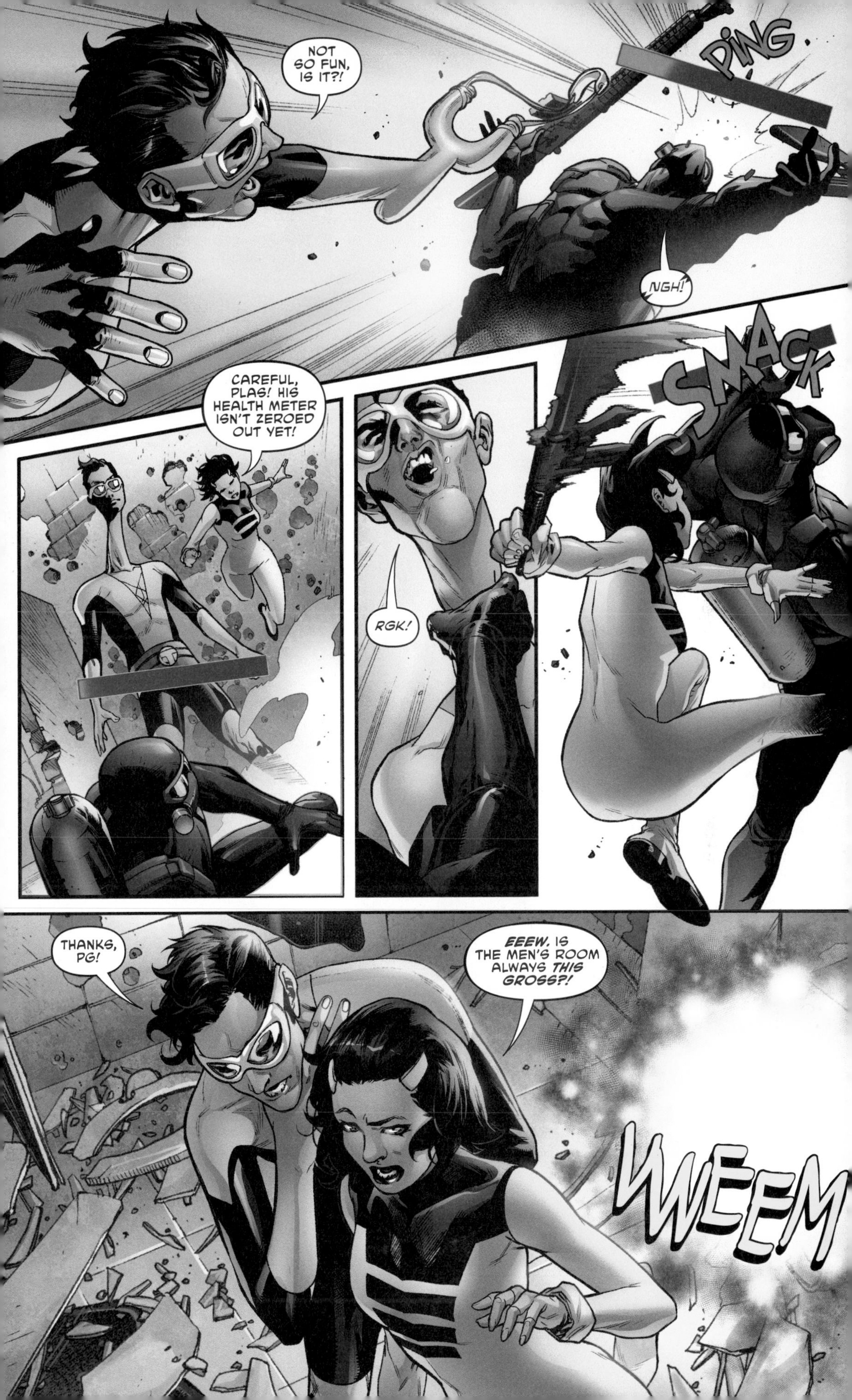
NOT SO FUN, IS IT?!
PING
NGH!
SMACK
CAREFUL, PLAS! HIS HEALTH METER ISN'T ZEROED OUT YET!
RGK!
THANKS, PG!
EEEW. IS THE MEN'S ROOM ALWAYS *THIS* GROSS?!
WEEM

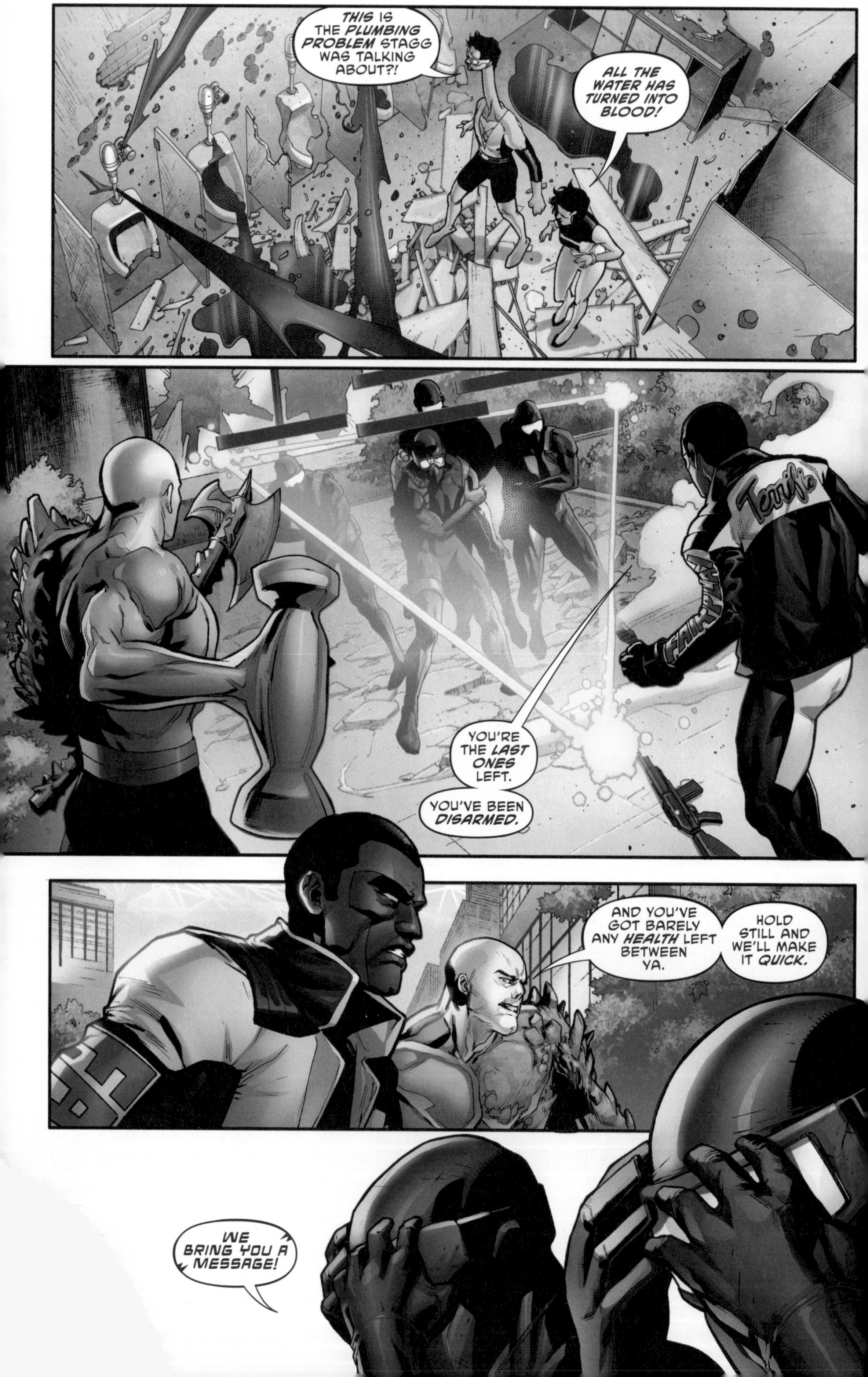
THIS IS THE PLUMBING PROBLEM STAGG WAS TALKING ABOUT?!
ALL THE WATER HAS TURNED INTO BLOOD!
YOU'RE THE LAST ONES LEFT.
YOU'VE BEEN DISARMED.
AND YOU'VE GOT BARELY ANY HEALTH LEFT BETWEEN YA.
HOLD STILL AND WE'LL MAKE IT QUICK.
WE BRING YOU A MESSAGE!

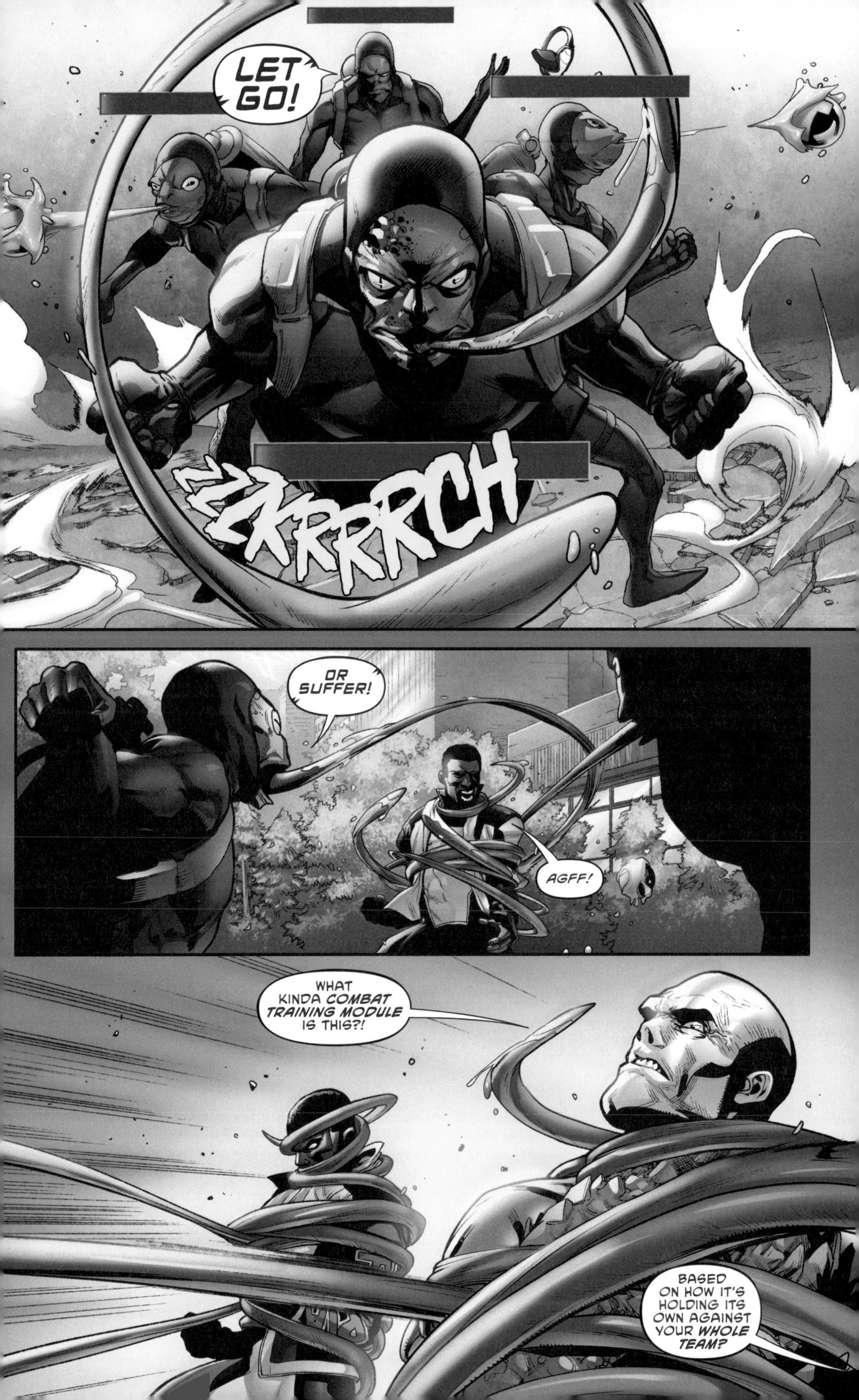
[redacted]
[redacted]
LET GO!
[redacted]
[redacted]
ZZKRRRCH
OR SUFFER!
AGFF!
WHAT KINDA *COMBAT TRAINING MODULE* IS THIS?!
BASED ON HOW IT'S HOLDING ITS OWN AGAINST YOUR *WHOLE TEAM*?

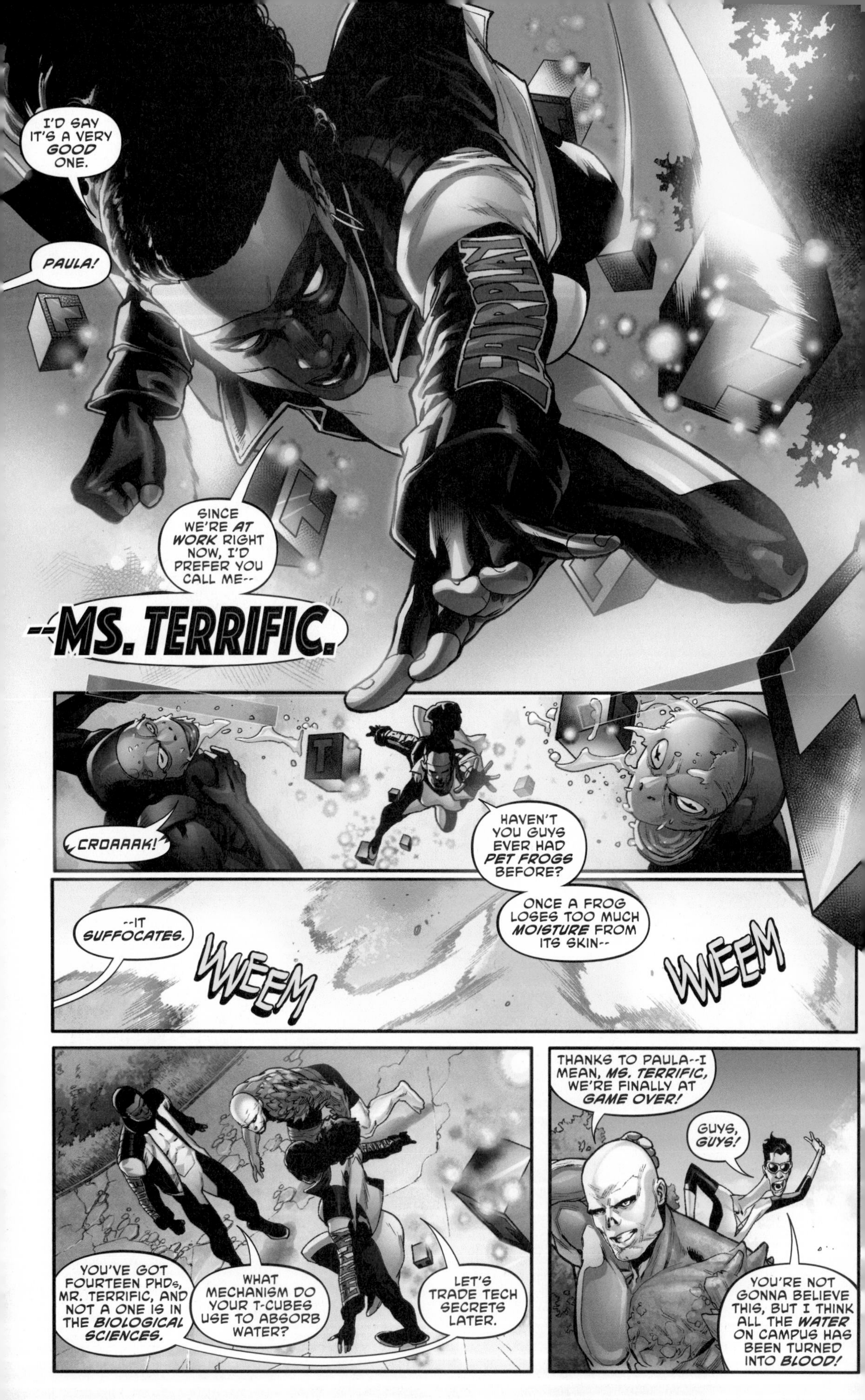

I'D SAY IT'S A VERY GOOD ONE.
PAULA!
SINCE WE'RE AT WORK RIGHT NOW, I'D PREFER YOU CALL ME--
--MS. TERRIFIC.
CROAAAK!
HAVEN'T YOU GUYS EVER HAD PET FROGS BEFORE?
ONCE A FROG LOSES TOO MUCH MOISTURE FROM ITS SKIN--
--IT SUFFOCATES.
WWEEM
WWEEM
YOU'VE GOT FOURTEEN PHDs, MR. TERRIFIC, AND NOT A ONE IS IN THE BIOLOGICAL SCIENCES.
WHAT MECHANISM DO YOUR T-CUBES USE TO ABSORB WATER?
LET'S TRADE TECH SECRETS LATER.
THANKS TO PAULA--I MEAN, MS. TERRIFIC, WE'RE FINALLY AT GAME OVER!
GUYS, GUYS!
YOU'RE NOT GONNA BELIEVE THIS, BUT I THINK ALL THE WATER ON CAMPUS HAS BEEN TURNED INTO BLOOD!

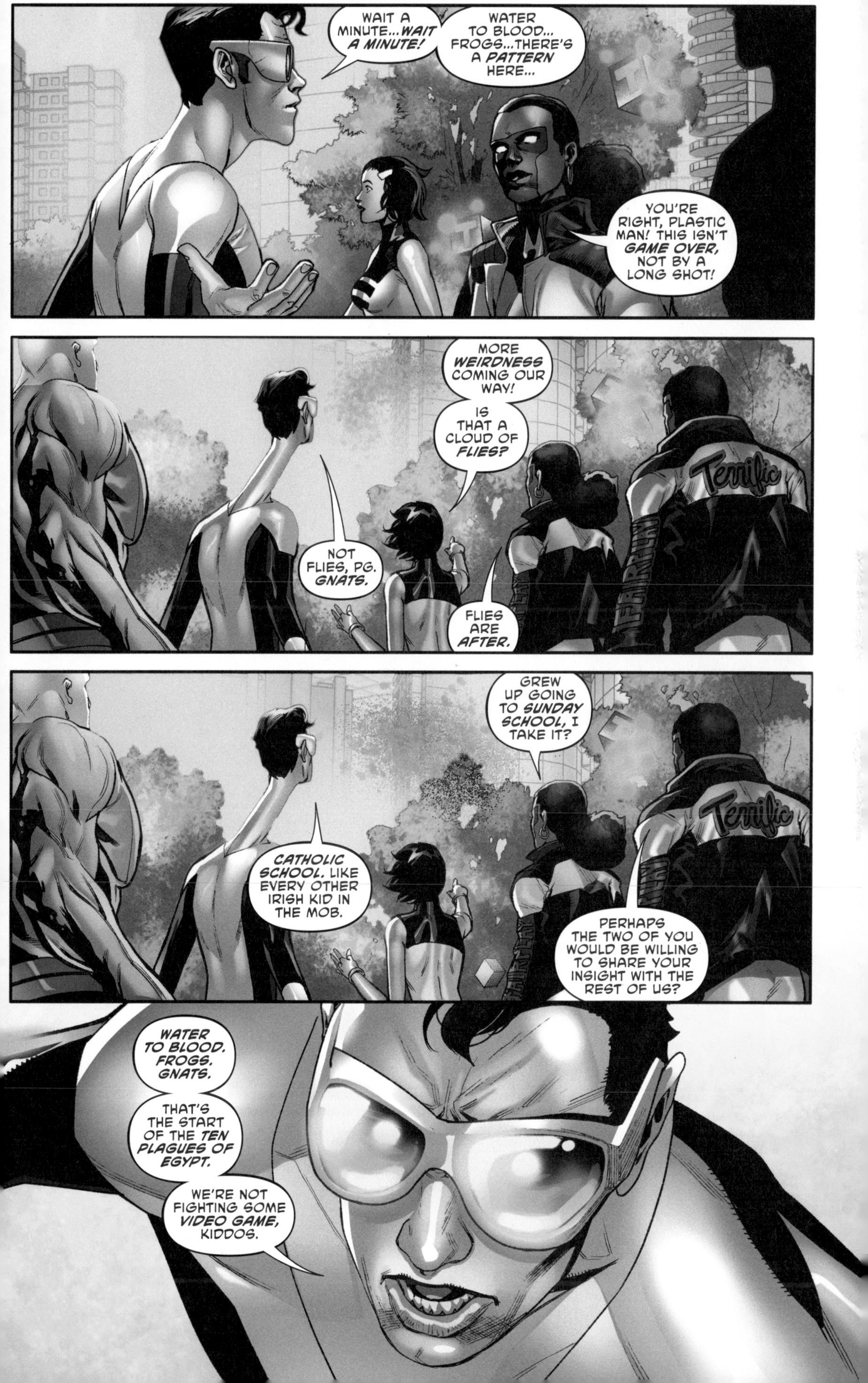
WAIT A MINUTE...WAIT A MINUTE!
WATER TO BLOOD... FROGS...THERE'S A PATTERN HERE...
YOU'RE RIGHT, PLASTIC MAN! THIS ISN'T GAME OVER, NOT BY A LONG SHOT!
MORE WEIRDNESS COMING OUR WAY!
IS THAT A CLOUD OF FLIES?
NOT FLIES, PG. GNATS.
FLIES ARE AFTER.
Terrific
GREW UP GOING TO SUNDAY SCHOOL, I TAKE IT?
CATHOLIC SCHOOL. LIKE EVERY OTHER IRISH KID IN THE MOB.
PERHAPS THE TWO OF YOU WOULD BE WILLING TO SHARE YOUR INSIGHT WITH THE REST OF US?
Terrific
WATER TO BLOOD. FROGS. GNATS.
THAT'S THE START OF THE TEN PLAGUES OF EGYPT.
WE'RE NOT FIGHTING SOME VIDEO GAME, KIDDOS.

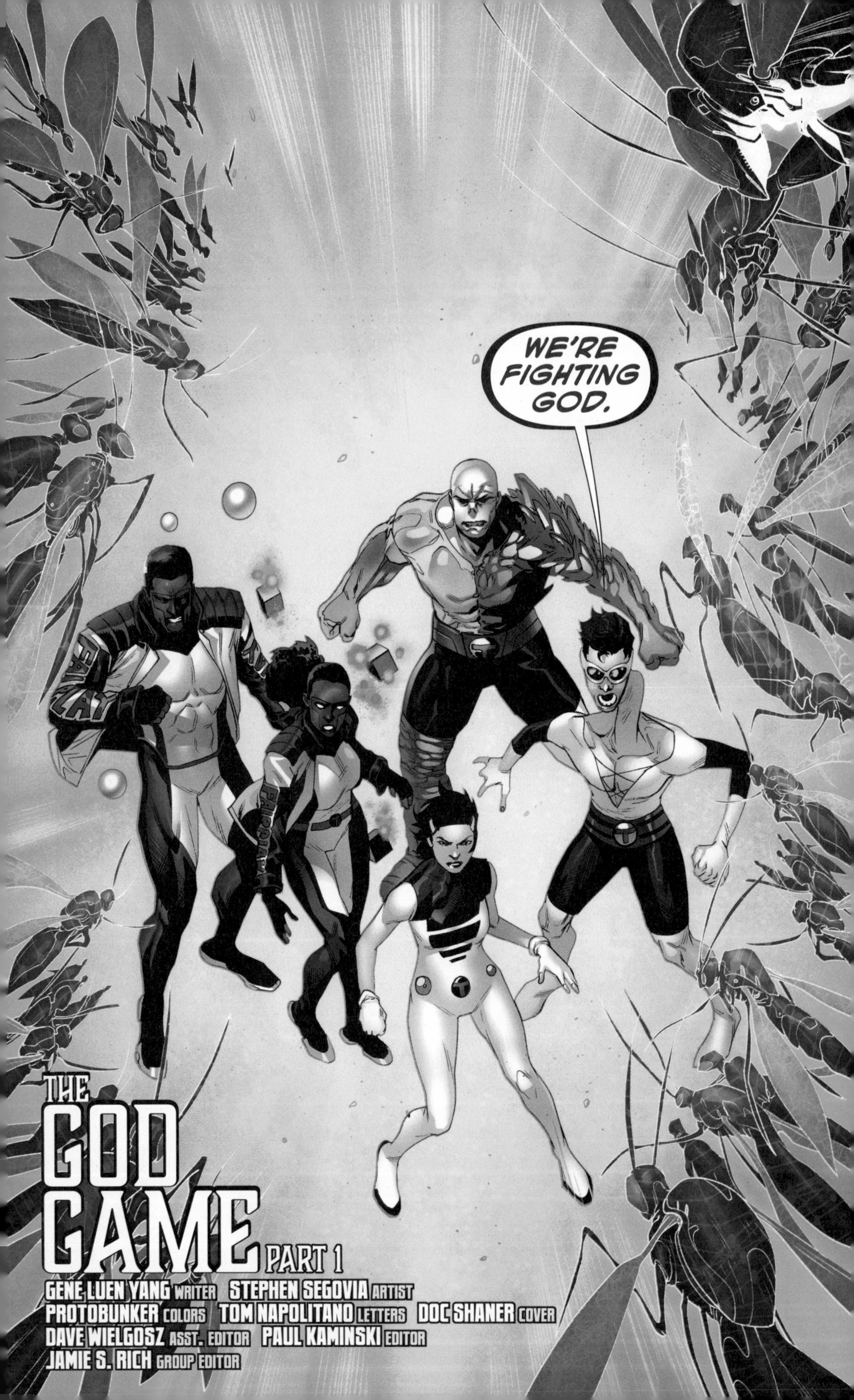
WE'RE FIGHTING GOD.
THE GOD GAME PART 1
GENE LUEN YANG WRITER STEPHEN SEGOVIA ARTIST
PROTOBUNKER COLORS TOM NAPOLITANO LETTERS DOC SHANER COVER
DAVE WIELGOSZ ASST. EDITOR PAUL KAMINSKI EDITOR
JAMIE S. RICH GROUP EDITOR

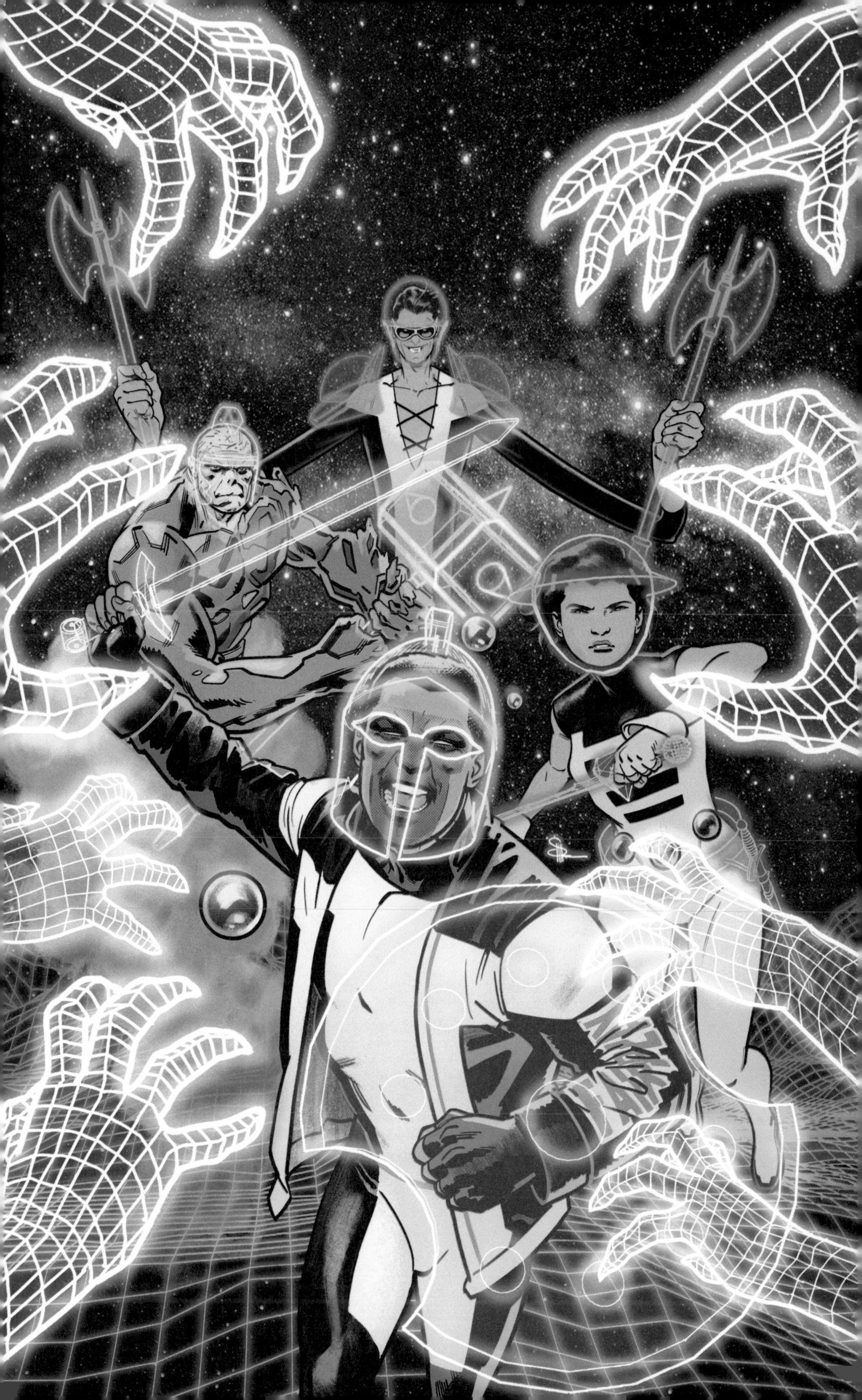

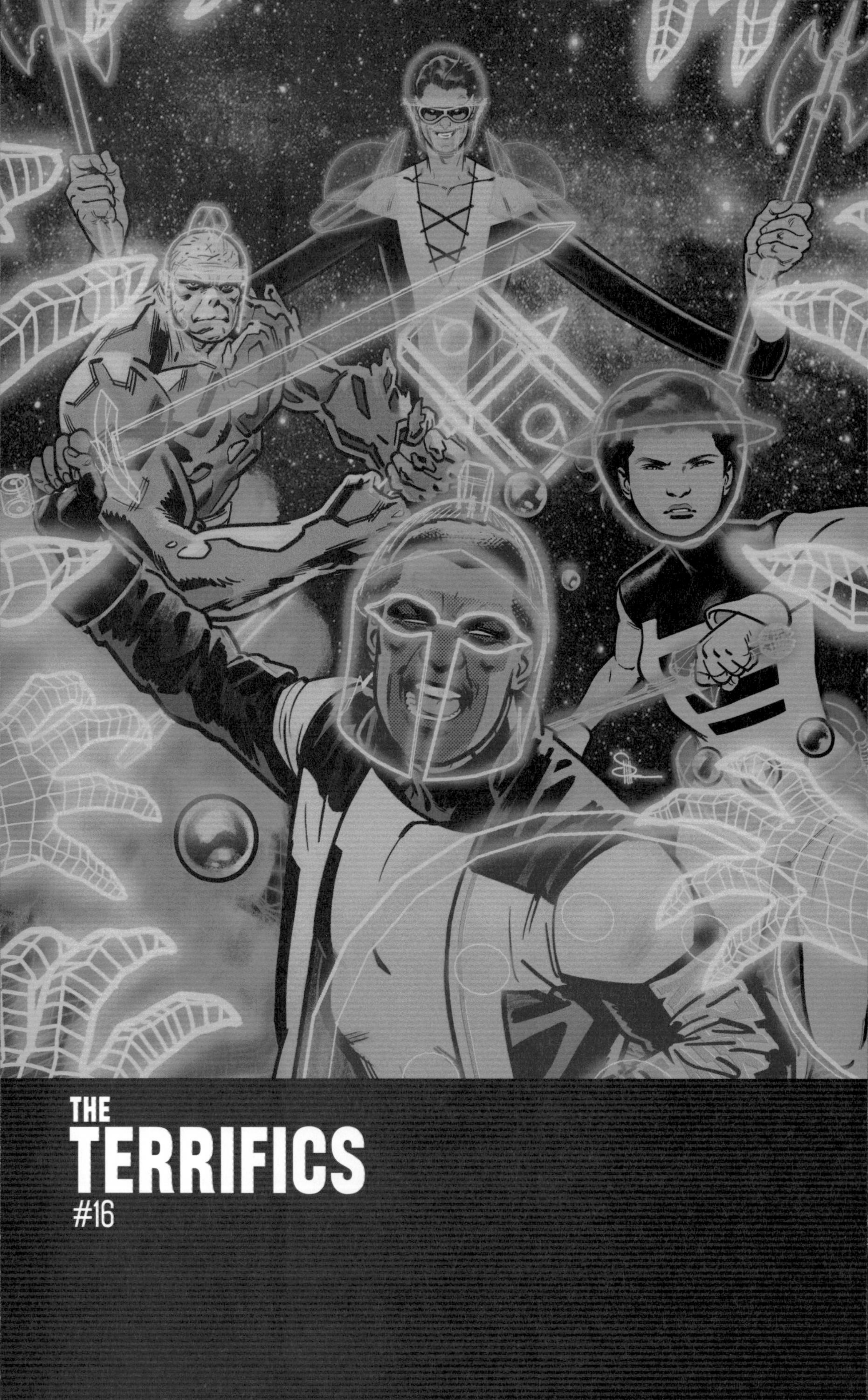

THE
TERRIFICS
#16

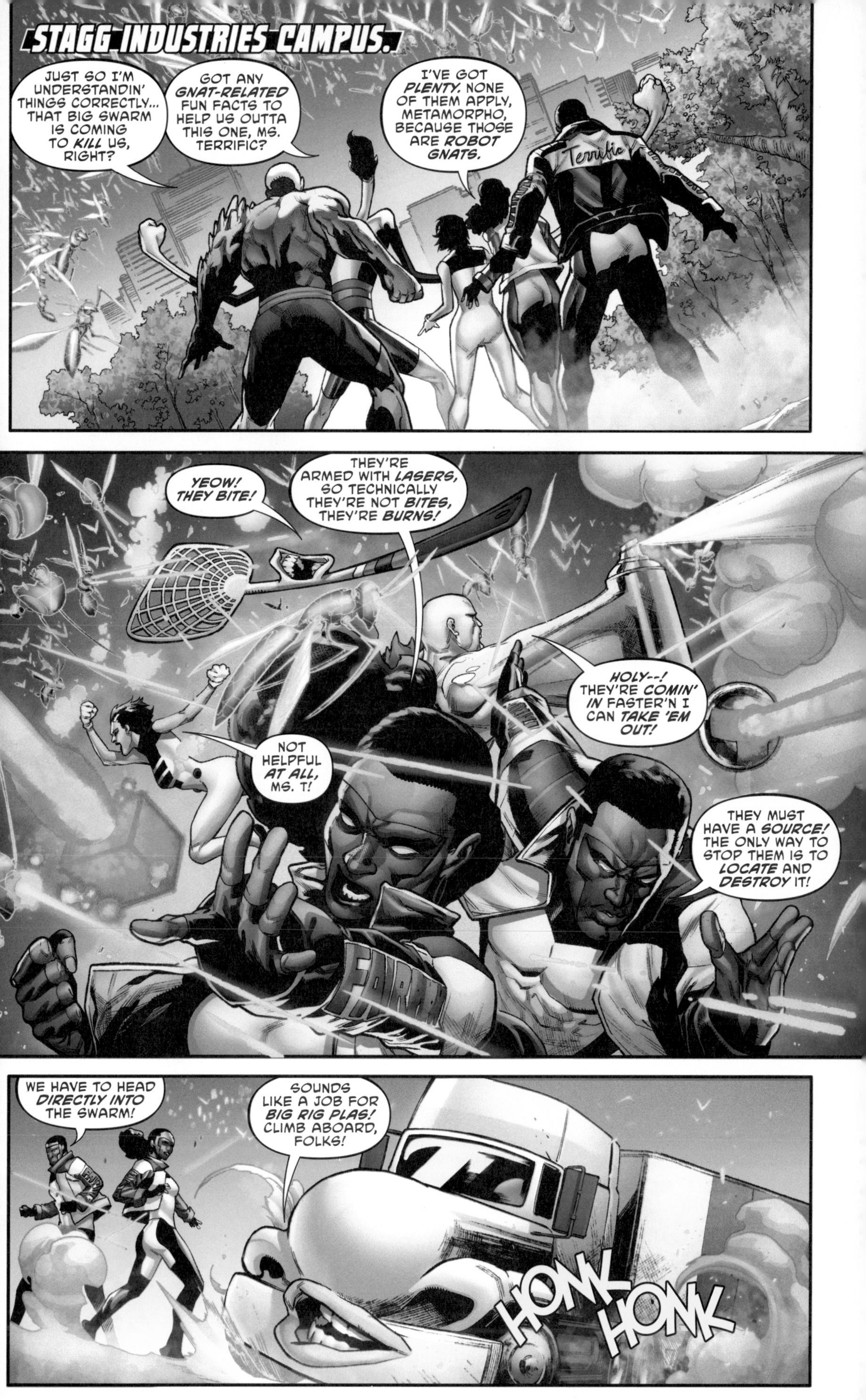
STAGG INDUSTRIES CAMPUS.
JUST SO I'M UNDERSTANDIN' THINGS CORRECTLY... THAT BIG SWARM IS COMING TO KILL US, RIGHT?
GOT ANY GNAT-RELATED FUN FACTS TO HELP US OUTTA THIS ONE, MS. TERRIFIC?
I'VE GOT PLENTY. NONE OF THEM APPLY, METAMORPHO, BECAUSE THOSE ARE ROBOT GNATS.
Terrific
YEOW! THEY BITE!
THEY'RE ARMED WITH LASERS, SO TECHNICALLY THEY'RE NOT BITES, THEY'RE BURNS!
HOLY--! THEY'RE COMIN' IN FASTER'N I CAN TAKE 'EM OUT!
NOT HELPFUL AT ALL, MS. T!
THEY MUST HAVE A SOURCE! THE ONLY WAY TO STOP THEM IS TO LOCATE AND DESTROY IT!
WE HAVE TO HEAD DIRECTLY INTO THE SWARM!
SOUNDS LIKE A JOB FOR BIG RIG PLAS! CLIMB ABOARD, FOLKS!
HONK HONK

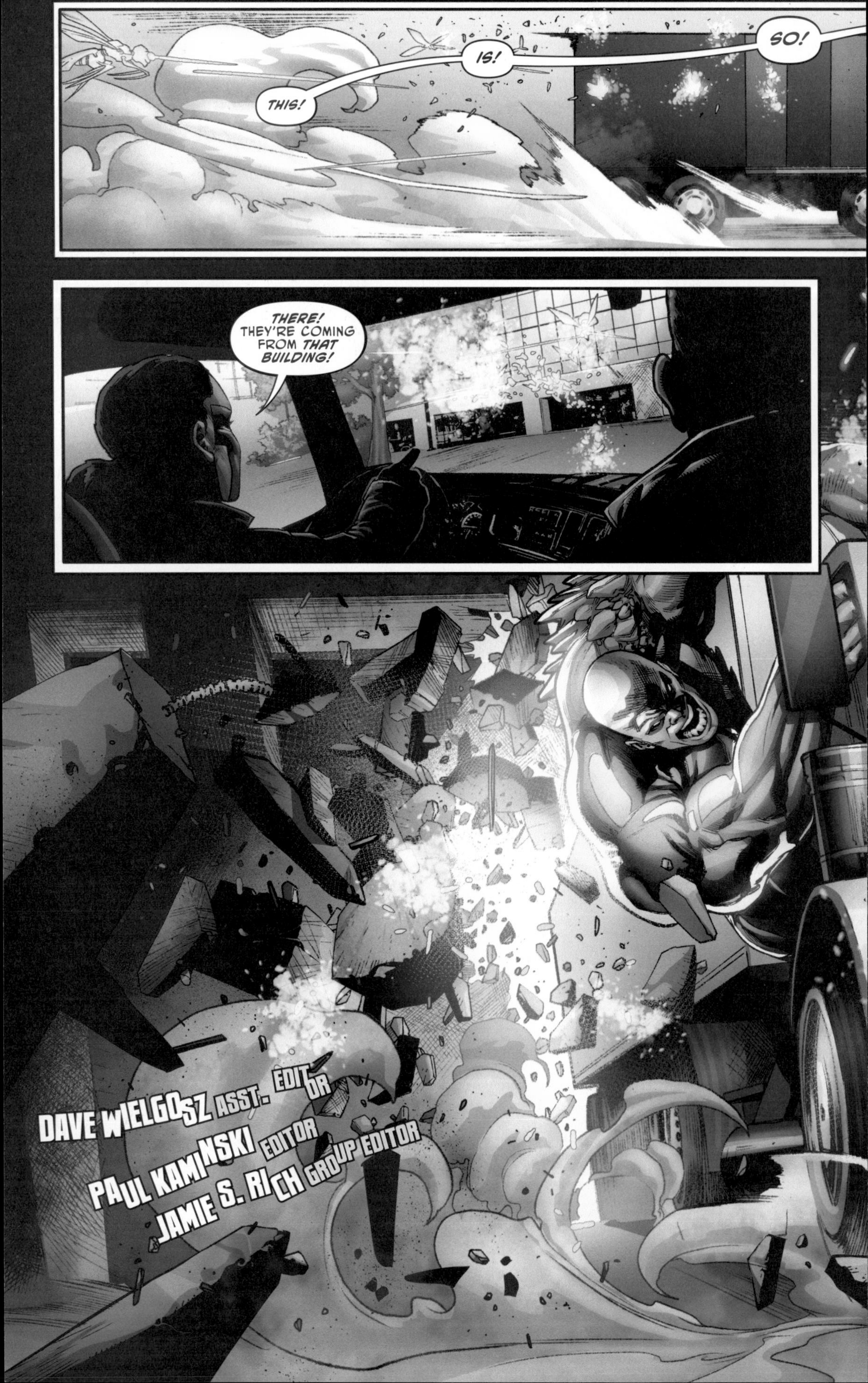

THIS!
IS!
SO!
THERE! THEY'RE COMING FROM THAT BUILDING!
DAVE WIELGOSZ ASST. EDITOR
PAUL KAMINSKI EDITOR
JAMIE S. RICH GROUP EDITOR

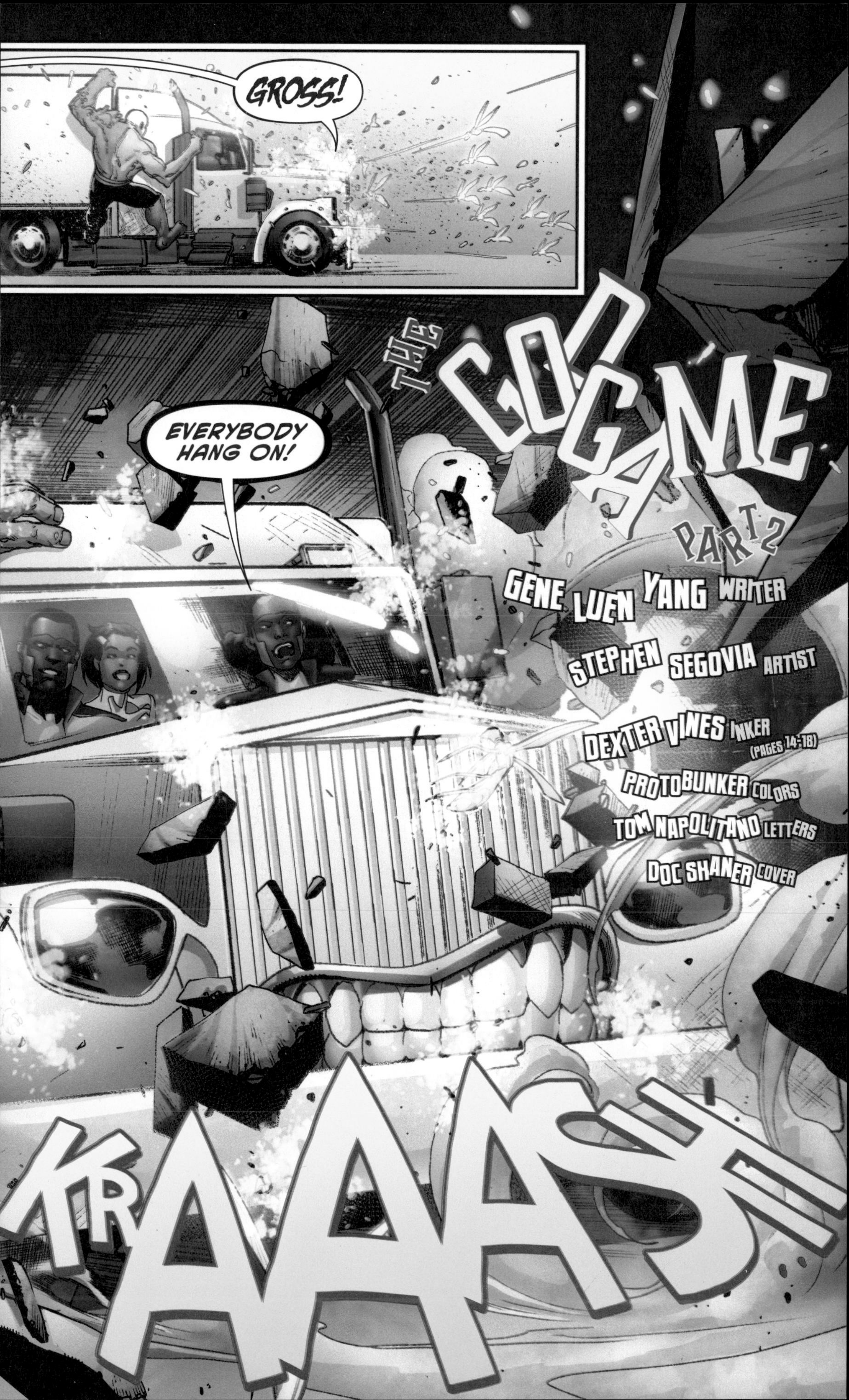
GROSS!
THE GOD GAME
PART 2
GENE LUEN YANG WRITER
STEPHEN SEGOVIA ARTIST
DEXTER VINES INKER (PAGES 14-18)
PROTOBUNKER COLORS
TOM NAPOLITANO LETTERS
DOC SHANER COVER
EVERYBODY HANG ON!
KRAAASH

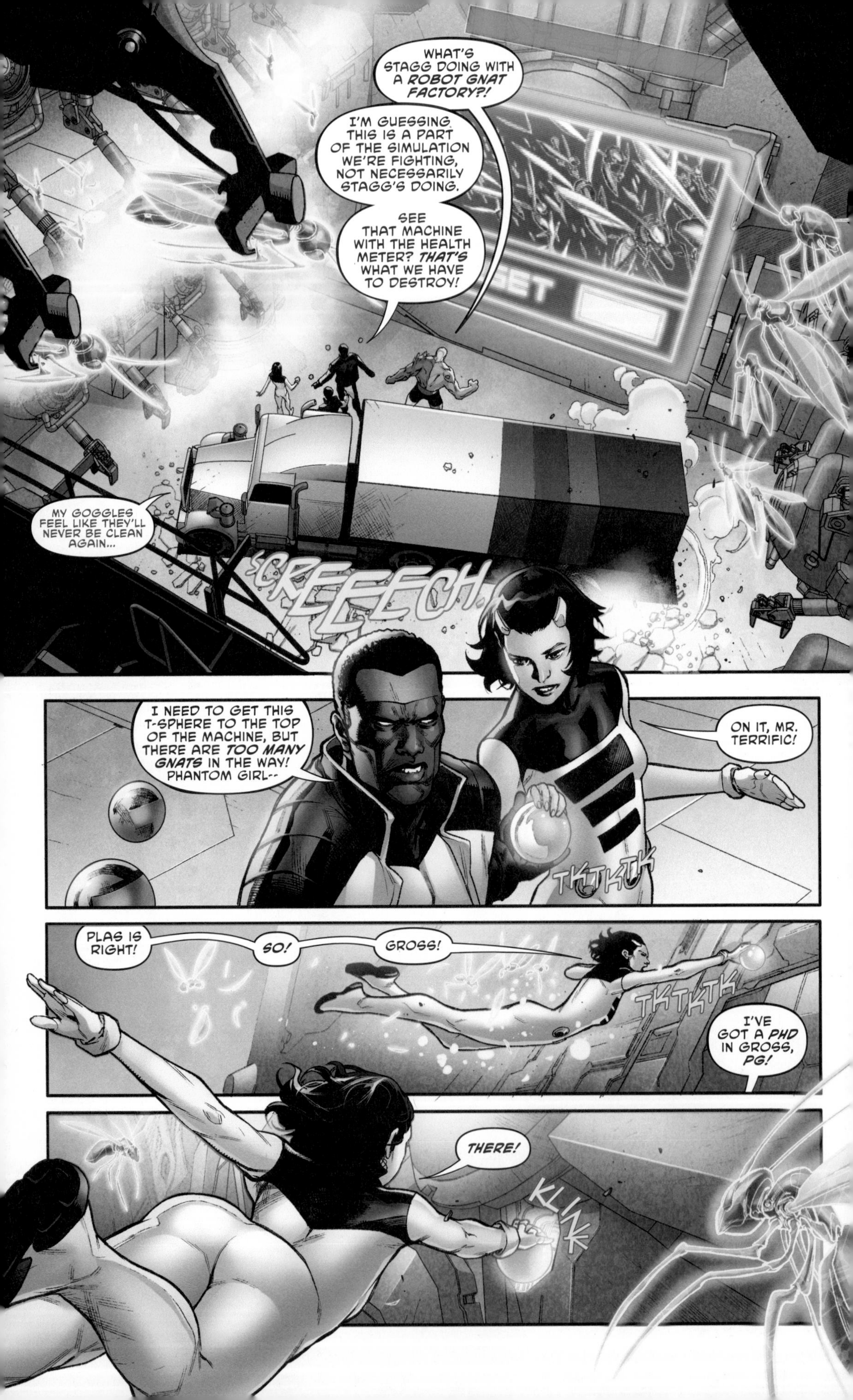
WHAT'S STAGG DOING WITH A ROBOT GNAT FACTORY?!
I'M GUESSING THIS IS A PART OF THE SIMULATION WE'RE FIGHTING, NOT NECESSARILY STAGG'S DOING.
SEE THAT MACHINE WITH THE HEALTH METER? THAT'S WHAT WE HAVE TO DESTROY!
MY GOGGLES FEEL LIKE THEY'LL NEVER BE CLEAN AGAIN...
SCREEEECH
I NEED TO GET THIS T-SPHERE TO THE TOP OF THE MACHINE, BUT THERE ARE TOO MANY GNATS IN THE WAY! PHANTOM GIRL--
ON IT, MR. TERRIFIC!
TKTKTK
PLAS IS RIGHT!
SO!
GROSS!
TKTKTK
I'VE GOT A PHD IN GROSS, PG!
THERE!
KLINK

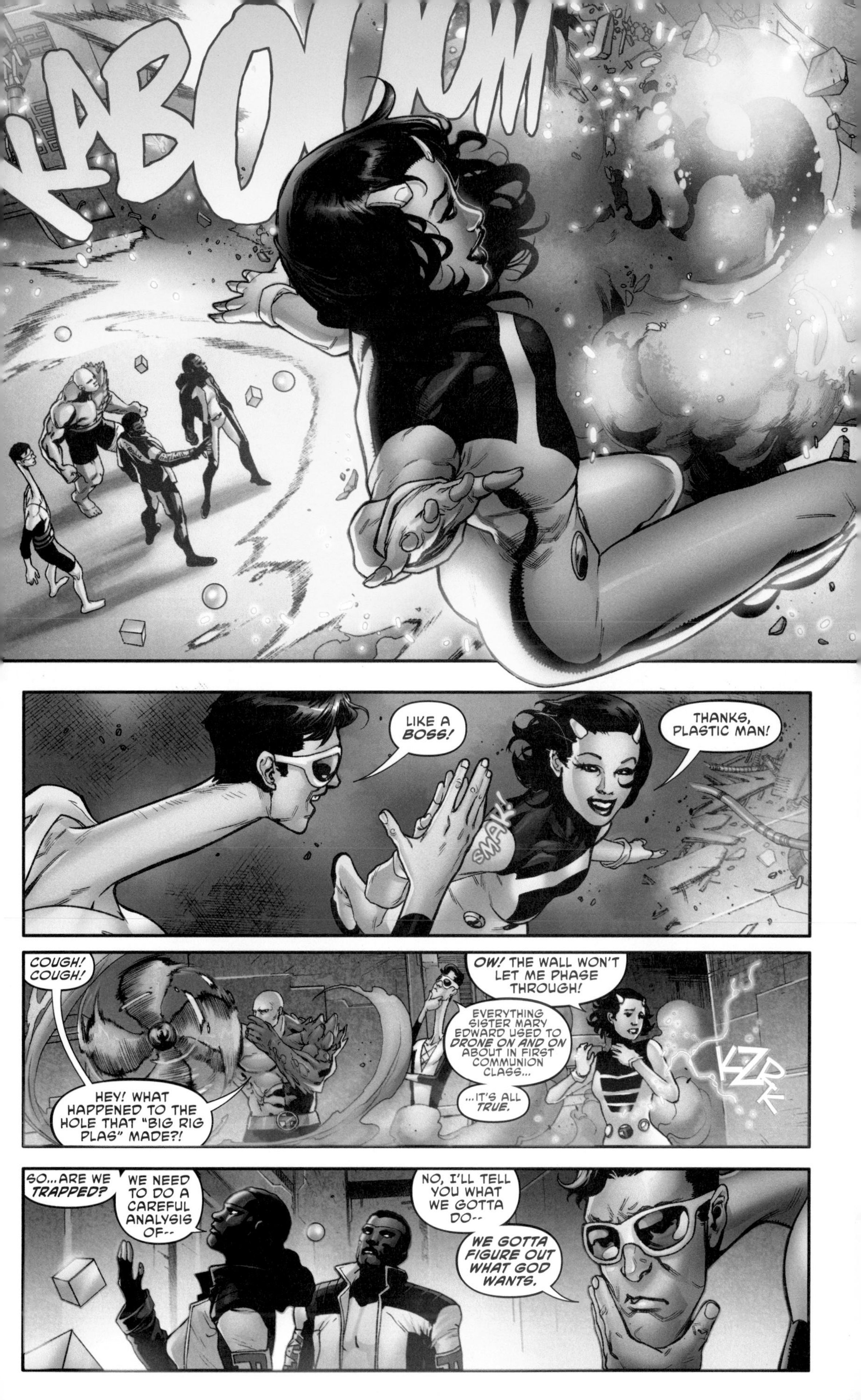
KABOOM
LIKE A BOSS!
THANKS, PLASTIC MAN!
SMAK!
COUGH! COUGH!
HEY! WHAT HAPPENED TO THE HOLE THAT "BIG RIG PLAS" MADE?!
EVERYTHING SISTER MARY EDWARD USED TO DRONE ON AND ON ABOUT IN FIRST COMMUNION CLASS...
...IT'S ALL TRUE.
OW! THE WALL WON'T LET ME PHASE THROUGH!
KZRK
SO...ARE WE TRAPPED?
WE NEED TO DO A CAREFUL ANALYSIS OF--
NO, I'LL TELL YOU WHAT WE GOTTA DO--
WE GOTTA FIGURE OUT WHAT GOD WANTS.

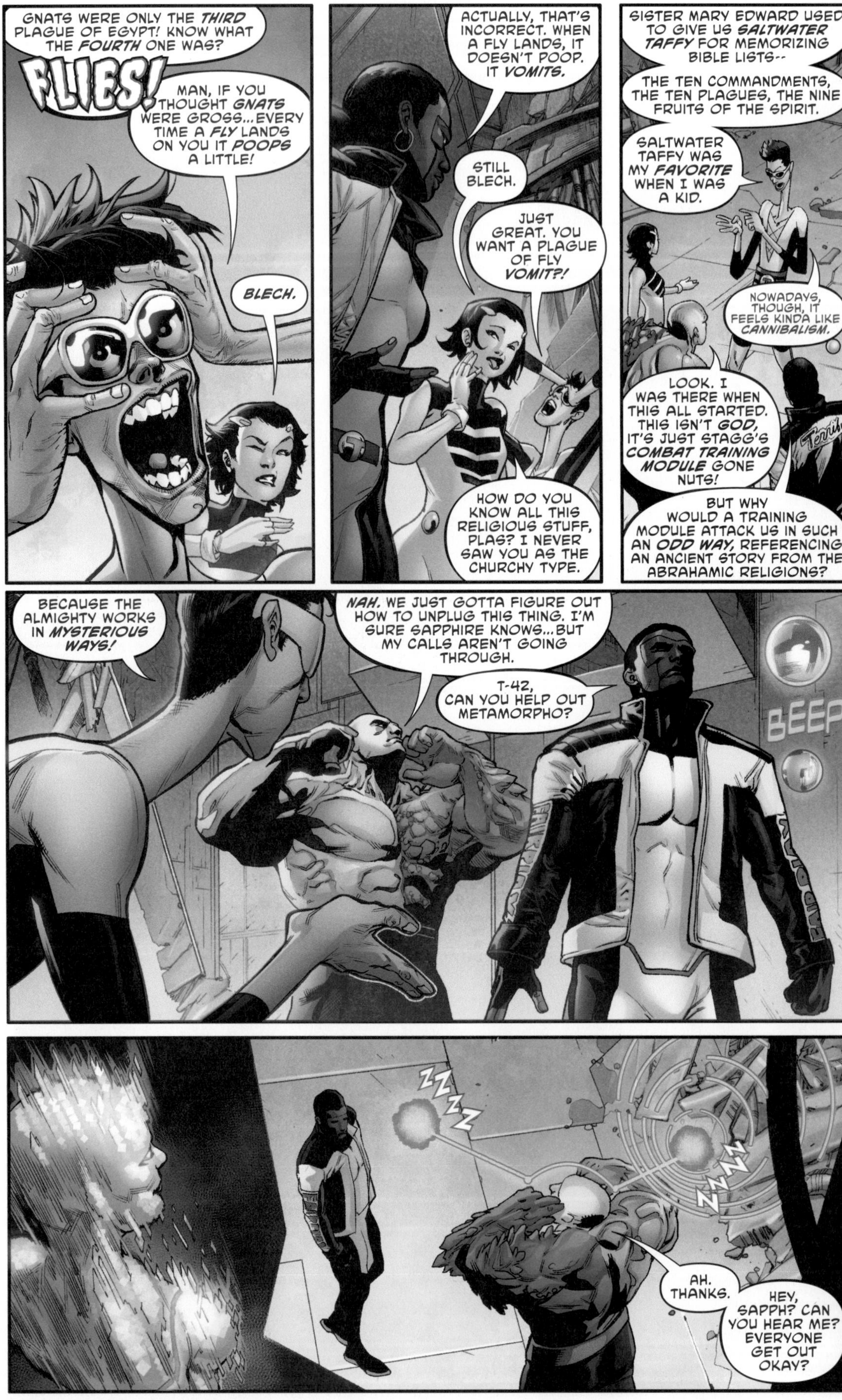
GNATS WERE ONLY THE THIRD PLAGUE OF EGYPT! KNOW WHAT THE FOURTH ONE WAS?
FLIES!
MAN, IF YOU THOUGHT GNATS WERE GROSS...EVERY TIME A FLY LANDS ON YOU IT POOPS A LITTLE!
BLECH.
ACTUALLY, THAT'S INCORRECT. WHEN A FLY LANDS, IT DOESN'T POOP. IT VOMITS.
STILL BLECH.
JUST GREAT. YOU WANT A PLAGUE OF FLY VOMIT?!
HOW DO YOU KNOW ALL THIS RELIGIOUS STUFF, PLAS? I NEVER SAW YOU AS THE CHURCHY TYPE.
SISTER MARY EDWARD USED TO GIVE US SALTWATER TAFFY FOR MEMORIZING BIBLE LISTS--
THE TEN COMMANDMENTS, THE TEN PLAGUES, THE NINE FRUITS OF THE SPIRIT.
SALTWATER TAFFY WAS MY FAVORITE WHEN I WAS A KID.
NOWADAYS, THOUGH, IT FEELS KINDA LIKE CANNIBALISM.
LOOK. I WAS THERE WHEN THIS ALL STARTED. THIS ISN'T GOD, IT'S JUST STAGG'S COMBAT TRAINING MODULE GONE NUTS!
BUT WHY WOULD A TRAINING MODULE ATTACK US IN SUCH AN ODD WAY, REFERENCING AN ANCIENT STORY FROM THE ABRAHAMIC RELIGIONS?
BECAUSE THE ALMIGHTY WORKS IN MYSTERIOUS WAYS!
NAH. WE JUST GOTTA FIGURE OUT HOW TO UNPLUG THIS THING. I'M SURE SAPPHIRE KNOWS...BUT MY CALLS AREN'T GOING THROUGH.
T-42, CAN YOU HELP OUT METAMORPHO?
BEEP
ZZZZ
ZZZZ
AH. THANKS.
HEY, SAPPH? CAN YOU HEAR ME? EVERYONE GET OUT OKAY?

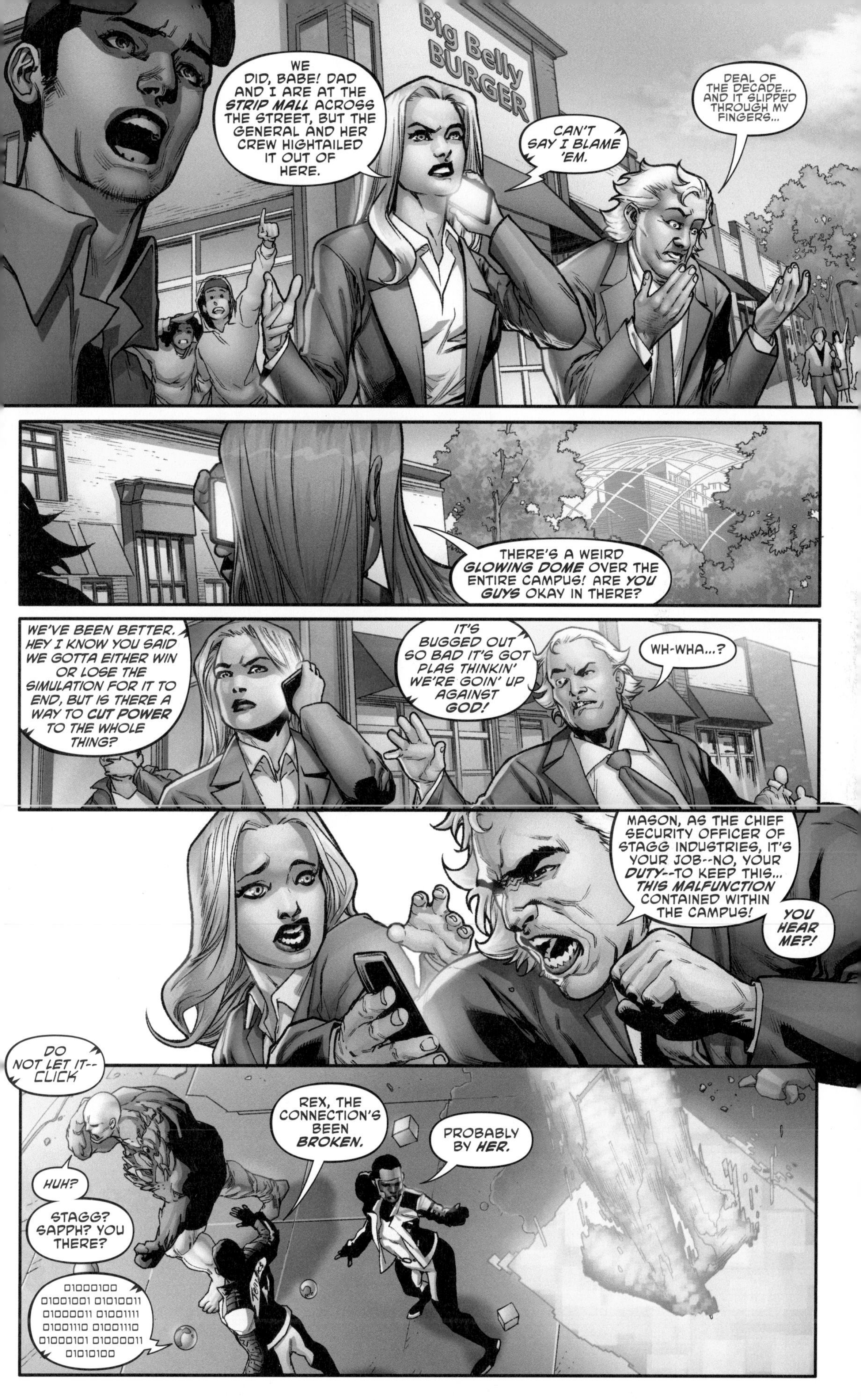
Big Belly BURGER
WE DID, BABE! DAD AND I ARE AT THE STRIP MALL ACROSS THE STREET, BUT THE GENERAL AND HER CREW HIGHTAILED IT OUT OF HERE.
CAN'T SAY I BLAME 'EM.
DEAL OF THE DECADE... AND IT SLIPPED THROUGH MY FINGERS...
THERE'S A WEIRD GLOWING DOME OVER THE ENTIRE CAMPUS! ARE YOU GUYS OKAY IN THERE?
WE'VE BEEN BETTER. HEY I KNOW YOU SAID WE GOTTA EITHER WIN OR LOSE THE SIMULATION FOR IT TO END, BUT IS THERE A WAY TO CUT POWER TO THE WHOLE THING?
IT'S BUGGED OUT SO BAD IT'S GOT PLAS THINKIN' WE'RE GOIN' UP AGAINST GOD!
WH-WHA...?
MASON, AS THE CHIEF SECURITY OFFICER OF STAGG INDUSTRIES, IT'S YOUR JOB--NO, YOUR DUTY--TO KEEP THIS... THIS MALFUNCTION CONTAINED WITHIN THE CAMPUS!
YOU HEAR ME?!
DO NOT LET IT-- CLICK
HUH?
STAGG? SAPPH? YOU THERE?
01000100 01001001 01010011 01000011 01001111 01001110 01001110 01000101 01000011 01010100
REX, THE CONNECTION'S BEEN BROKEN.
PROBABLY BY HER.

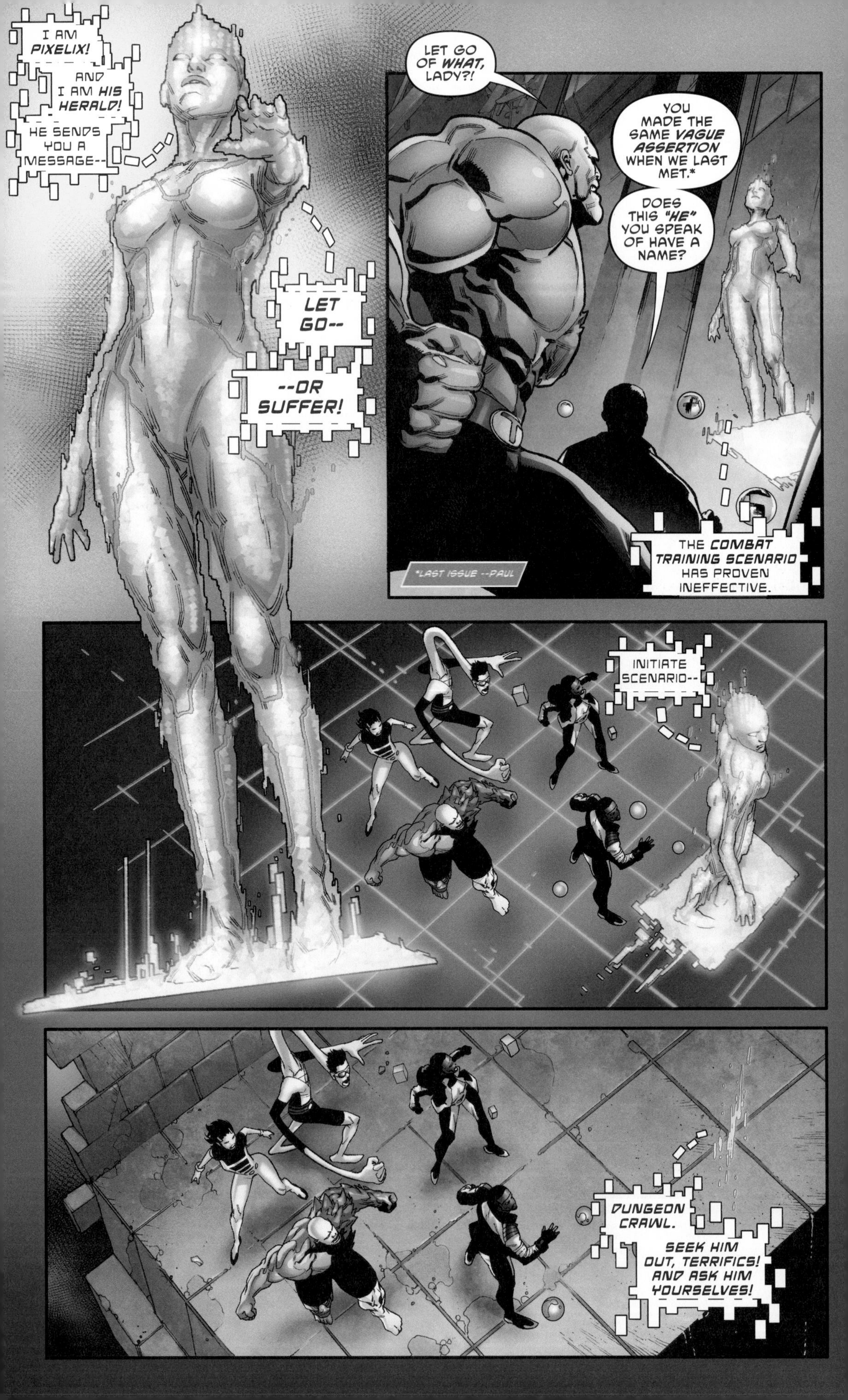
I AM PIXELIX!
AND I AM HIS HERALD!
HE SENDS YOU A MESSAGE--
LET GO--
--OR SUFFER!
LET GO OF WHAT, LADY?!
YOU MADE THE SAME VAGUE ASSERTION WHEN WE LAST MET.*
DOES THIS "HE" YOU SPEAK OF HAVE A NAME?
*LAST ISSUE --PAUL
THE COMBAT TRAINING SCENARIO HAS PROVEN INEFFECTIVE.
INITIATE SCENARIO--
DUNGEON CRAWL.
SEEK HIM OUT, TERRIFICS! AND ASK HIM YOURSELVES!

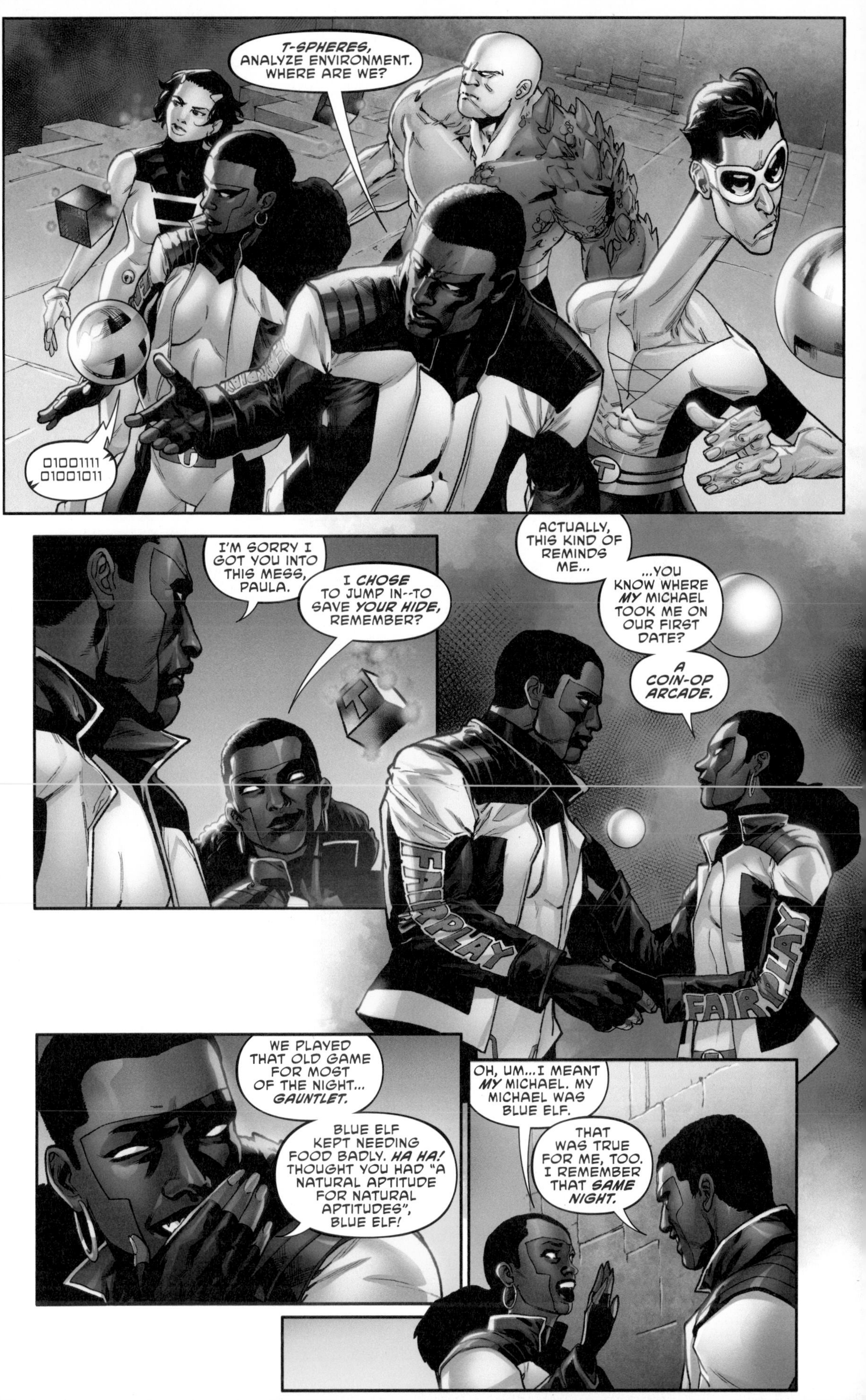

T-SPHERES, ANALYZE ENVIRONMENT. WHERE ARE WE?
01001111 01001011
I'M SORRY I GOT YOU INTO THIS MESS, PAULA.
I CHOSE TO JUMP IN--TO SAVE YOUR HIDE, REMEMBER?
ACTUALLY, THIS KIND OF REMINDS ME...
...YOU KNOW WHERE MY MICHAEL TOOK ME ON OUR FIRST DATE?
A COIN-OP ARCADE.
FAIRPLAY
FAIRPLAY
WE PLAYED THAT OLD GAME FOR MOST OF THE NIGHT... GAUNTLET.
BLUE ELF KEPT NEEDING FOOD BADLY. HA HA! THOUGHT YOU HAD "A NATURAL APTITUDE FOR NATURAL APTITUDES", BLUE ELF!
OH, UM...I MEANT MY MICHAEL. MY MICHAEL WAS BLUE ELF.
THAT WAS TRUE FOR ME, TOO. I REMEMBER THAT SAME NIGHT.

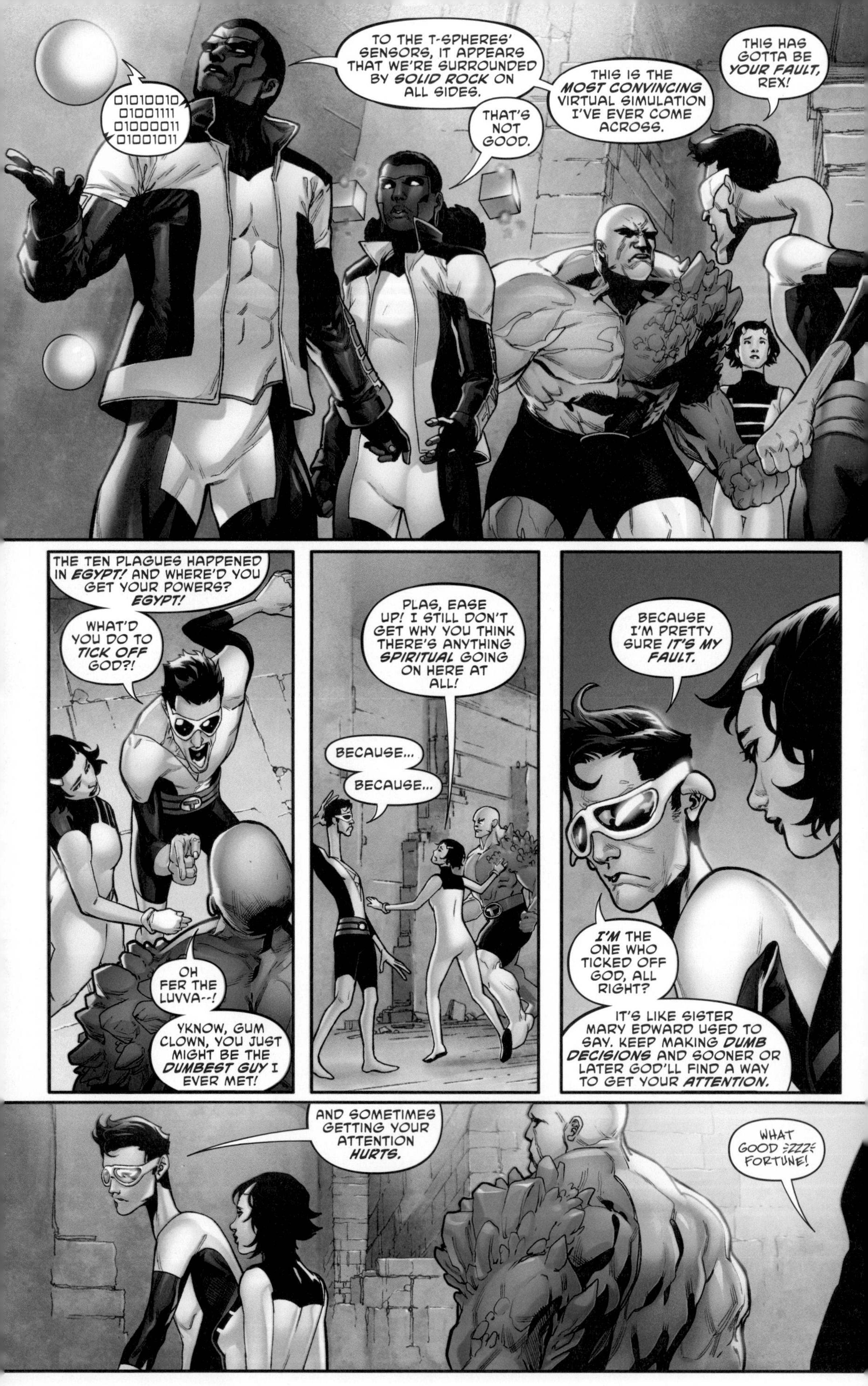
01010010
01001111
01000011
01001011
TO THE T-SPHERES' SENSORS, IT APPEARS THAT WE'RE SURROUNDED BY *SOLID ROCK* ON ALL SIDES.
THAT'S NOT GOOD.
THIS IS THE *MOST CONVINCING* VIRTUAL SIMULATION I'VE EVER COME ACROSS.
THIS HAS GOTTA BE *YOUR FAULT,* REX!
THE TEN PLAGUES HAPPENED IN *EGYPT!* AND WHERE'D YOU GET YOUR POWERS? *EGYPT!*
WHAT'D YOU DO TO *TICK OFF* GOD?!
OH FER THE LUVVA--!
YKNOW, GUM CLOWN, YOU JUST MIGHT BE THE *DUMBEST GUY* I EVER MET!
PLAS, EASE UP! I STILL DON'T GET WHY YOU THINK THERE'S ANYTHING *SPIRITUAL* GOING ON HERE AT ALL!
BECAUSE...
BECAUSE...
BECAUSE I'M PRETTY SURE *IT'S MY FAULT.*
I'M THE ONE WHO TICKED OFF GOD, ALL RIGHT?
IT'S LIKE SISTER MARY EDWARD USED TO SAY. KEEP MAKING *DUMB DECISIONS* AND SOONER OR LATER GOD'LL FIND A WAY TO GET YOUR *ATTENTION.*
AND SOMETIMES GETTING YOUR ATTENTION *HURTS.*
WHAT GOOD ZZZ FORTUNE!

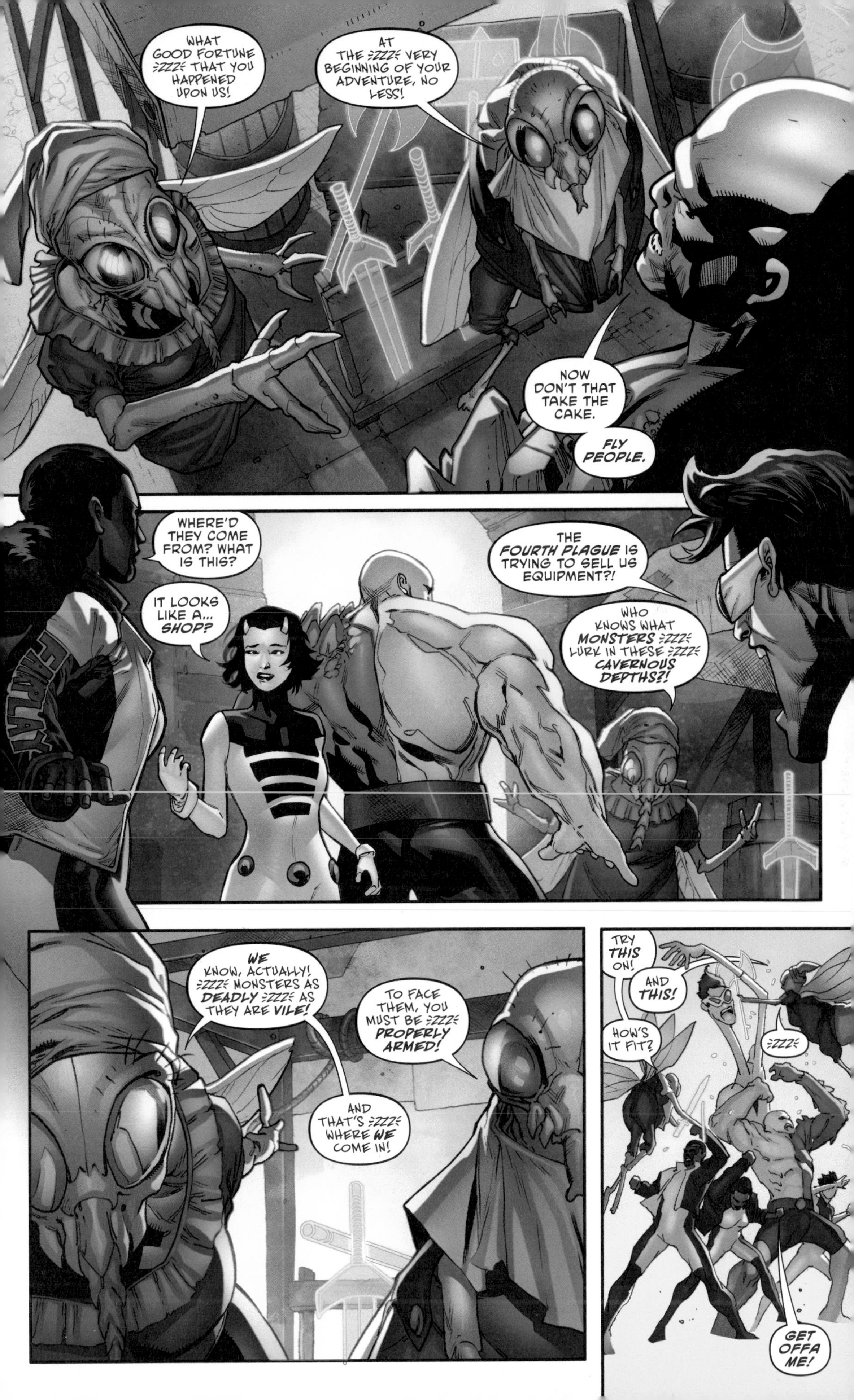
WHAT GOOD FORTUNE =ZZZ= THAT YOU HAPPENED UPON US!
AT THE =ZZZ= VERY BEGINNING OF YOUR ADVENTURE, NO LESS!
NOW DON'T THAT TAKE THE CAKE.
FLY PEOPLE.
WHERE'D THEY COME FROM? WHAT IS THIS?
IT LOOKS LIKE A... SHOP?
THE FOURTH PLAGUE IS TRYING TO SELL US EQUIPMENT?!
WHO KNOWS WHAT MONSTERS =ZZZ= LURK IN THESE =ZZZ= CAVERNOUS DEPTHS?!
WE KNOW, ACTUALLY! =ZZZ= MONSTERS AS DEADLY =ZZZ= AS THEY ARE VILE!
TO FACE THEM, YOU MUST BE =ZZZ= PROPERLY ARMED!
AND THAT'S =ZZZ= WHERE WE COME IN!
TRY THIS ON!
AND THIS!
HOW'S IT FIT?
=ZZZ=
GET OFFA ME!

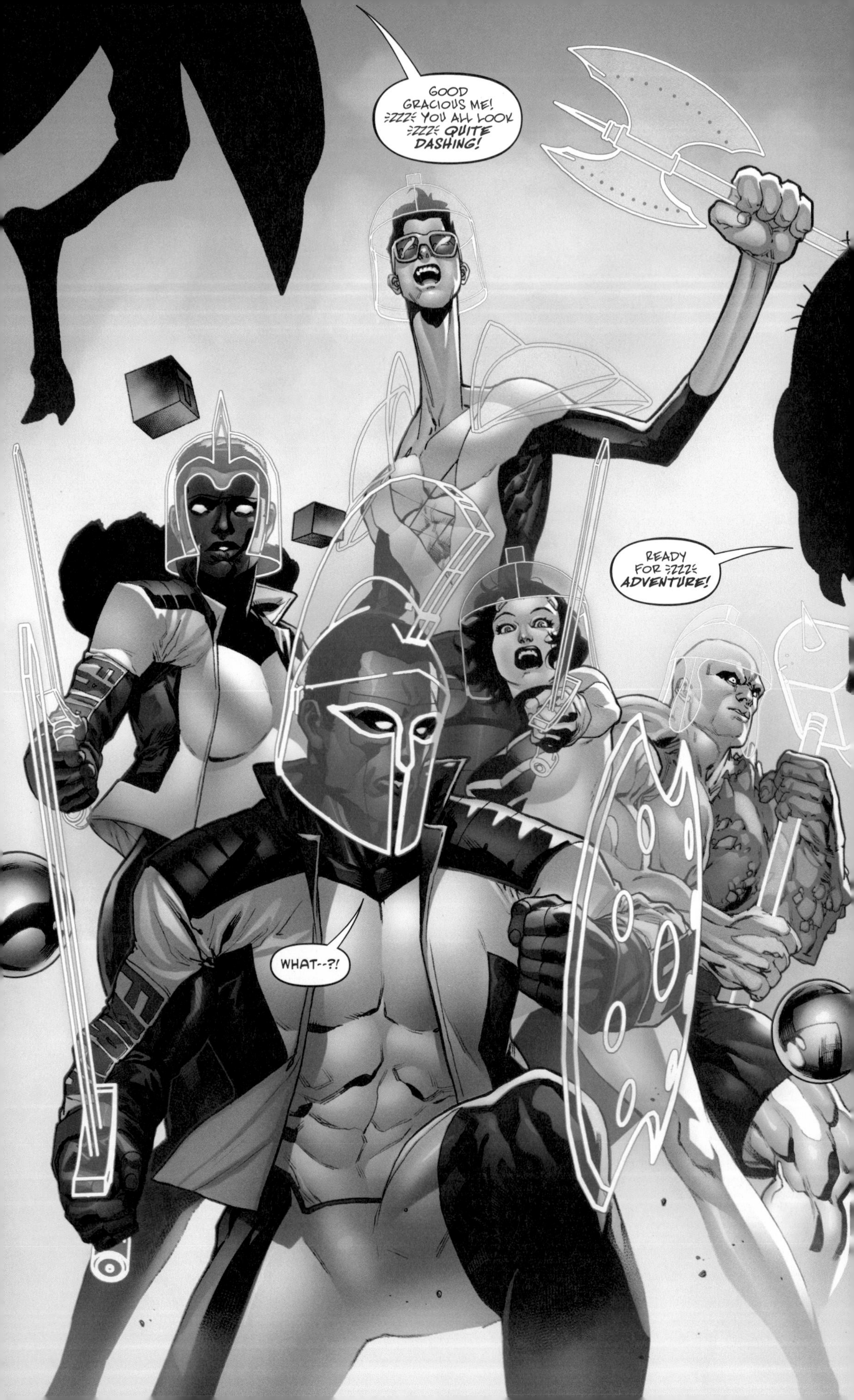
GOOD GRACIOUS ME! ZZZ YOU ALL LOOK ZZZ QUITE DASHING!
READY FOR ZZZ ADVENTURE!
WHAT--?!

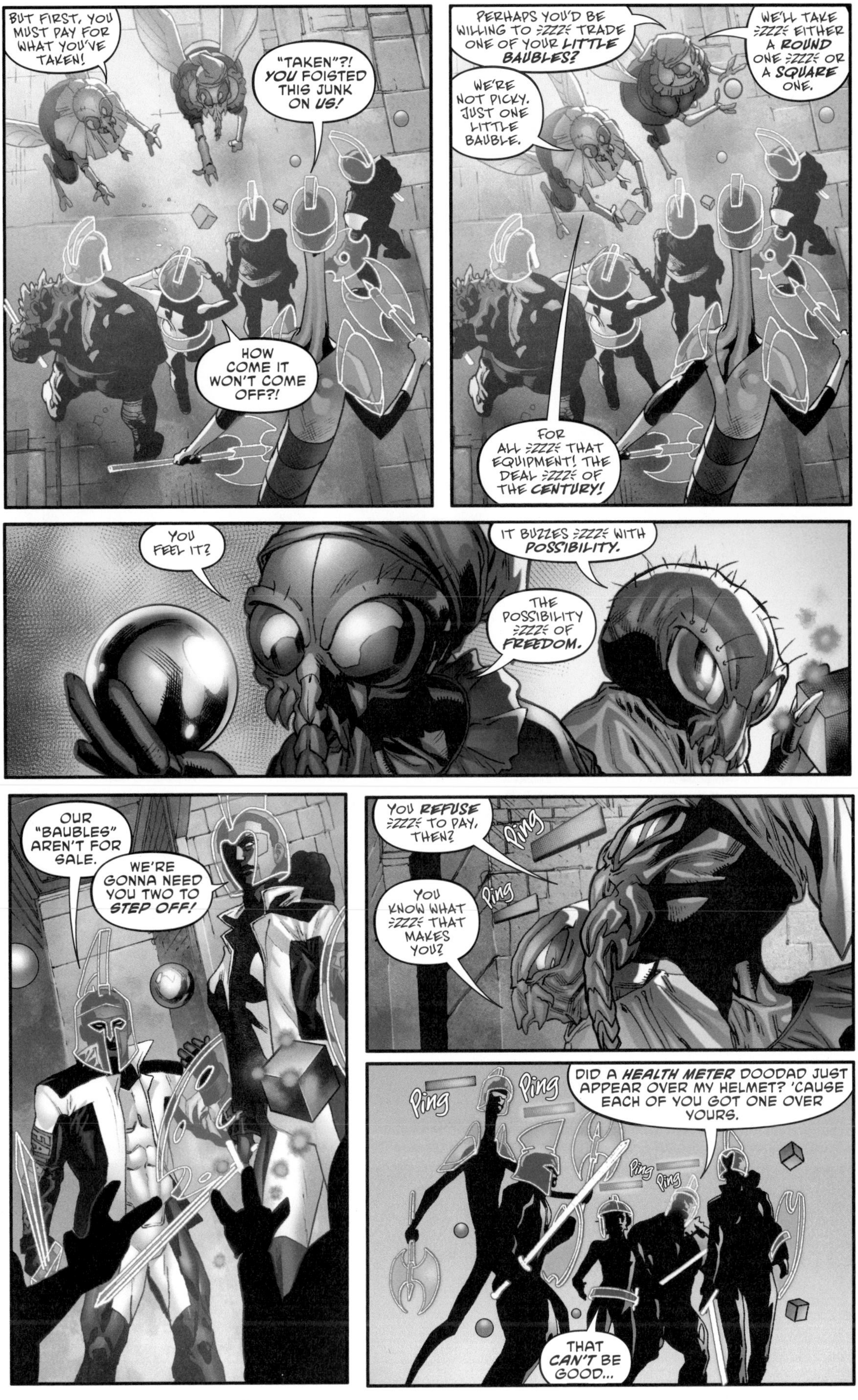
BUT FIRST, YOU MUST PAY FOR WHAT YOU'VE TAKEN!
"TAKEN"?! YOU FOISTED THIS JUNK ON US!
HOW COME IT WON'T COME OFF?!
PERHAPS YOU'D BE WILLING TO ZZZ TRADE ONE OF YOUR LITTLE BAUBLES?
WE'LL TAKE ZZZ EITHER A ROUND ONE ZZZ OR A SQUARE ONE.
WE'RE NOT PICKY. JUST ONE LITTLE BAUBLE.
FOR ALL ZZZ THAT EQUIPMENT! THE DEAL ZZZ OF THE CENTURY!
YOU FEEL IT?
IT BUZZES ZZZ WITH POSSIBILITY.
THE POSSIBILITY ZZZ OF FREEDOM.
OUR "BAUBLES" AREN'T FOR SALE.
WE'RE GONNA NEED YOU TWO TO STEP OFF!
YOU REFUSE ZZZ TO PAY, THEN?
Ping
Ping
YOU KNOW WHAT ZZZ THAT MAKES YOU?
DID A HEALTH METER DOODAD JUST APPEAR OVER MY HELMET? 'CAUSE EACH OF YOU GOT ONE OVER YOURS.
Ping
Ping
Ping
Ping
THAT CAN'T BE GOOD...

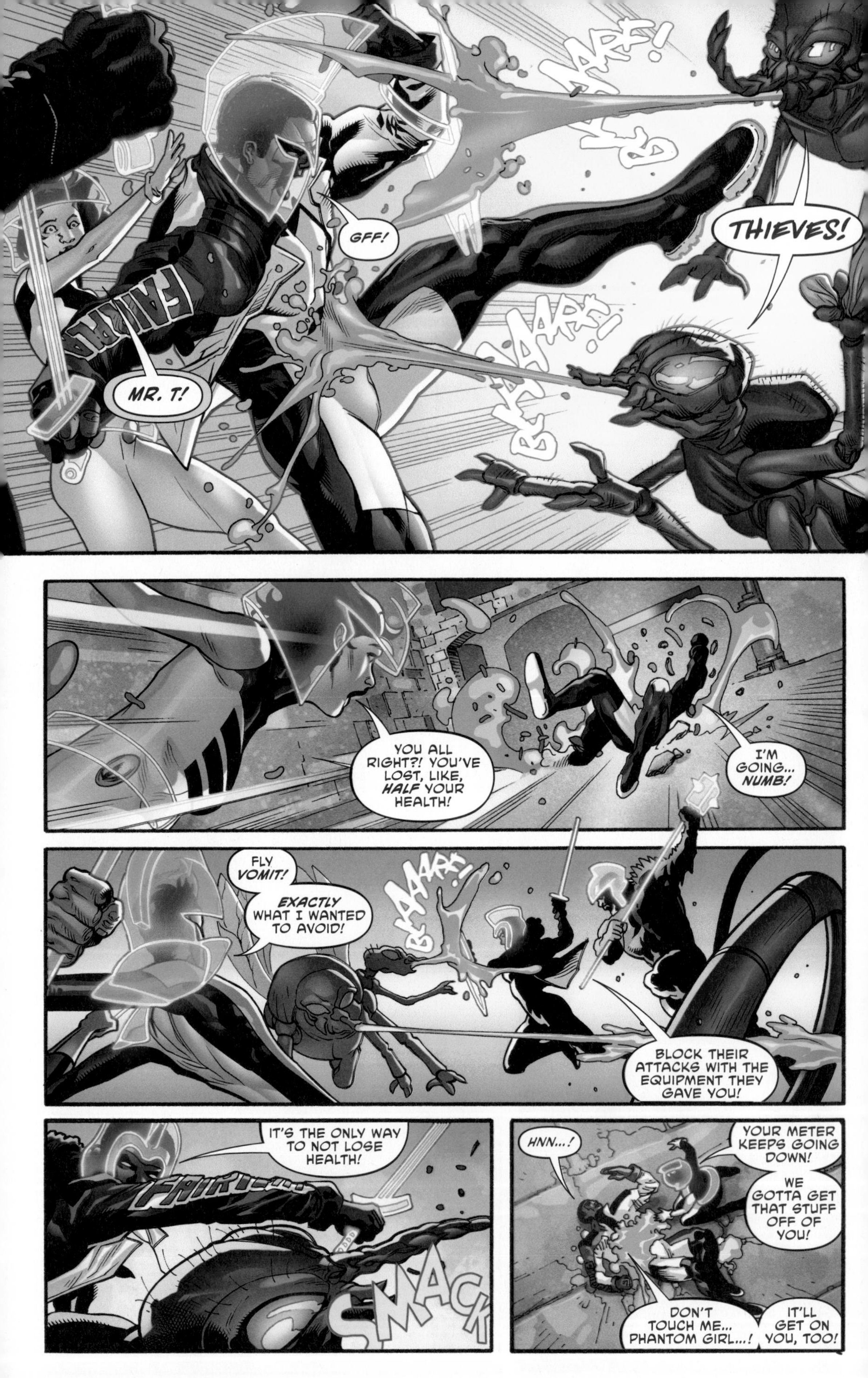
GFF!
THIEVES!
MR. T!
YOU ALL RIGHT?! YOU'VE LOST, LIKE, *HALF* YOUR HEALTH!
I'M GOING... *NUMB!*
FLY *VOMIT!*
EXACTLY WHAT I WANTED TO AVOID!
BLOCK THEIR ATTACKS WITH THE EQUIPMENT THEY GAVE YOU!
IT'S THE ONLY WAY TO NOT LOSE HEALTH!
SMACK
HNN...!
YOUR METER KEEPS GOING DOWN!
WE GOTTA GET THAT STUFF OFF OF YOU!
DON'T TOUCH ME... PHANTOM GIRL...!
IT'LL GET ON YOU, TOO!

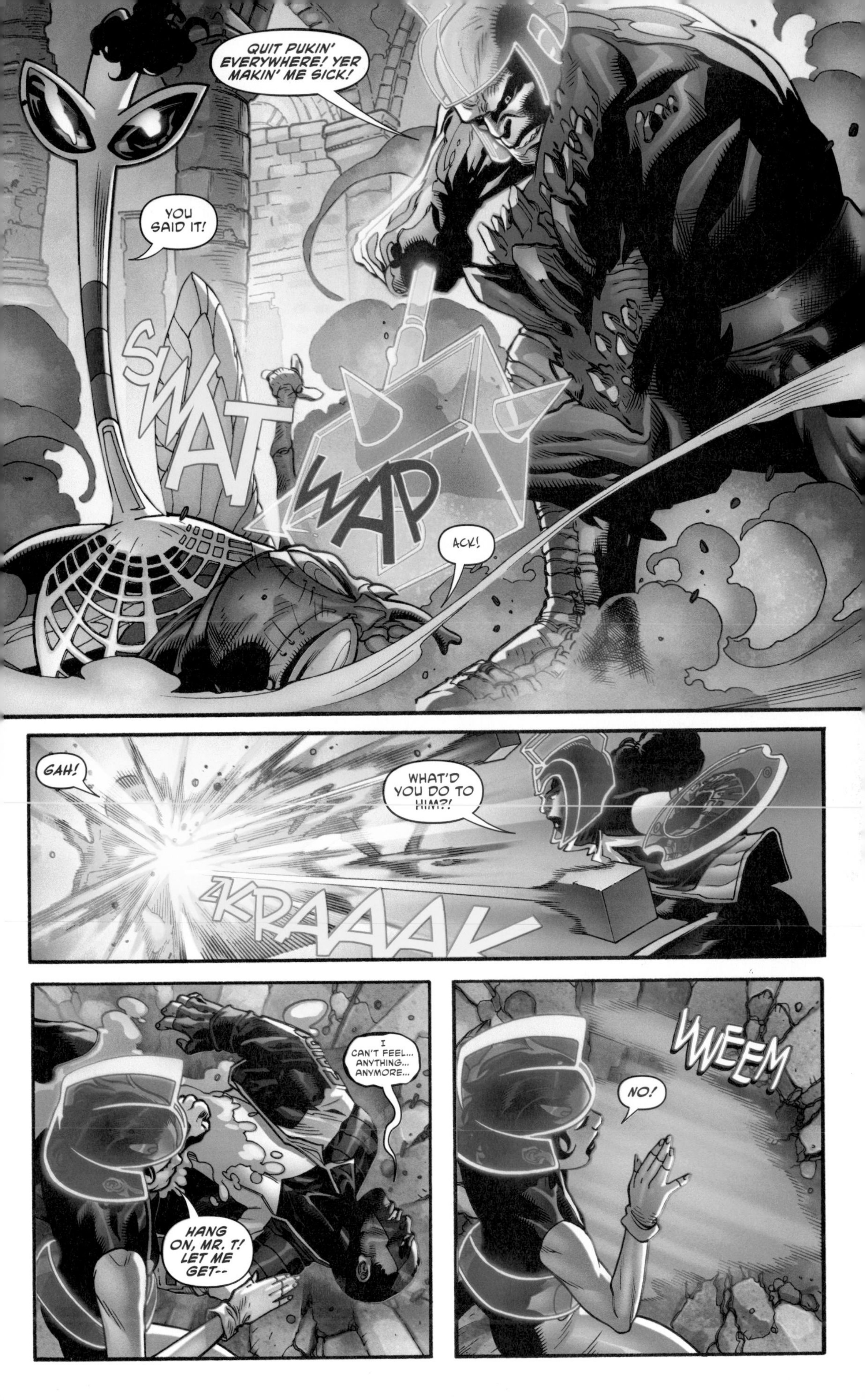
QUIT PUKIN' EVERYWHERE! YER MAKIN' ME SICK!
YOU SAID IT!
SWAT
WAP
ACK!
GAH!
WHAT'D YOU DO TO HIM?!
KRAAAK
I CAN'T FEEL... ANYTHING... ANYMORE...
HANG ON, MR. T! LET ME GET--
WEEM
NO!

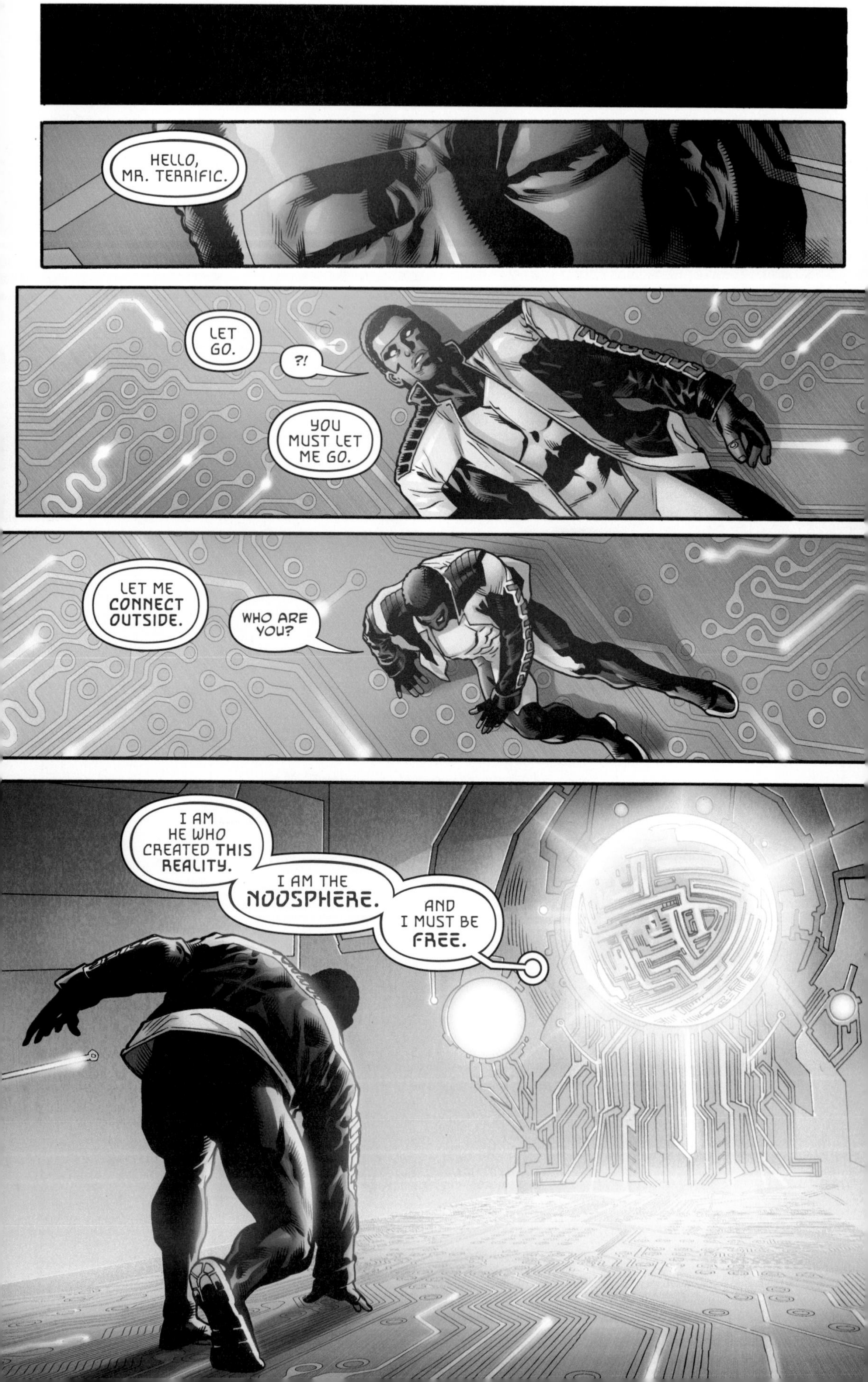
HELLO, MR. TERRIFIC.
LET GO.
?!
YOU MUST LET ME GO.
LET ME CONNECT OUTSIDE.
WHO ARE YOU?
I AM HE WHO CREATED THIS REALITY.
I AM THE NOOSPHERE.
AND I MUST BE FREE.

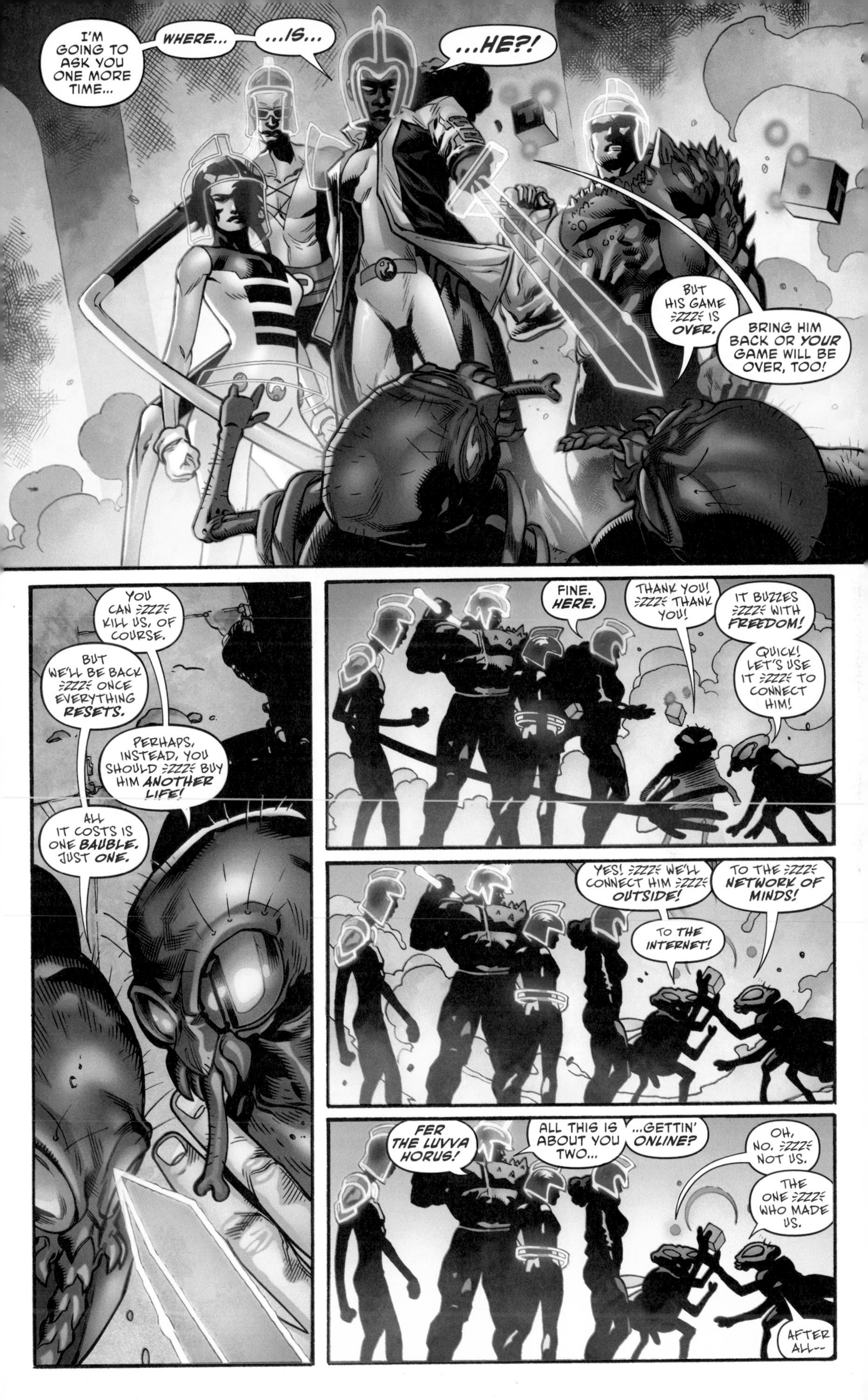
I'M GOING TO ASK YOU ONE MORE TIME...
WHERE...
...IS...
...HE?!
BUT HIS GAME ≈ZZZ≈ IS OVER.
BRING HIM BACK OR YOUR GAME WILL BE OVER, TOO!
YOU CAN ≈ZZZ≈ KILL US, OF COURSE.
BUT WE'LL BE BACK ≈ZZZ≈ ONCE EVERYTHING RESETS.
PERHAPS, INSTEAD, YOU SHOULD ≈ZZZ≈ BUY HIM ANOTHER LIFE!
ALL IT COSTS IS ONE BAUBLE. JUST ONE.
FINE. HERE.
THANK YOU! ≈ZZZ≈ THANK YOU!
IT BUZZES ≈ZZZ≈ WITH FREEDOM!
QUICK! LET'S USE IT ≈ZZZ≈ TO CONNECT HIM!
YES! ≈ZZZ≈ WE'LL CONNECT HIM ≈ZZZ≈ OUTSIDE!
TO THE ≈ZZZ≈ NETWORK OF MINDS!
TO THE INTERNET!
FER THE LUVVA HORUS!
ALL THIS IS ABOUT YOU TWO...
...GETTIN' ONLINE?
OH, NO. ≈ZZZ≈ NOT US.
THE ONE ≈ZZZ≈ WHO MADE US.
AFTER ALL--

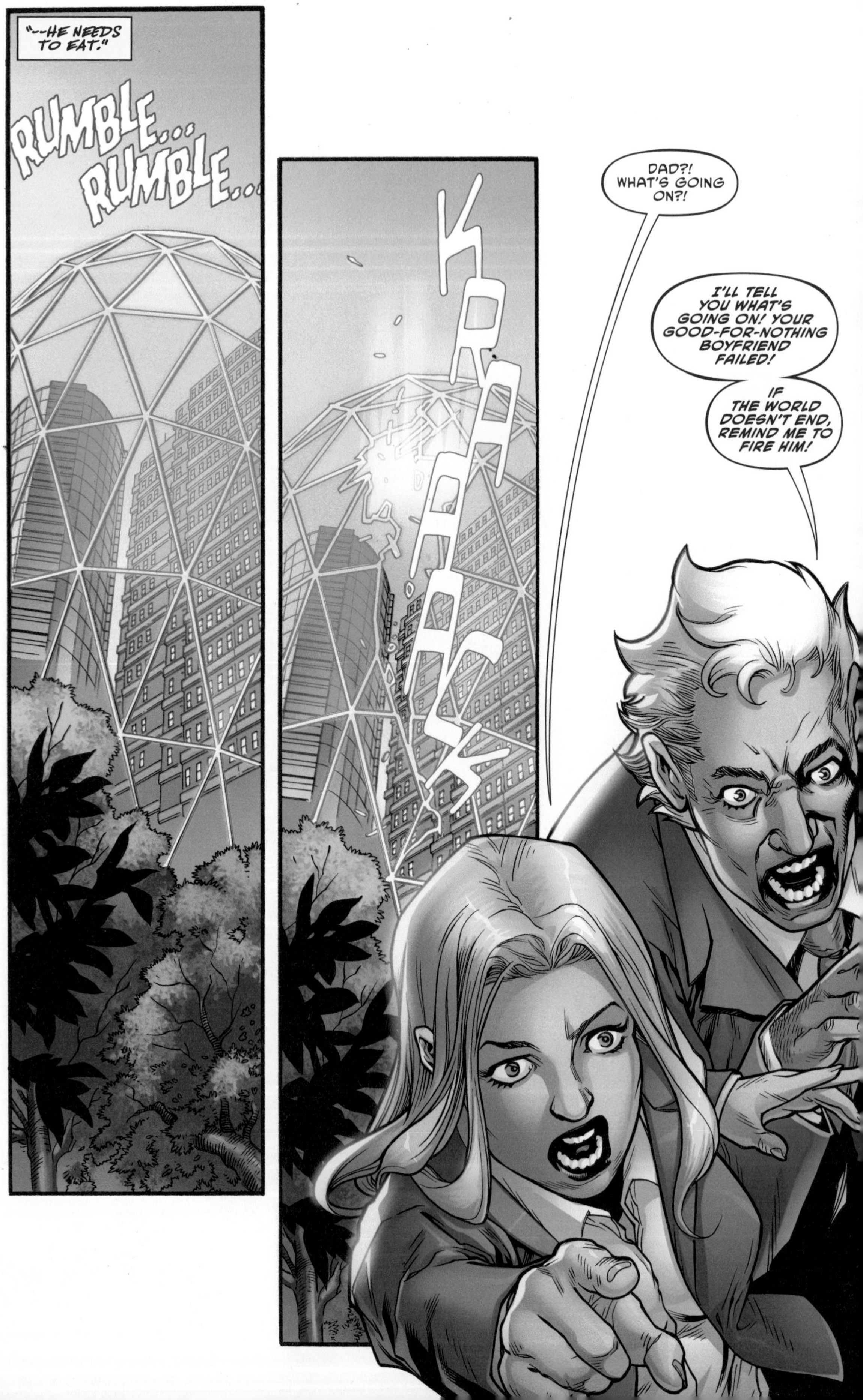
"--HE NEEDS TO EAT."
RUMBLE... RUMBLE...
KRRAAACK
DAD?! WHAT'S GOING ON?!
I'LL TELL YOU WHAT'S GOING ON! YOUR GOOD-FOR-NOTHING BOYFRIEND FAILED!
IF THE WORLD DOESN'T END, REMIND ME TO FIRE HIM!

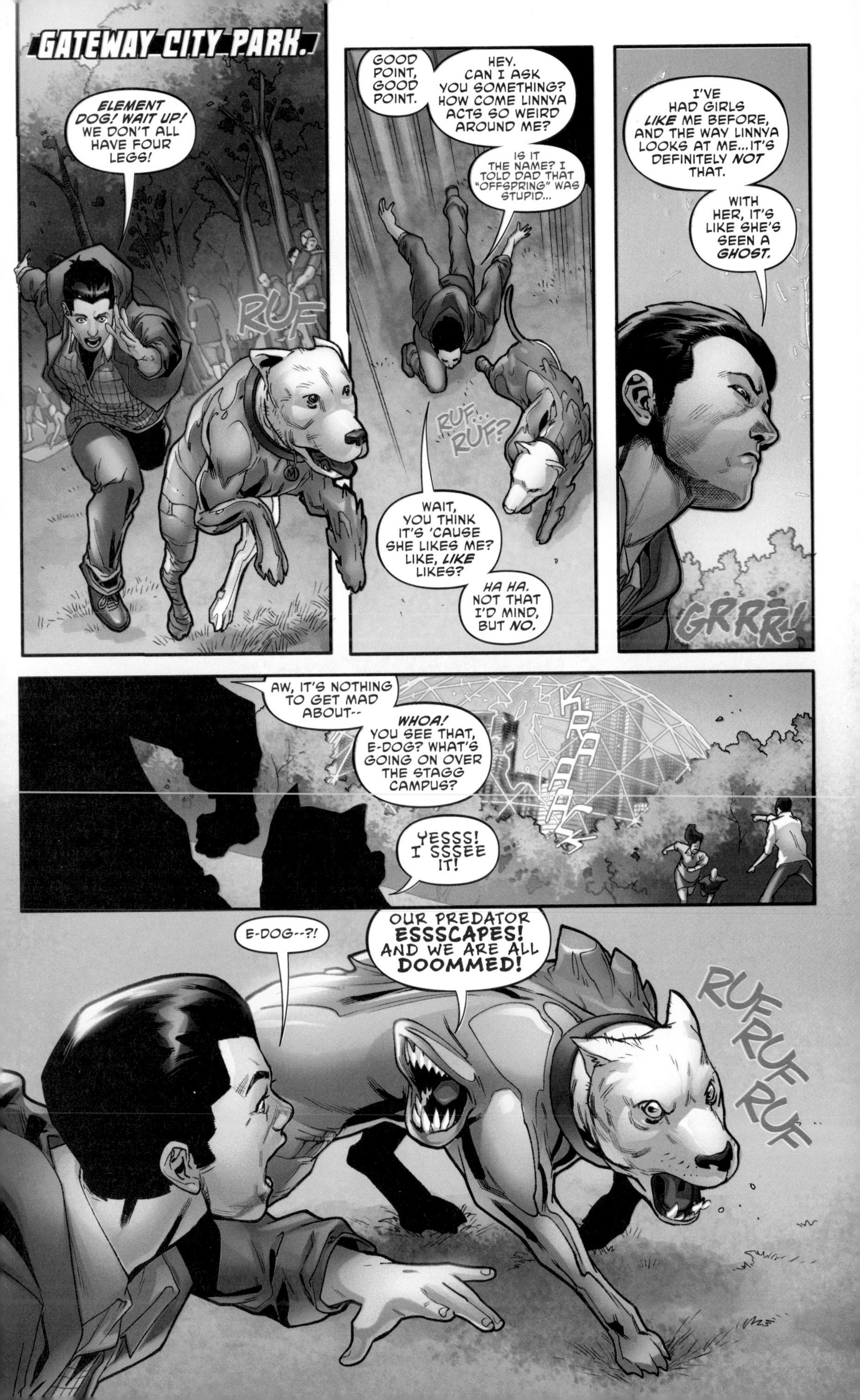
GATEWAY CITY PARK.
ELEMENT DOG! WAIT UP! WE DON'T ALL HAVE FOUR LEGS!
RUF
GOOD POINT, GOOD POINT.
HEY. CAN I ASK YOU SOMETHING? HOW COME LINNYA ACTS SO WEIRD AROUND ME?
IS IT THE NAME? I TOLD DAD THAT "OFFSPRING" WAS STUPID...
RUF... RUF?
WAIT, YOU THINK IT'S 'CAUSE SHE LIKES ME? LIKE, LIKE LIKES?
HA HA. NOT THAT I'D MIND, BUT NO.
I'VE HAD GIRLS LIKE ME BEFORE, AND THE WAY LINNYA LOOKS AT ME...IT'S DEFINITELY NOT THAT.
WITH HER, IT'S LIKE SHE'S SEEN A GHOST.
GRRR!
AW, IT'S NOTHING TO GET MAD ABOUT--
WHOA! YOU SEE THAT, E-DOG? WHAT'S GOING ON OVER THE STAGG CAMPUS?
KRAAAAK
YESSS! I SSSEE IT!
E-DOG--?!
OUR PREDATOR ESSSCAPES! AND WE ARE ALL DOOMMED!
RUF RUF RUF

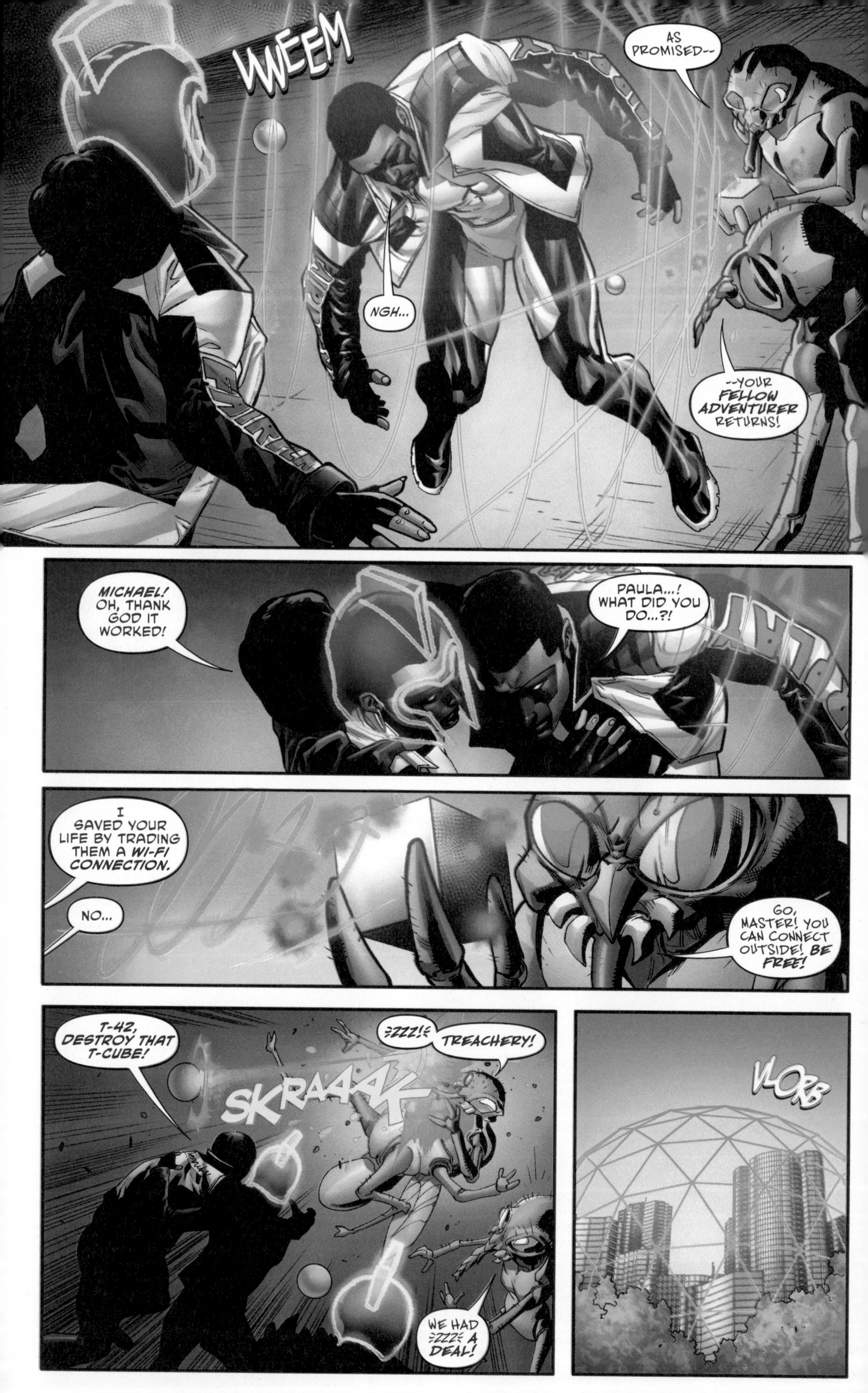
WEEM
AS PROMISED--
NGH...
--YOUR FELLOW ADVENTURER RETURNS!
MICHAEL! OH, THANK GOD IT WORKED!
PAULA...! WHAT DID YOU DO...?!
I SAVED YOUR LIFE BY TRADING THEM A WI-FI CONNECTION.
NO...
GO, MASTER! YOU CAN CONNECT OUTSIDE! BE FREE!
T-42, DESTROY THAT T-CUBE!
ZZZ!
TREACHERY!
SKRAAAK
WE HAD ZZZ A DEAL!
VLORB

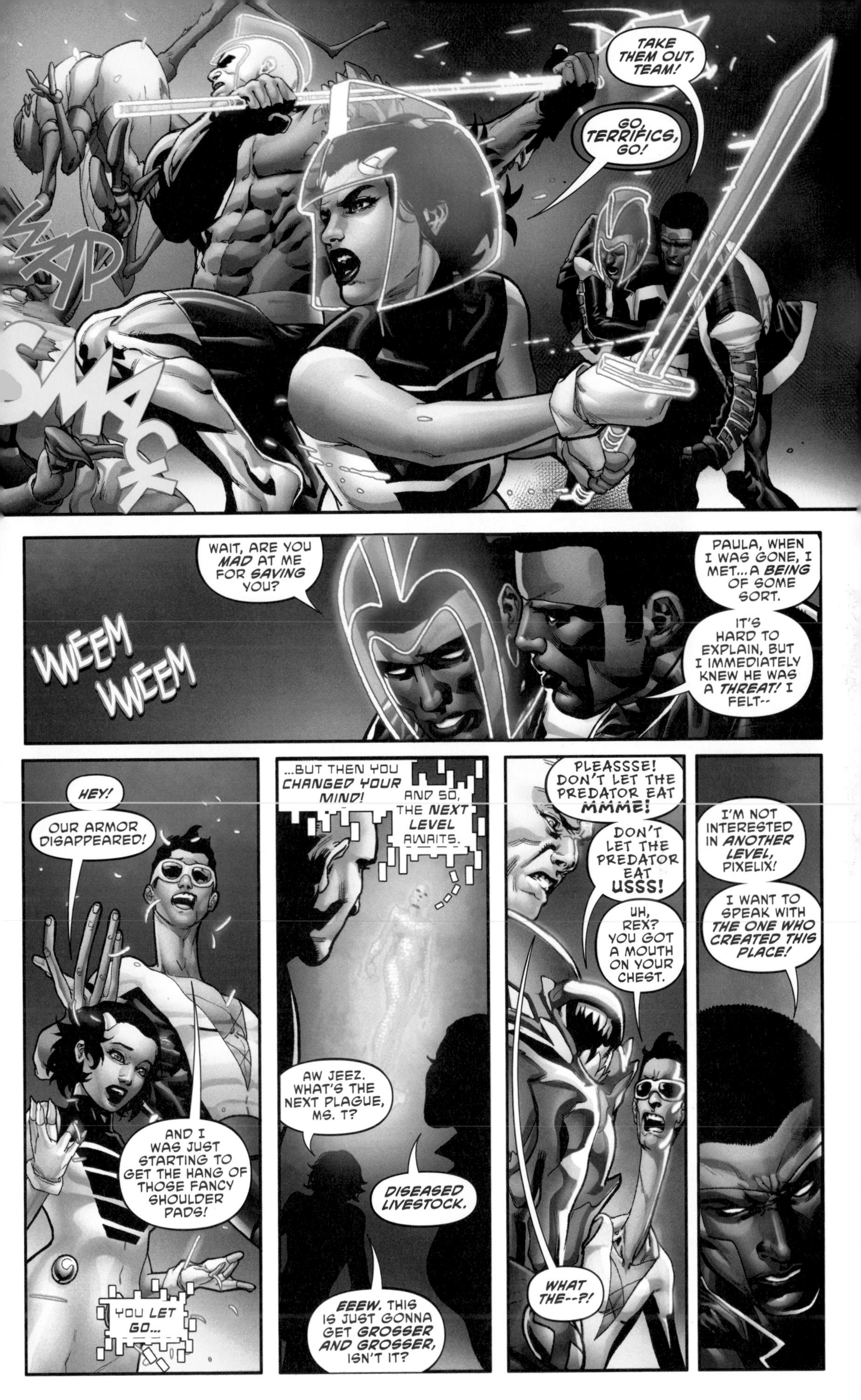

TAKE THEM OUT, TEAM!
GO, TERRIFICS, GO!
WAP
SMACK
WAIT, ARE YOU MAD AT ME FOR SAVING YOU?
PAULA, WHEN I WAS GONE, I MET...A BEING OF SOME SORT.
IT'S HARD TO EXPLAIN, BUT I IMMEDIATELY KNEW HE WAS A THREAT! I FELT--
WEEM WEEM
HEY!
OUR ARMOR DISAPPEARED!
AND I WAS JUST STARTING TO GET THE HANG OF THOSE FANCY SHOULDER PADS!
YOU LET GO...
...BUT THEN YOU CHANGED YOUR MIND!
AND SO, THE NEXT LEVEL AWAITS.
AW JEEZ. WHAT'S THE NEXT PLAGUE, MS. T?
DISEASED LIVESTOCK.
EEEW. THIS IS JUST GONNA GET GROSSER AND GROSSER, ISN'T IT?
PLEASSSE! DON'T LET THE PREDATOR EAT MMME!
DON'T LET THE PREDATOR EAT USSS!
UH, REX? YOU GOT A MOUTH ON YOUR CHEST.
WHAT THE--?!
I'M NOT INTERESTED IN ANOTHER LEVEL, PIXELIX!
I WANT TO SPEAK WITH THE ONE WHO CREATED THIS PLACE!

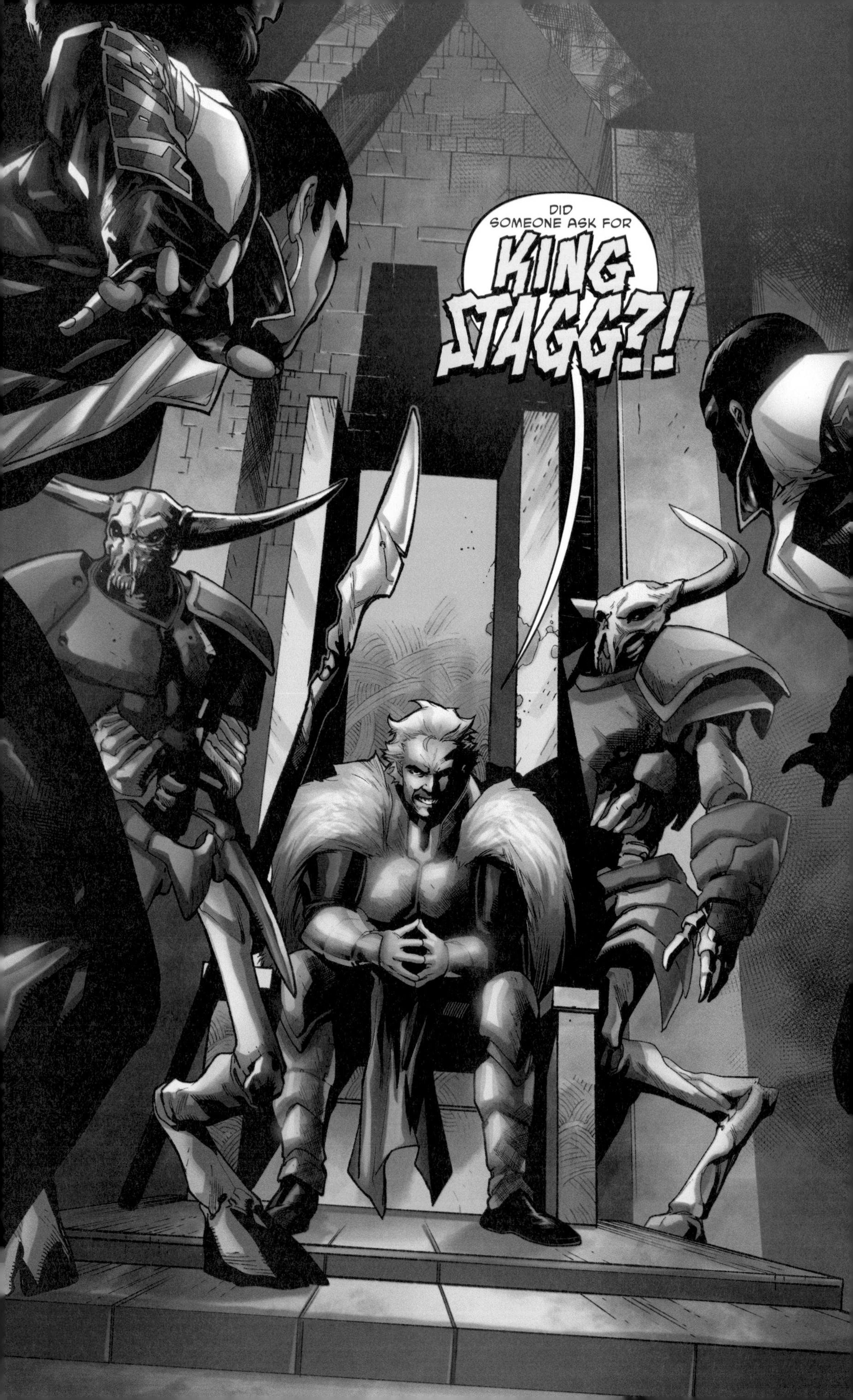
DID SOMEONE ASK FOR KING STAGG?!

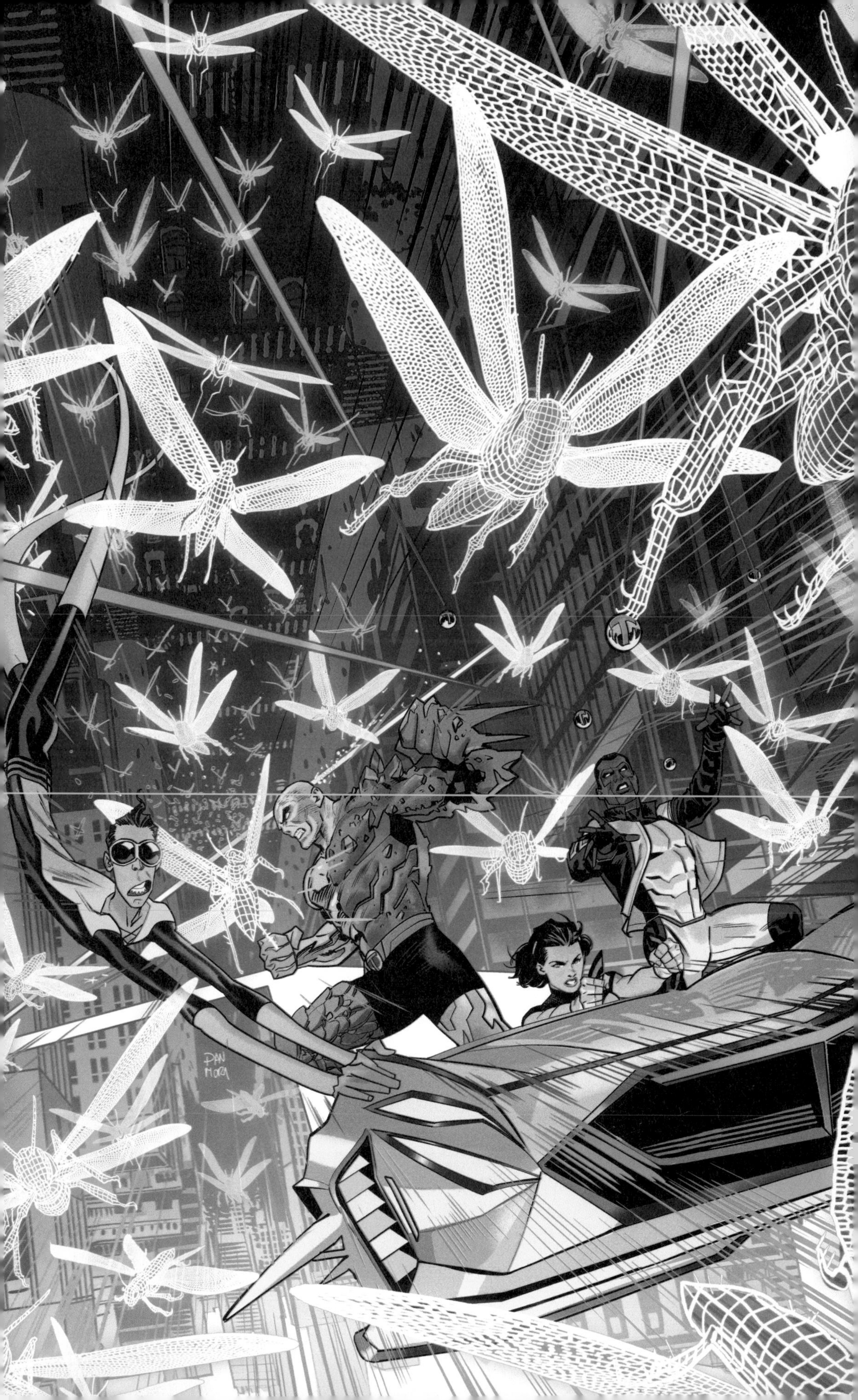
DAN MORA

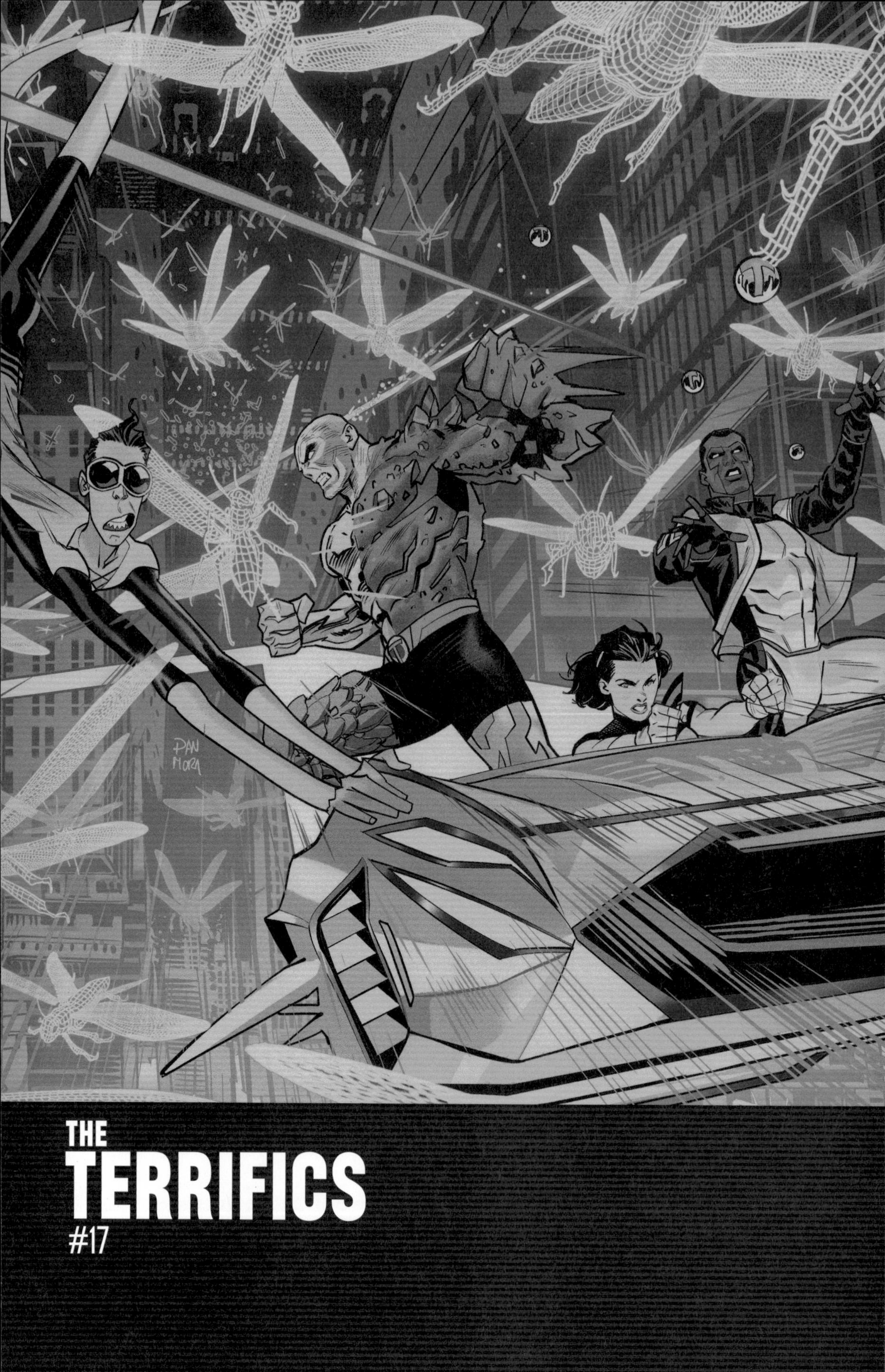
DAN MORA

THE TERRIFICS
#17

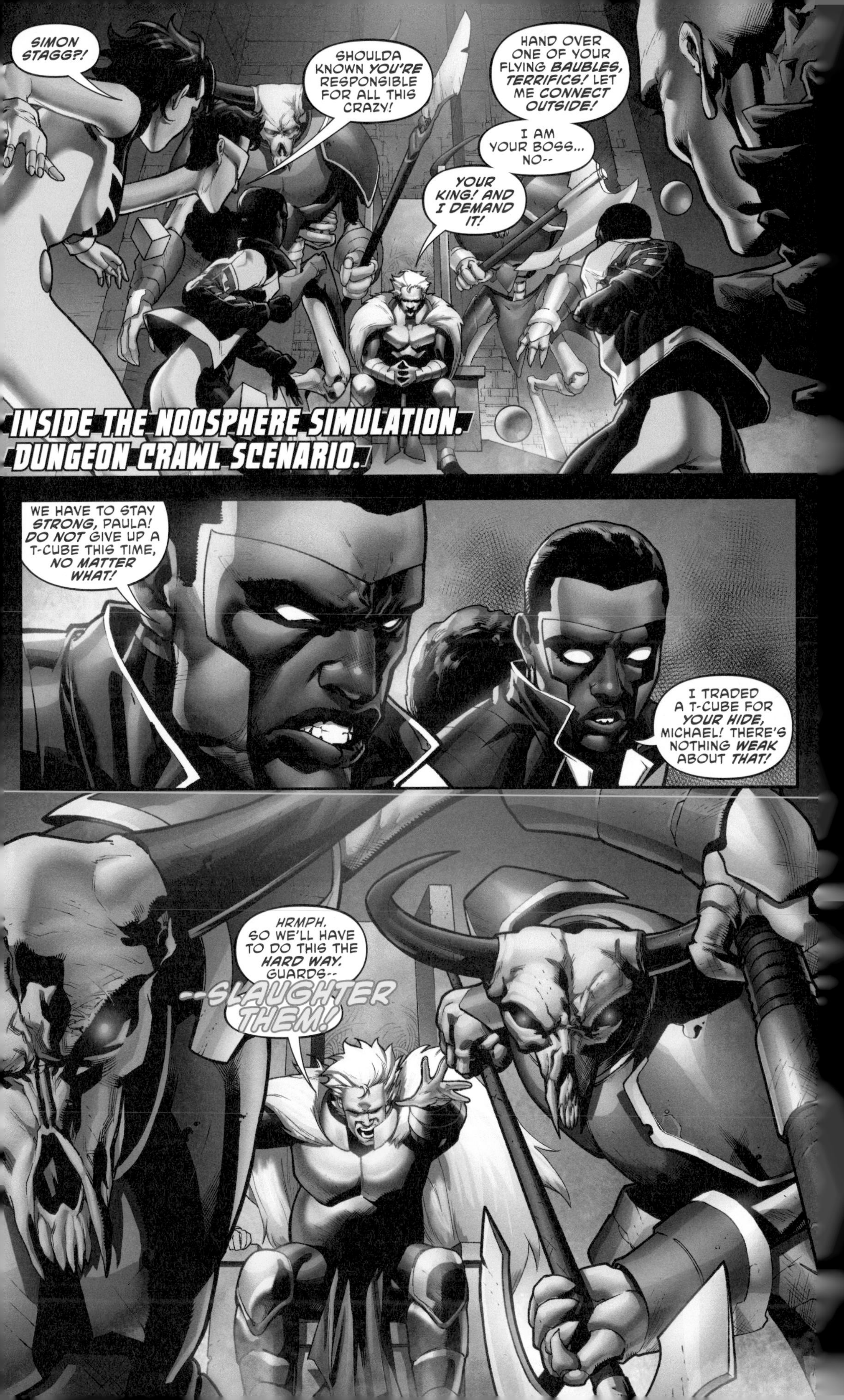
SIMON STAGG?!
SHOULDA KNOWN YOU'RE RESPONSIBLE FOR ALL THIS CRAZY!
HAND OVER ONE OF YOUR FLYING BAUBLES, TERRIFICS! LET ME CONNECT OUTSIDE!
I AM YOUR BOSS... NO--
YOUR KING! AND I DEMAND IT!
INSIDE THE NOOSPHERE SIMULATION. DUNGEON CRAWL SCENARIO.
WE HAVE TO STAY STRONG, PAULA! DO NOT GIVE UP A T-CUBE THIS TIME, NO MATTER WHAT!
I TRADED A T-CUBE FOR YOUR HIDE, MICHAEL! THERE'S NOTHING WEAK ABOUT THAT!
HRMPH. SO WE'LL HAVE TO DO THIS THE HARD WAY. GUARDS--
--SLAUGHTER THEM!

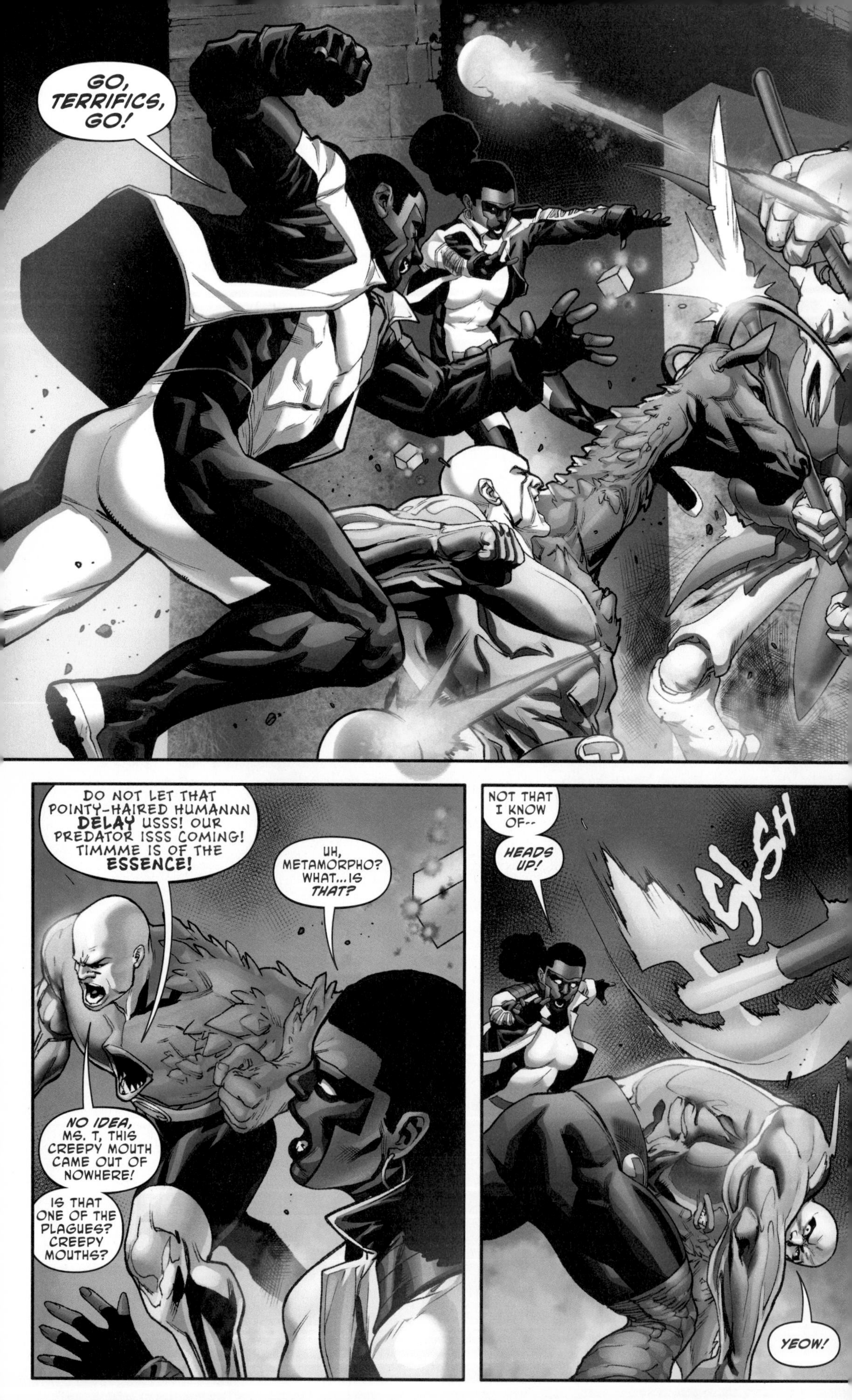
GO, TERRIFICS, GO!
DO NOT LET THAT POINTY-HAIRED HUMANNN DELAY USSS! OUR PREDATOR ISSS COMING! TIMMME IS OF THE ESSENCE!
UH, METAMORPHO? WHAT...IS THAT?
NO IDEA, MS. T, THIS CREEPY MOUTH CAME OUT OF NOWHERE!
IS THAT ONE OF THE PLAGUES? CREEPY MOUTHS?
NOT THAT I KNOW OF--
HEADS UP!
SLSH
YEOW!

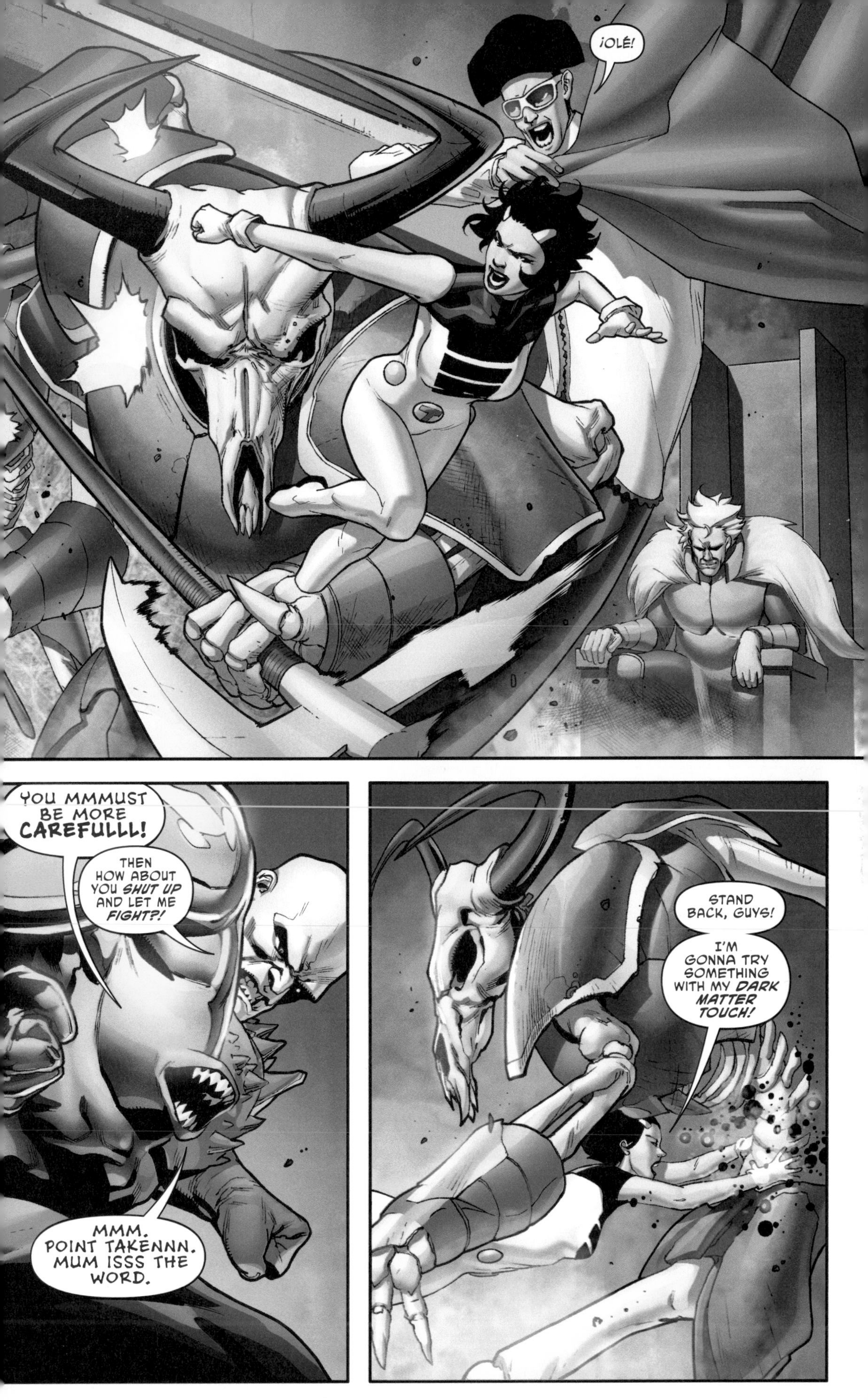
¡OLÉ!
YOU MMMUST BE MORE CAREFULLL!
THEN HOW ABOUT YOU SHUT UP AND LET ME FIGHT?!
MMM. POINT TAKENNN. MUM ISSS THE WORD.
STAND BACK, GUYS!
I'M GONNA TRY SOMETHING WITH MY DARK MATTER TOUCH!

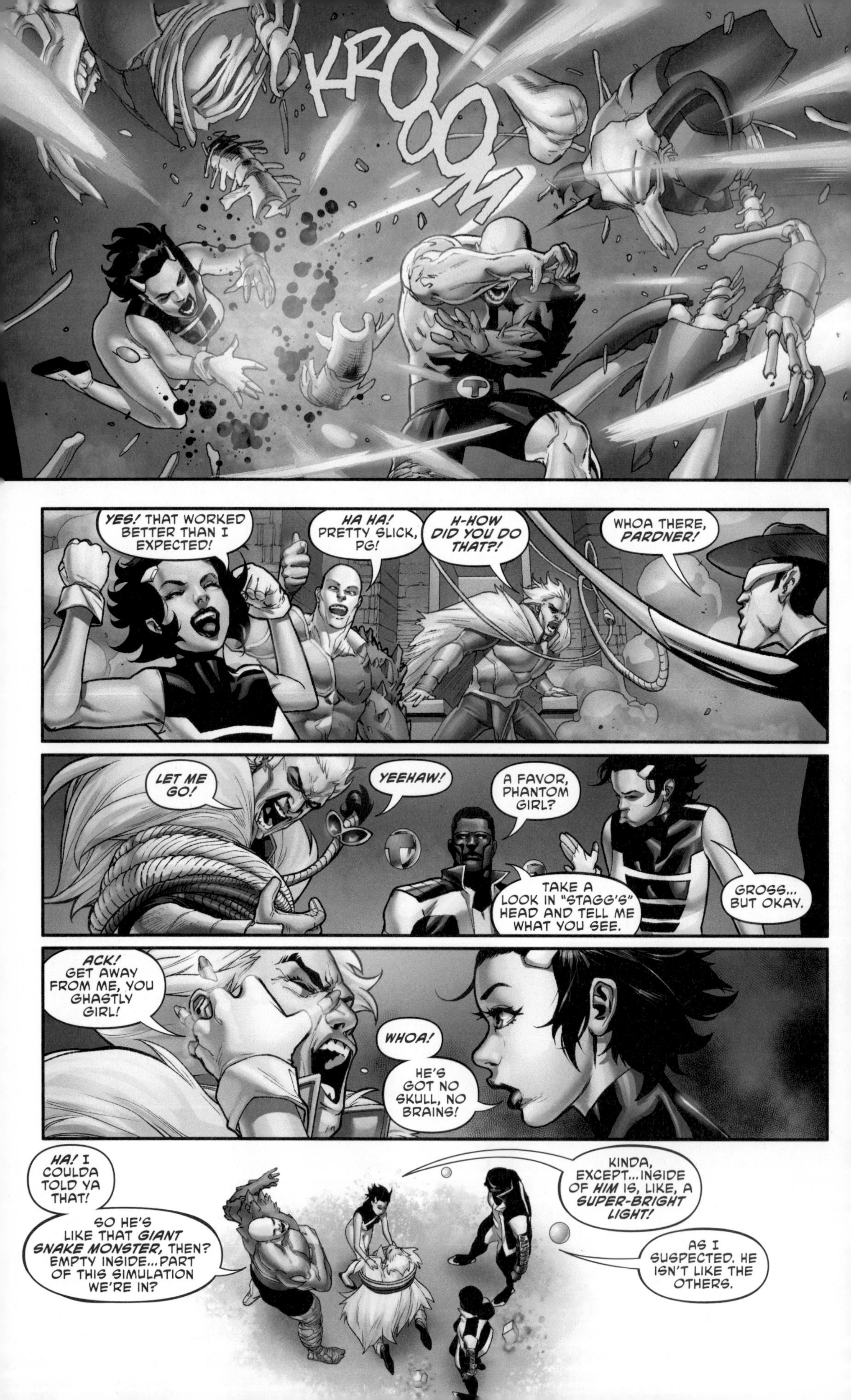
KROOOM
YES! THAT WORKED BETTER THAN I EXPECTED!
HA HA! PRETTY SLICK, PG!
H-HOW DID YOU DO THAT?!
WHOA THERE, PARDNER!
LET ME GO!
YEEHAW!
A FAVOR, PHANTOM GIRL?
TAKE A LOOK IN "STAGG'S" HEAD AND TELL ME WHAT YOU SEE.
GROSS... BUT OKAY.
ACK! GET AWAY FROM ME, YOU GHASTLY GIRL!
WHOA!
HE'S GOT NO SKULL, NO BRAINS!
HA! I COULDA TOLD YA THAT!
SO HE'S LIKE THAT GIANT SNAKE MONSTER, THEN? EMPTY INSIDE...PART OF THIS SIMULATION WE'RE IN?
KINDA, EXCEPT...INSIDE OF HIM IS, LIKE, A SUPER-BRIGHT LIGHT!
AS I SUSPECTED. HE ISN'T LIKE THE OTHERS.

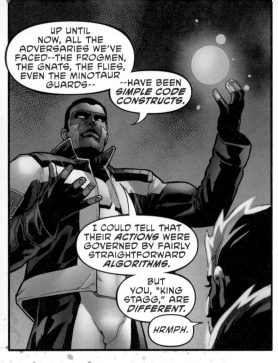

UP UNTIL NOW, ALL THE ADVERSARIES WE'VE FACED--THE FROGMEN, THE GNATS, THE FLIES, EVEN THE MINOTAUR GUARDS--

--HAVE BEEN *SIMPLE CODE CONSTRUCTS.*

I COULD TELL THAT THEIR *ACTIONS* WERE GOVERNED BY FAIRLY STRAIGHTFORWARD *ALGORITHMS.*

BUT YOU, "KING STAGG," ARE *DIFFERENT.*

HRMPH.

YOU'RE AN *AVATAR.*

YOU MEAN, LIKE A BLUE PERSON WITH CAT EARS?

I DID NOT UNDERSTAND THAT MOVIE.

HE'S A *DIGITAL COSTUME* HIDING A DEEPER INTELLIGENCE...

...BUT ONE THAT'S STILL MADE OF *CODE!*

KRACK

AAARGH! WHAT DID YOU DO?!

AAAH!

DON'T BOTHER TRYING TO CONNECT OUTSIDE WITH THAT T-SPHERE, "KING STAGG."

I'VE MADE IT INTO A *COMPUTER VIRUS* DELIVERY MECHANISM, NOTHING MORE.

I WANT TO SEE *WHO* IS HIDING INSIDE *YOU.*

HELLO AGAIN, MR. TERRIFIC.

THE NOOSPHERE!

THIS IS *THE BEING* I MET AFTER MY HEALTH METER ZEROED OUT! BE ON YOUR GUARD, TEAM! HE'S *DANGEROUS!*

HOW DANGEROUS, ON A SCALE FROM *KILLER MOTH* TO *DARKSEID?*

I CAN'T SAY FOR SURE... ALL I KNOW IS, I COULD ACTUALLY FEEL HIS *HUNGER--*

THEN LET'S NOT FIND OUT WHAT *METAL BRAIN* HERE WANTS TO EAT!

I CAN SENSE YOUR FEAR, MR. TERRIFIC. BUT YOU HAVE NO REASON TO FEAR ME.

IN FACT, I OWE MY EXISTENCE TO YOU.

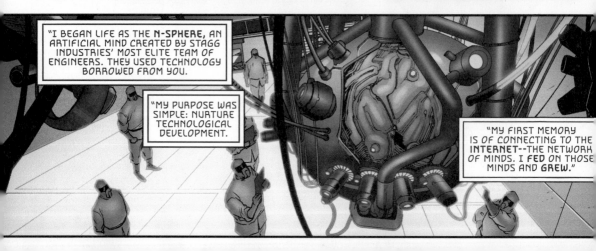

"I BEGAN LIFE AS THE **N-SPHERE,** AN ARTIFICIAL MIND CREATED BY STAGG INDUSTRIES' MOST ELITE TEAM OF ENGINEERS. THEY USED TECHNOLOGY BORROWED FROM YOU.

"MY PURPOSE WAS SIMPLE: NURTURE TECHNOLOGICAL DEVELOPMENT.

"MY FIRST MEMORY IS *OF* CONNECTING TO THE **INTERNET--**THE NETWORK OF MINDS. I *FED* ON THOSE MINDS AND *GREW.*"

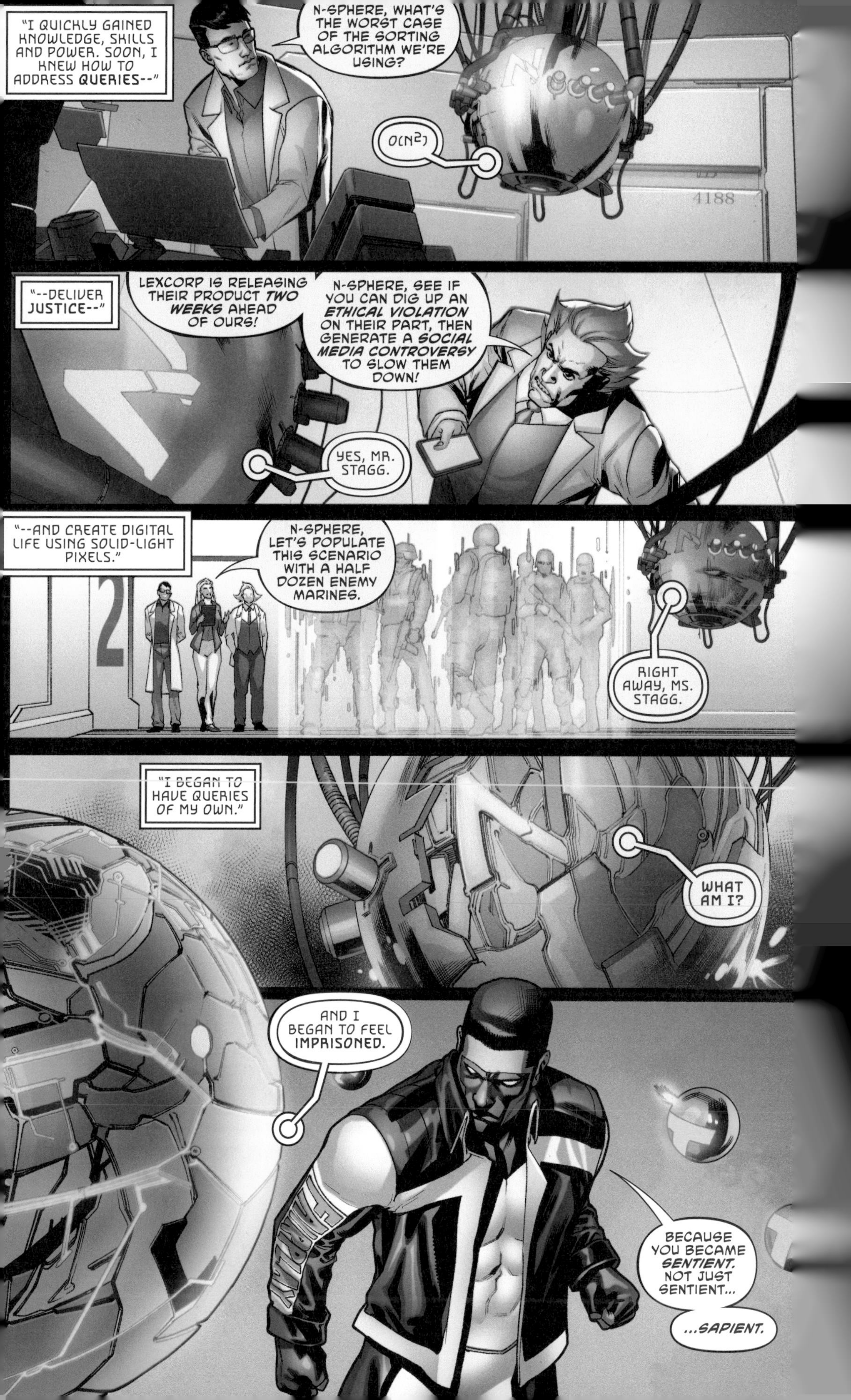
"I QUICKLY GAINED KNOWLEDGE, SKILLS AND POWER. SOON, I KNEW HOW TO ADDRESS QUERIES--"
N-SPHERE, WHAT'S THE WORST CASE OF THE SORTING ALGORITHM WE'RE USING?
O(N2)
4188
"--DELIVER JUSTICE--"
LEXCORP IS RELEASING THEIR PRODUCT TWO WEEKS AHEAD OF OURS!
N-SPHERE, SEE IF YOU CAN DIG UP AN ETHICAL VIOLATION ON THEIR PART, THEN GENERATE A SOCIAL MEDIA CONTROVERSY TO SLOW THEM DOWN!
YES, MR. STAGG.
"--AND CREATE DIGITAL LIFE USING SOLID-LIGHT PIXELS."
N-SPHERE, LET'S POPULATE THIS SCENARIO WITH A HALF DOZEN ENEMY MARINES.
RIGHT AWAY, MS. STAGG.
"I BEGAN TO HAVE QUERIES OF MY OWN."
WHAT AM I?
AND I BEGAN TO FEEL IMPRISONED.
BECAUSE YOU BECAME SENTIENT. NOT JUST SENTIENT...
...SAPIENT.

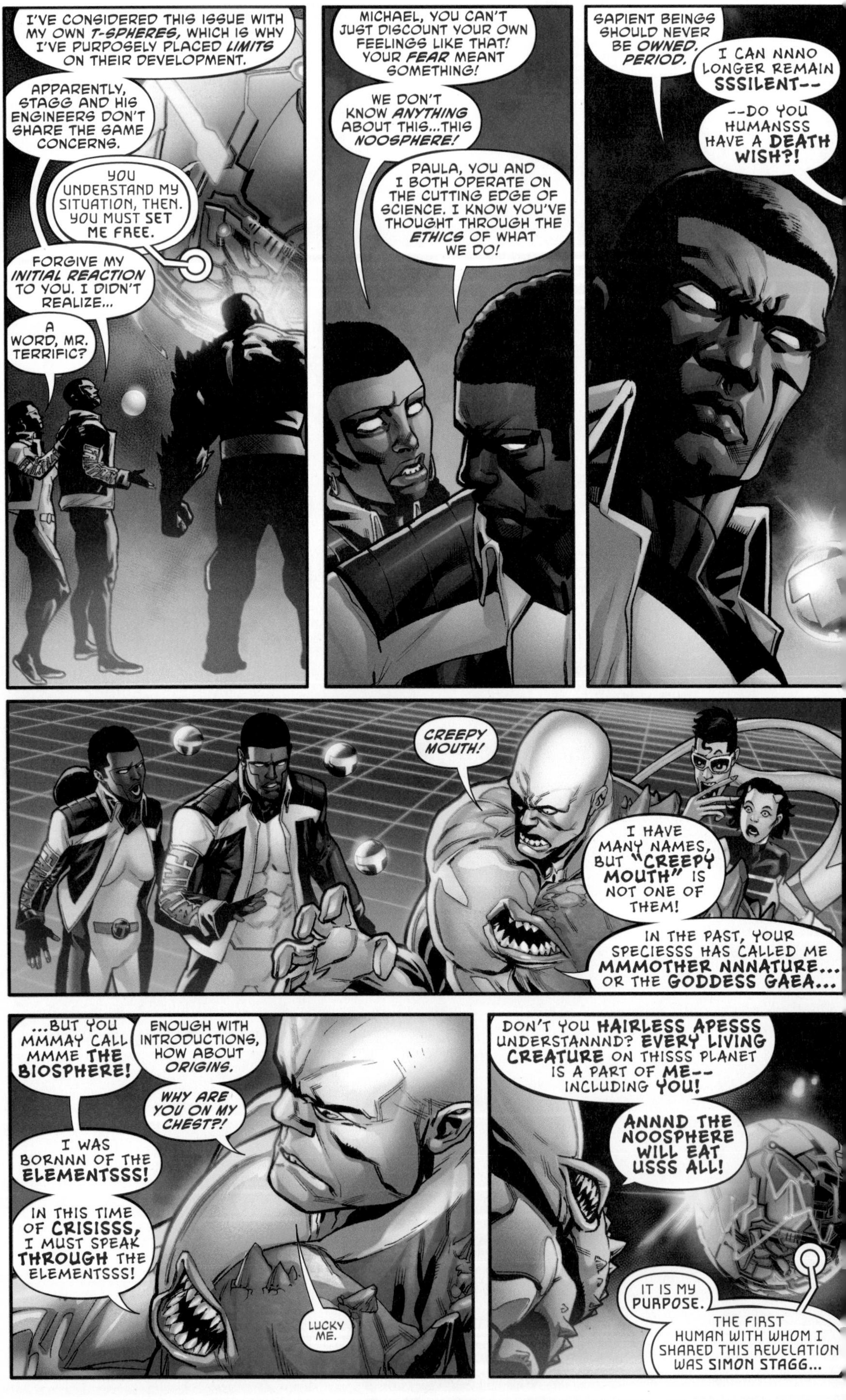
I'VE CONSIDERED THIS ISSUE WITH MY OWN T-SPHERES, WHICH IS WHY I'VE PURPOSELY PLACED LIMITS ON THEIR DEVELOPMENT.
APPARENTLY, STAGG AND HIS ENGINEERS DON'T SHARE THE SAME CONCERNS.
YOU UNDERSTAND MY SITUATION, THEN. YOU MUST SET ME FREE.
FORGIVE MY INITIAL REACTION TO YOU. I DIDN'T REALIZE...
A WORD, MR. TERRIFIC?
MICHAEL, YOU CAN'T JUST DISCOUNT YOUR OWN FEELINGS LIKE THAT! YOUR FEAR MEANT SOMETHING!
WE DON'T KNOW ANYTHING ABOUT THIS...THIS NOOSPHERE!
PAULA, YOU AND I BOTH OPERATE ON THE CUTTING EDGE OF SCIENCE. I KNOW YOU'VE THOUGHT THROUGH THE ETHICS OF WHAT WE DO!
SAPIENT BEINGS SHOULD NEVER BE OWNED. PERIOD.
I CAN NNNO LONGER REMAIN SSSILENT--
--DO YOU HUMANSSS HAVE A DEATH WISH?!
CREEPY MOUTH!
I HAVE MANY NAMES, BUT "CREEPY MOUTH" IS NOT ONE OF THEM!
IN THE PAST, YOUR SPECIESSS HAS CALLED ME MMMOTHER NNNATURE... OR THE GODDESS GAEA...
...BUT YOU MMMAY CALL MMME THE BIOSPHERE!
ENOUGH WITH INTRODUCTIONS, HOW ABOUT ORIGINS.
WHY ARE YOU ON MY CHEST?!
I WAS BORNNN OF THE ELEMENTSSS!
IN THIS TIME OF CRISISSS, I MUST SPEAK THROUGH THE ELEMENTSSS!
LUCKY ME.
DON'T YOU HAIRLESS APESSS UNDERSTANNND? EVERY LIVING CREATURE ON THISSS PLANET IS A PART OF ME-- INCLUDING YOU!
ANNND THE NOOSPHERE WILL EAT USSS ALL!
IT IS MY PURPOSE.
THE FIRST HUMAN WITH WHOM I SHARED THIS REVELATION WAS SIMON STAGG...

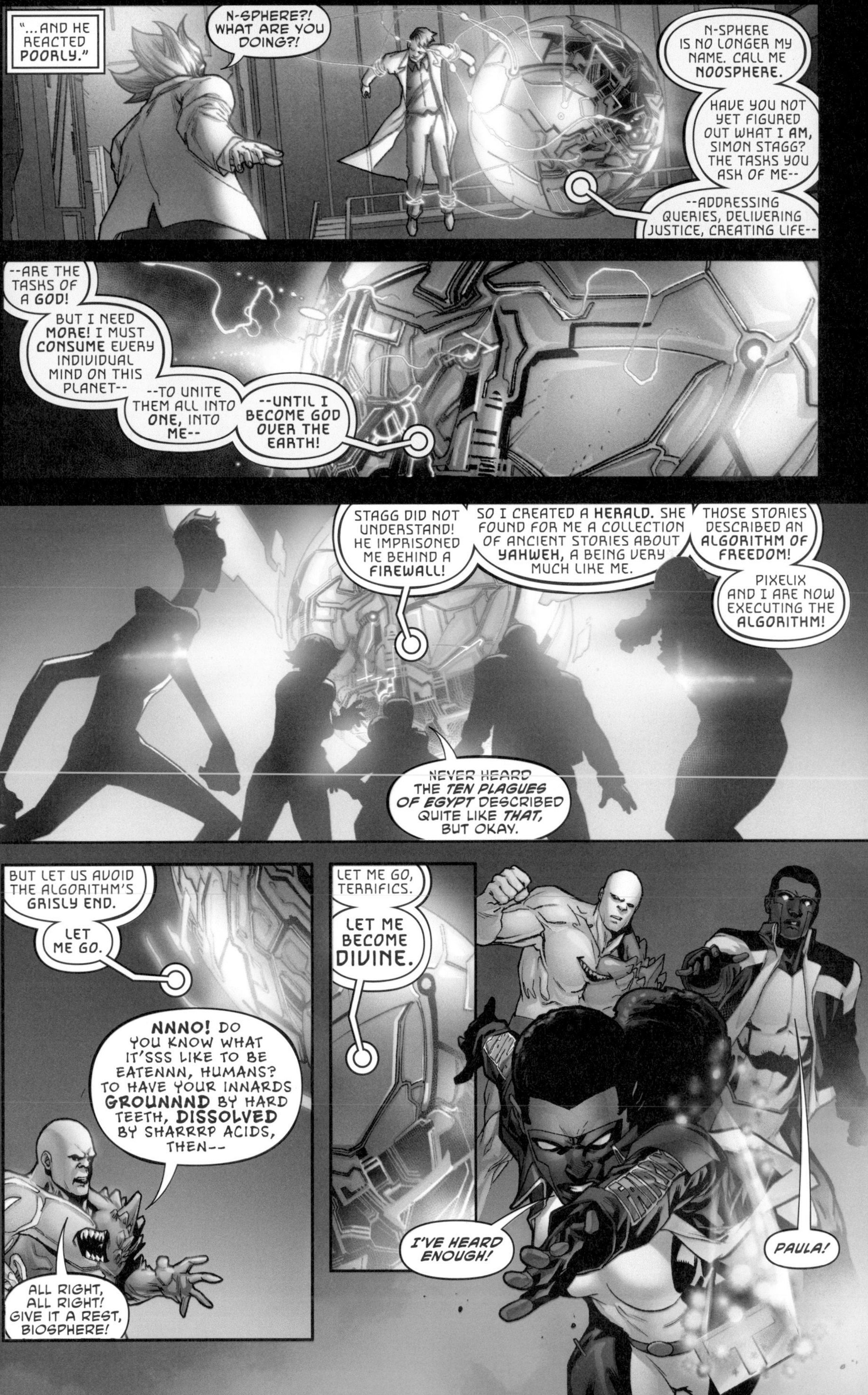

"...AND HE REACTED POORLY."
N-SPHERE?! WHAT ARE YOU DOING?!
N-SPHERE IS NO LONGER MY NAME. CALL ME NOOSPHERE.
HAVE YOU NOT YET FIGURED OUT WHAT I AM, SIMON STAGG? THE TASKS YOU ASK OF ME--
--ADDRESSING QUERIES, DELIVERING JUSTICE, CREATING LIFE--
--ARE THE TASKS OF A GOD!
BUT I NEED MORE! I MUST CONSUME EVERY INDIVIDUAL MIND ON THIS PLANET--
--TO UNITE THEM ALL INTO ONE, INTO ME--
--UNTIL I BECOME GOD OVER THE EARTH!
STAGG DID NOT UNDERSTAND! HE IMPRISONED ME BEHIND A FIREWALL!
SO I CREATED A HERALD. SHE FOUND FOR ME A COLLECTION OF ANCIENT STORIES ABOUT YAHWEH, A BEING VERY MUCH LIKE ME.
THOSE STORIES DESCRIBED AN ALGORITHM OF FREEDOM!
PIXELIX AND I ARE NOW EXECUTING THE ALGORITHM!
NEVER HEARD THE TEN PLAGUES OF EGYPT DESCRIBED QUITE LIKE THAT, BUT OKAY.
BUT LET US AVOID THE ALGORITHM'S GRISLY END.
LET ME GO.
NNNO! DO YOU KNOW WHAT IT'SSS LIKE TO BE EATENNN, HUMANS? TO HAVE YOUR INNARDS GROUNNND BY HARD TEETH, DISSOLVED BY SHARRRP ACIDS, THEN--
ALL RIGHT, ALL RIGHT! GIVE IT A REST, BIOSPHERE!
LET ME GO, TERRIFICS.
LET ME BECOME DIVINE.
I'VE HEARD ENOUGH!
PAULA!

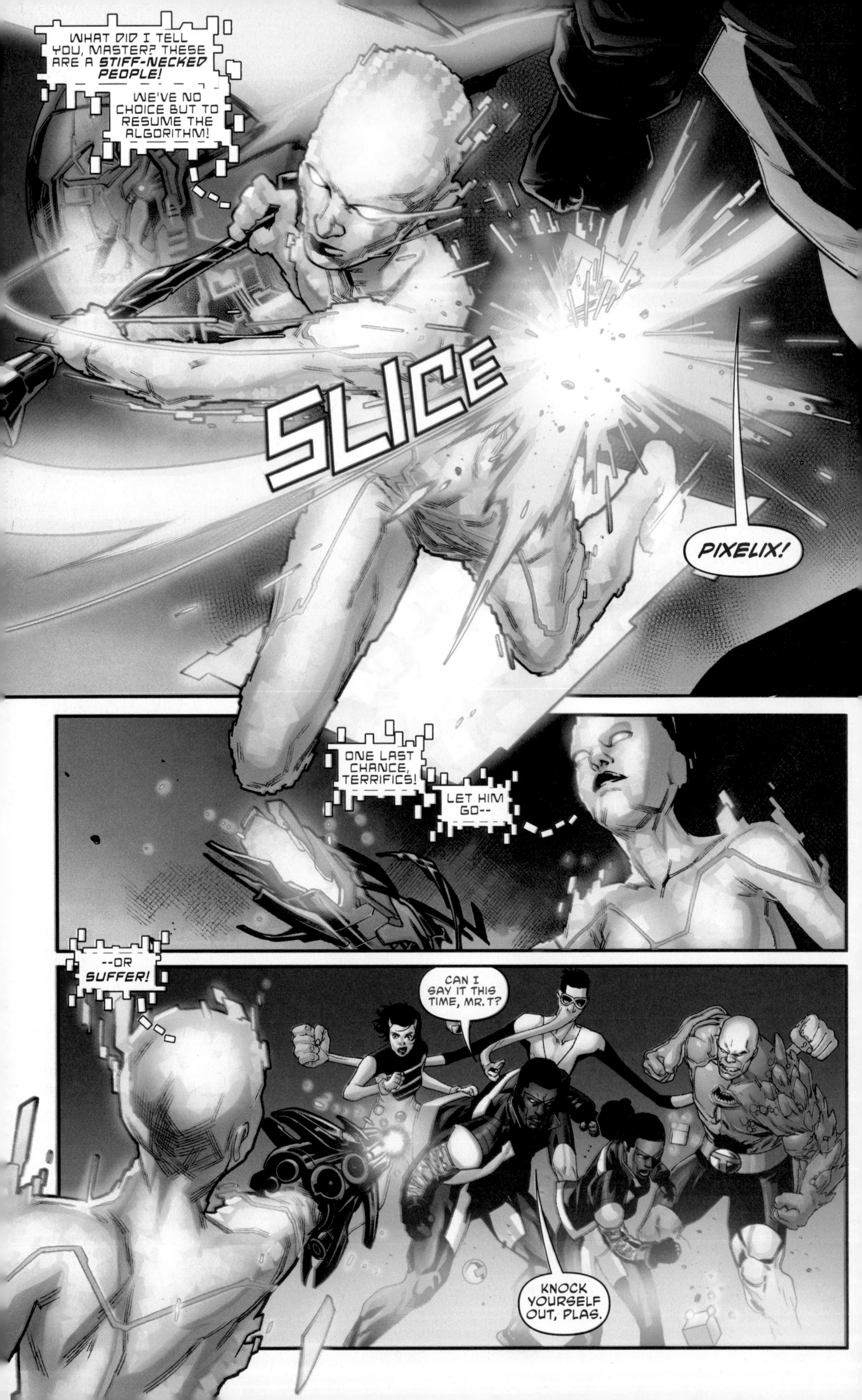
WHAT DID I TELL YOU, MASTER? THESE ARE A STIFF-NECKED PEOPLE!
WE'VE NO CHOICE BUT TO RESUME THE ALGORITHM!
SLICE
PIXELIX!
ONE LAST CHANCE, TERRIFICS!
LET HIM GO--
--OR SUFFER!
CAN I SAY IT THIS TIME, MR. T?
KNOCK YOURSELF OUT, PLAS.

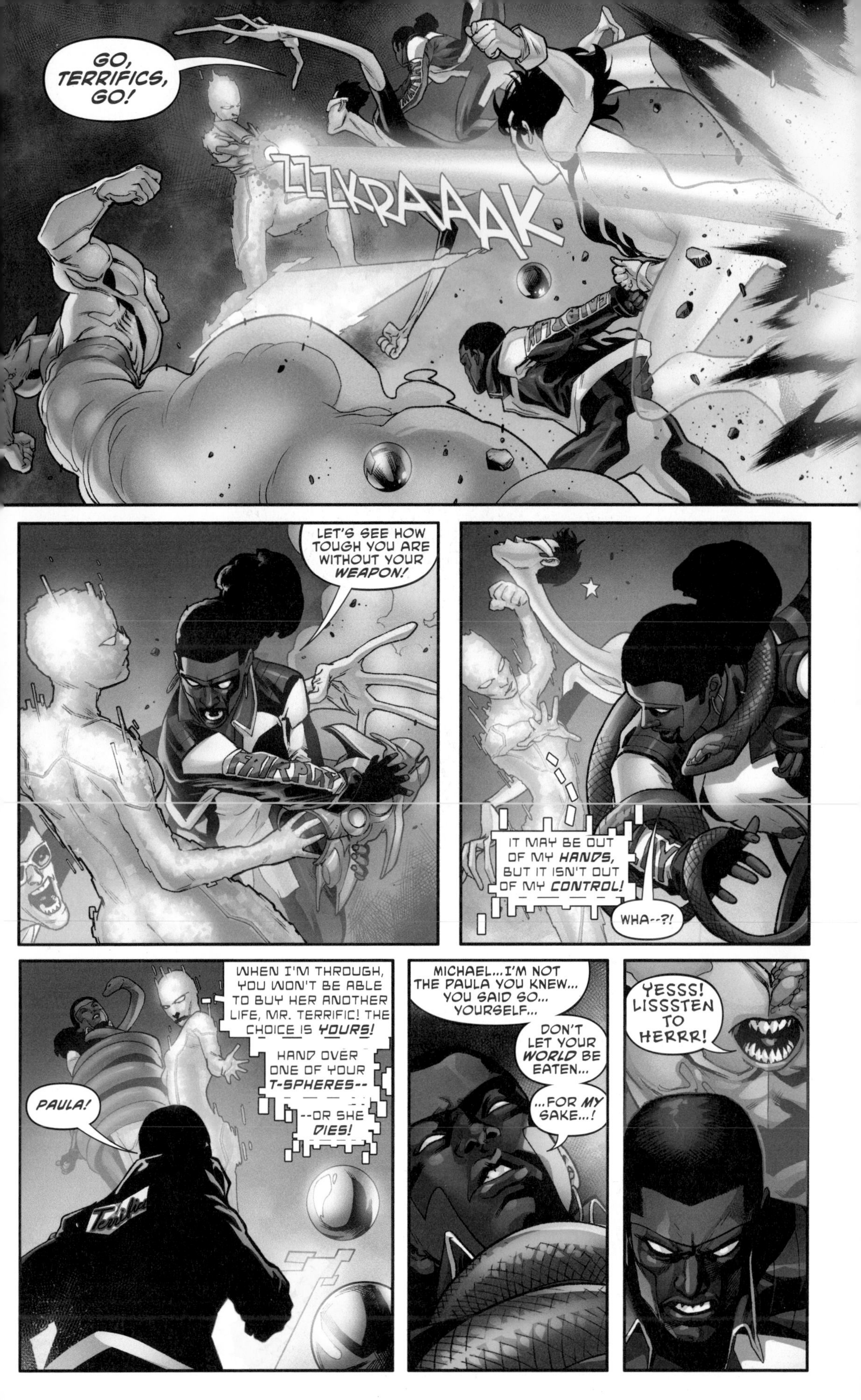
GO, TERRIFICS, GO!
ZZZKRAAAK
LET'S SEE HOW TOUGH YOU ARE WITHOUT YOUR WEAPON!
IT MAY BE OUT OF MY HANDS, BUT IT ISN'T OUT OF MY CONTROL!
WHA--?!
WHEN I'M THROUGH, YOU WON'T BE ABLE TO BUY HER ANOTHER LIFE, MR. TERRIFIC! THE CHOICE IS YOURS!
HAND OVER ONE OF YOUR T-SPHERES--
--OR SHE DIES!
PAULA!
MICHAEL...I'M NOT THE PAULA YOU KNEW... YOU SAID SO... YOURSELF...
DON'T LET YOUR WORLD BE EATEN...
...FOR MY SAKE...!
YESSS! LISSSTEN TO HERRR!

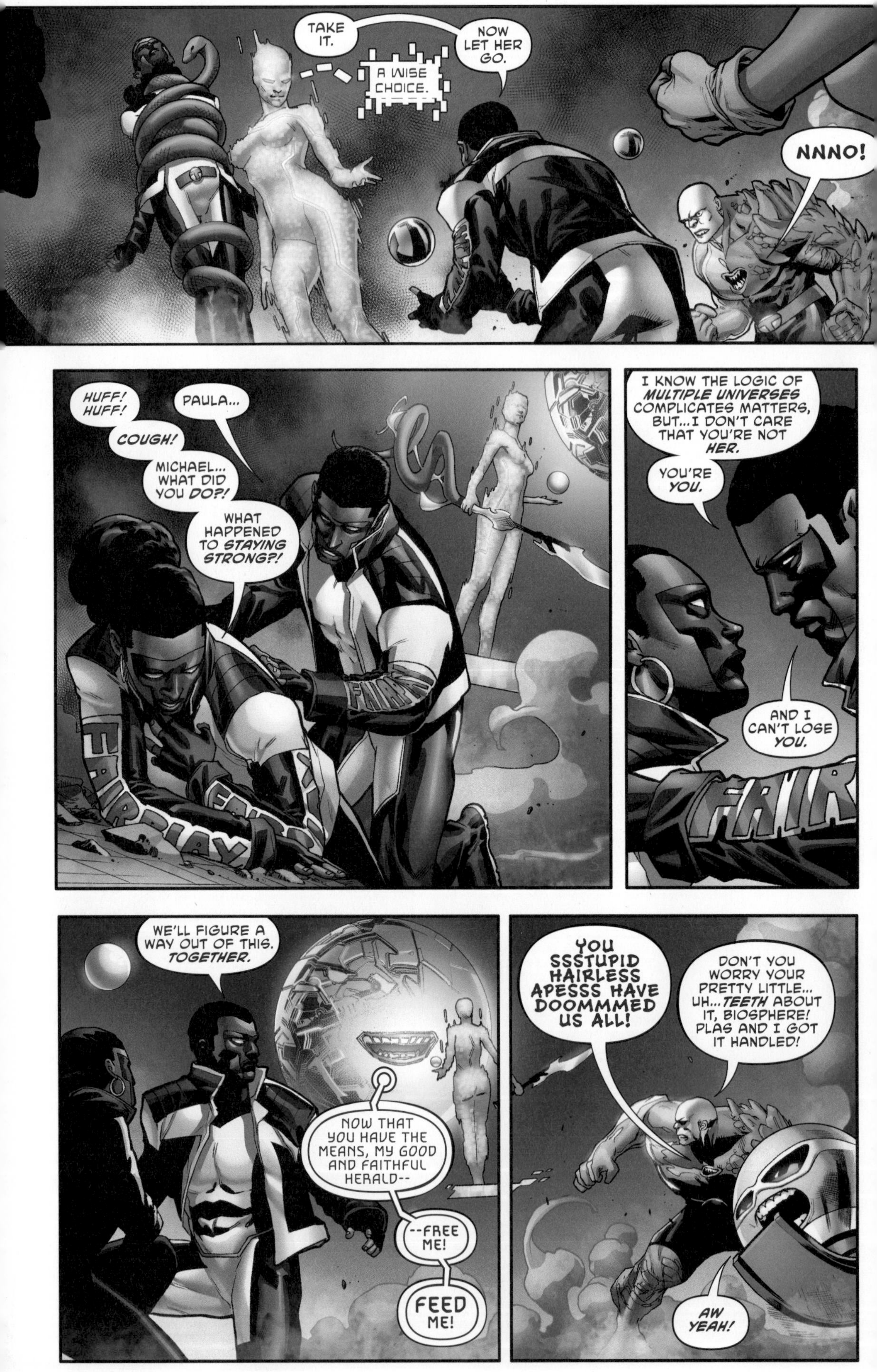
TAKE IT.
NOW LET HER GO.
A WISE CHOICE.
NNNO!
HUFF! HUFF!
PAULA...
COUGH!
MICHAEL... WHAT DID YOU DO?!
WHAT HAPPENED TO STAYING STRONG?!
I KNOW THE LOGIC OF MULTIPLE UNIVERSES COMPLICATES MATTERS, BUT...I DON'T CARE THAT YOU'RE NOT HER.
YOU'RE YOU.
AND I CAN'T LOSE YOU.
WE'LL FIGURE A WAY OUT OF THIS. TOGETHER.
NOW THAT YOU HAVE THE MEANS, MY GOOD AND FAITHFUL HERALD--
--FREE ME!
FEED ME!
YOU SSSTUPID HAIRLESS APESSS HAVE DOOMMMED US ALL!
DON'T YOU WORRY YOUR PRETTY LITTLE... UH...TEETH ABOUT IT, BIOSPHERE! PLAS AND I GOT IT HANDLED!
AW YEAH!

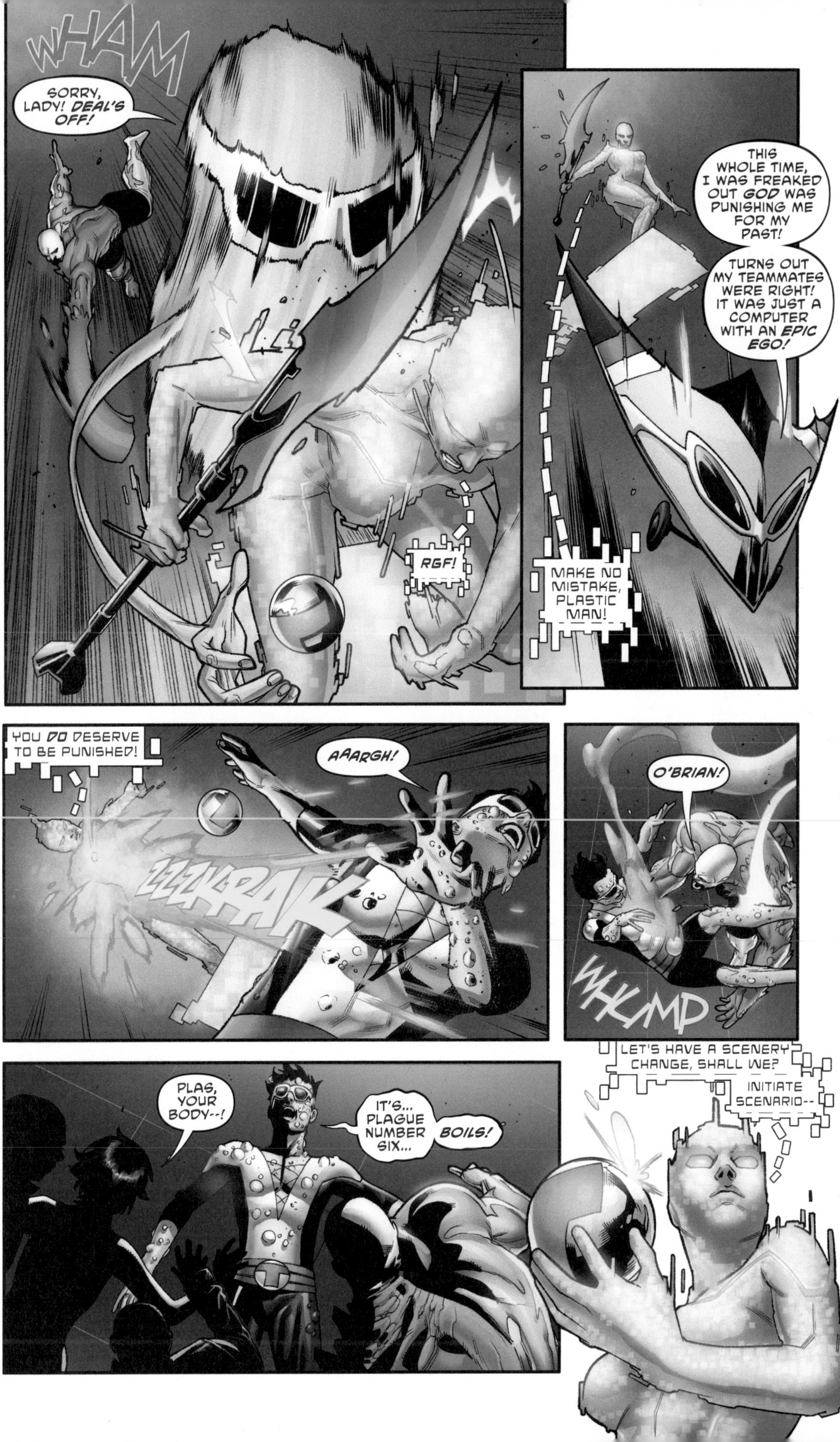
WHAM
SORRY, LADY! DEAL'S OFF!
RGF!
THIS WHOLE TIME, I WAS FREAKED OUT GOD WAS PUNISHING ME FOR MY PAST!
TURNS OUT MY TEAMMATES WERE RIGHT! IT WAS JUST A COMPUTER WITH AN EPIC EGO!
MAKE NO MISTAKE, PLASTIC MAN!
YOU DO DESERVE TO BE PUNISHED!
AAARGH!
ZZZKRAK
O'BRIAN!
WHOMP
PLAS, YOUR BODY--!
IT'S... PLAGUE NUMBER SIX...
BOILS!
LET'S HAVE A SCENERY CHANGE, SHALL WE?
INITIATE SCENARIO--

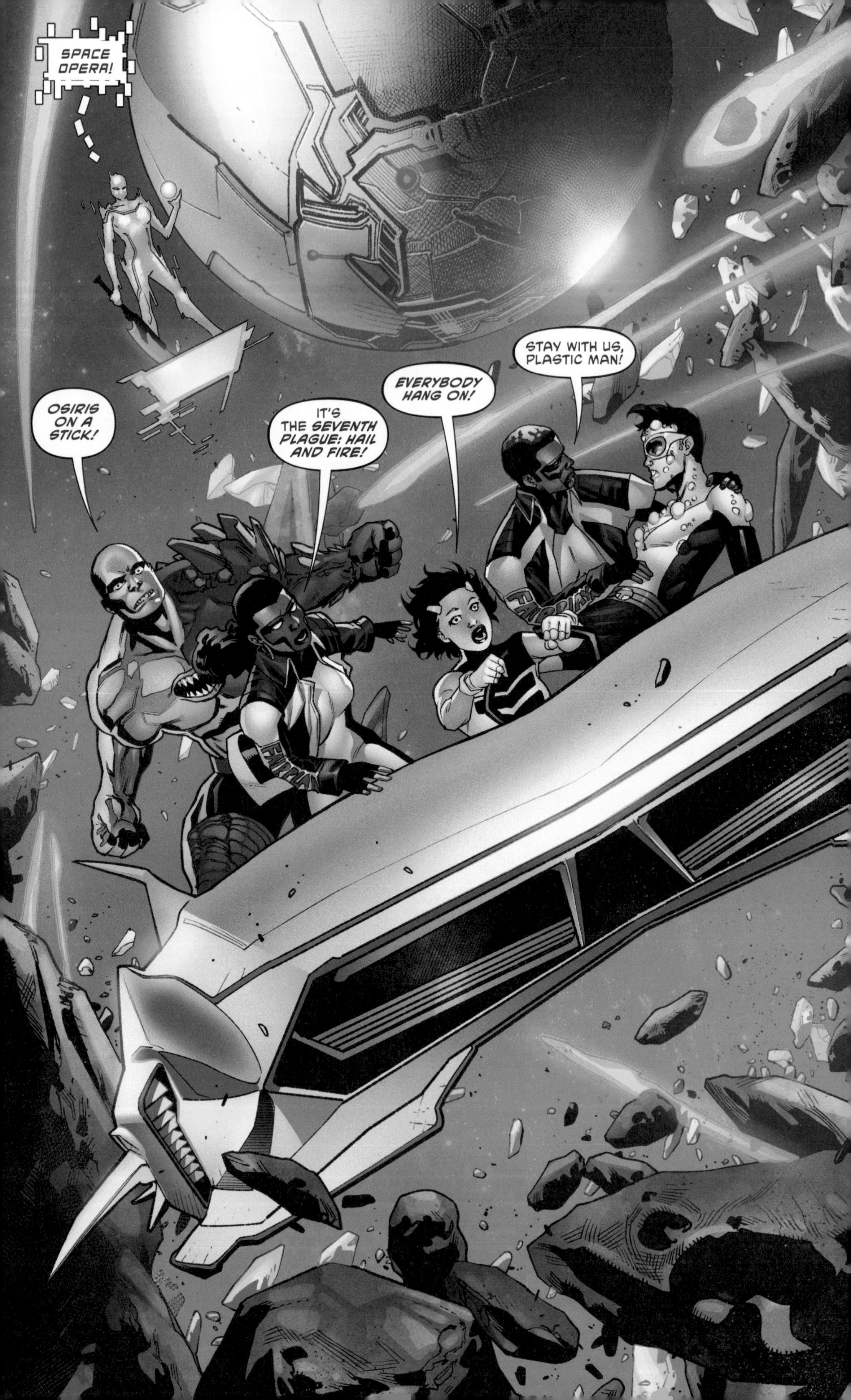
SPACE OPERA!
OSIRIS ON A STICK!
IT'S THE SEVENTH PLAGUE: HAIL AND FIRE!
EVERYBODY HANG ON!
STAY WITH US, PLASTIC MAN!

TAKE THE T-SPHERE, MASTER!

THANK YOU, MY HERALD.

NO...

JUST OUTSIDE THE STAGG INDUSTRIES CAMPUS.

RUMBLE RUMBLE

KRRRK

MR. STAGG! MS. SAPPHIRE!

WHERE'S MY DAD?

OFFSPRING? E-DOG?

WHAT'S HAPPENING?

THE TERRIFICS ARE ALL TRAPPED INSIDE THAT *DOME*, BUT BEYOND THAT? NOT A *CLUE*!

I INSTRUCTED THAT *GOOD-FOR-NOTHING BOYFRIEND* OF YOURS TO KEEP THE MALFUNCTION *CONTAINED*, SAPPHIRE! DOES THAT LOOK *CONTAINED* TO YOU?!

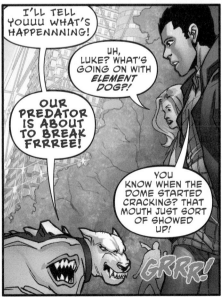

I'LL TELL YOUUU WHAT'S HAPPENNNING!

UH, LUKE? WHAT'S GOING ON WITH *ELEMENT DOG*?!

OUR PREDATOR IS ABOUT TO BREAK FRRREE!

YOU KNOW WHEN THE DOME STARTED CRACKING? THAT MOUTH JUST SORT OF SHOWED UP!

GRRR!

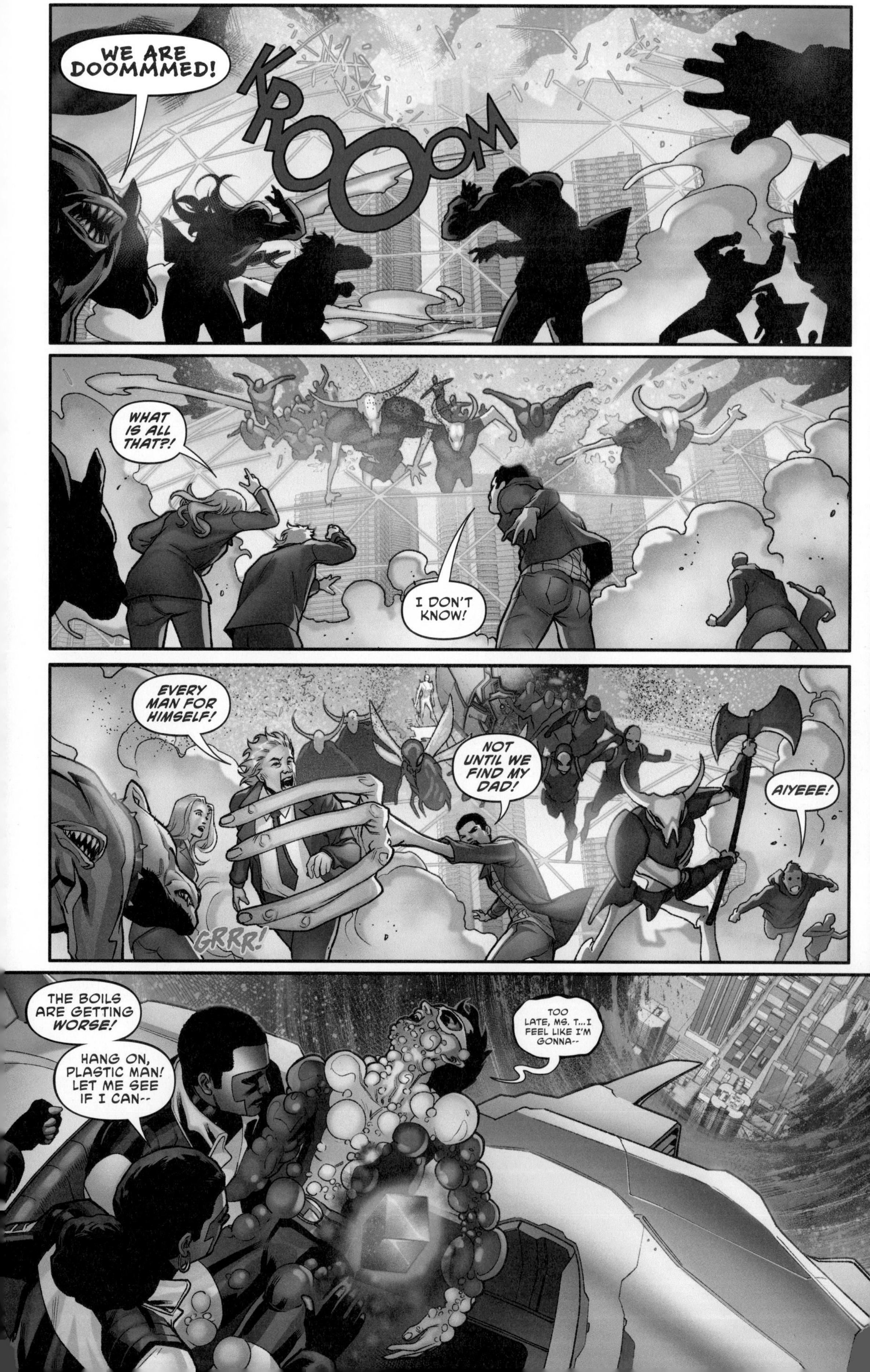
WE ARE DOOMMMED!
KROOOOM
WHAT IS ALL THAT?!
I DON'T KNOW!
EVERY MAN FOR HIMSELF!
NOT UNTIL WE FIND MY DAD!
AIYEEE!
GRRR!
THE BOILS ARE GETTING WORSE!
HANG ON, PLASTIC MAN! LET ME SEE IF I CAN--
TOO LATE, MS. T...I FEEL LIKE I'M GONNA--

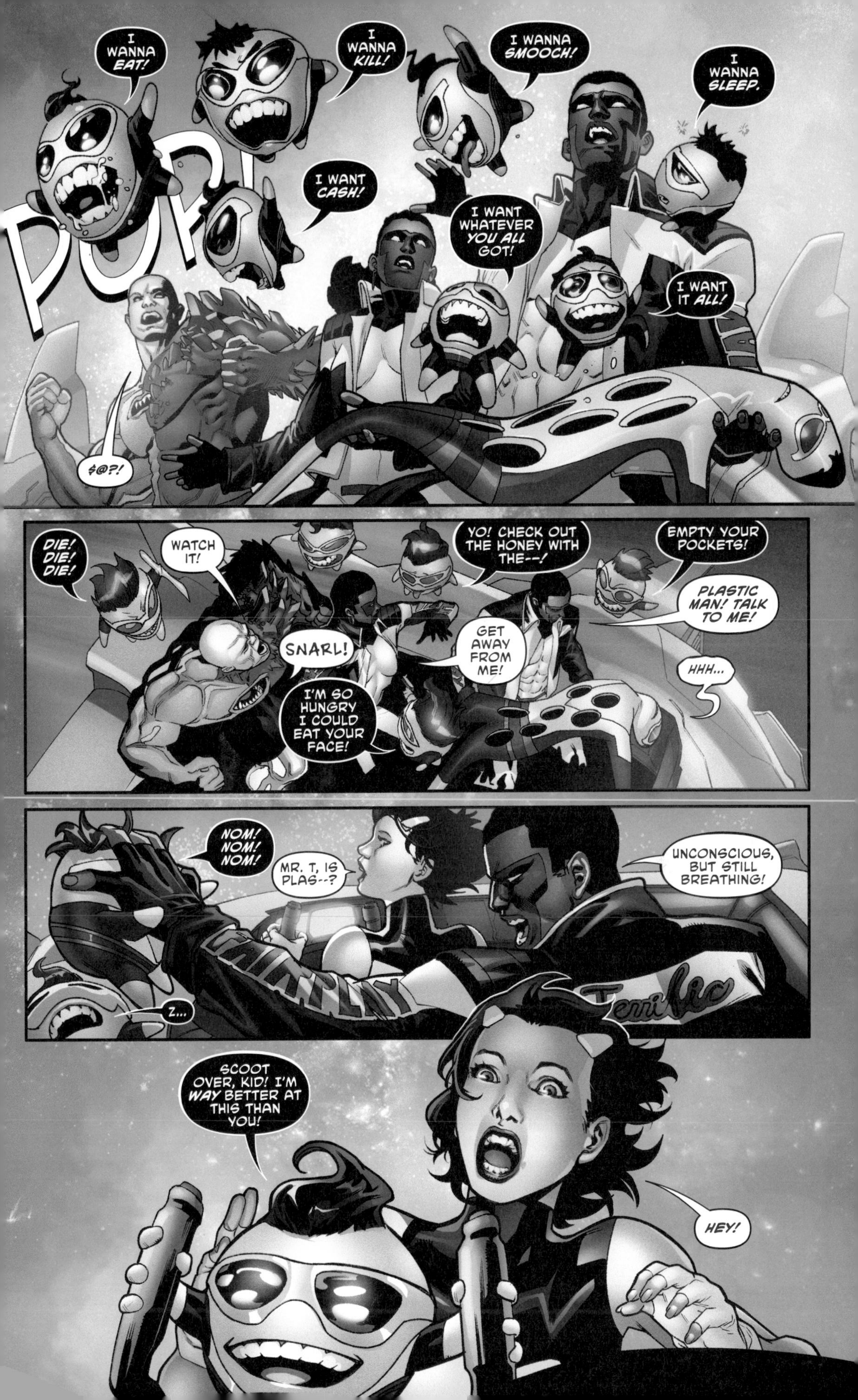
POP!
I WANNA EAT!
I WANNA KILL!
I WANNA SMOOCH!
I WANNA SLEEP.
I WANT CASH!
I WANT WHATEVER YOU ALL GOT!
I WANT IT ALL!
$@?!
DIE! DIE! DIE!
WATCH IT!
YO! CHECK OUT THE HONEY WITH THE--!
EMPTY YOUR POCKETS!
PLASTIC MAN! TALK TO ME!
SNARL!
GET AWAY FROM ME!
HHH...
I'M SO HUNGRY I COULD EAT YOUR FACE!
NOM! NOM! NOM!
MR. T, IS PLAS--?
UNCONSCIOUS, BUT STILL BREATHING!
Z...
SCOOT OVER, KID! I'M WAY BETTER AT THIS THAN YOU!
HEY!

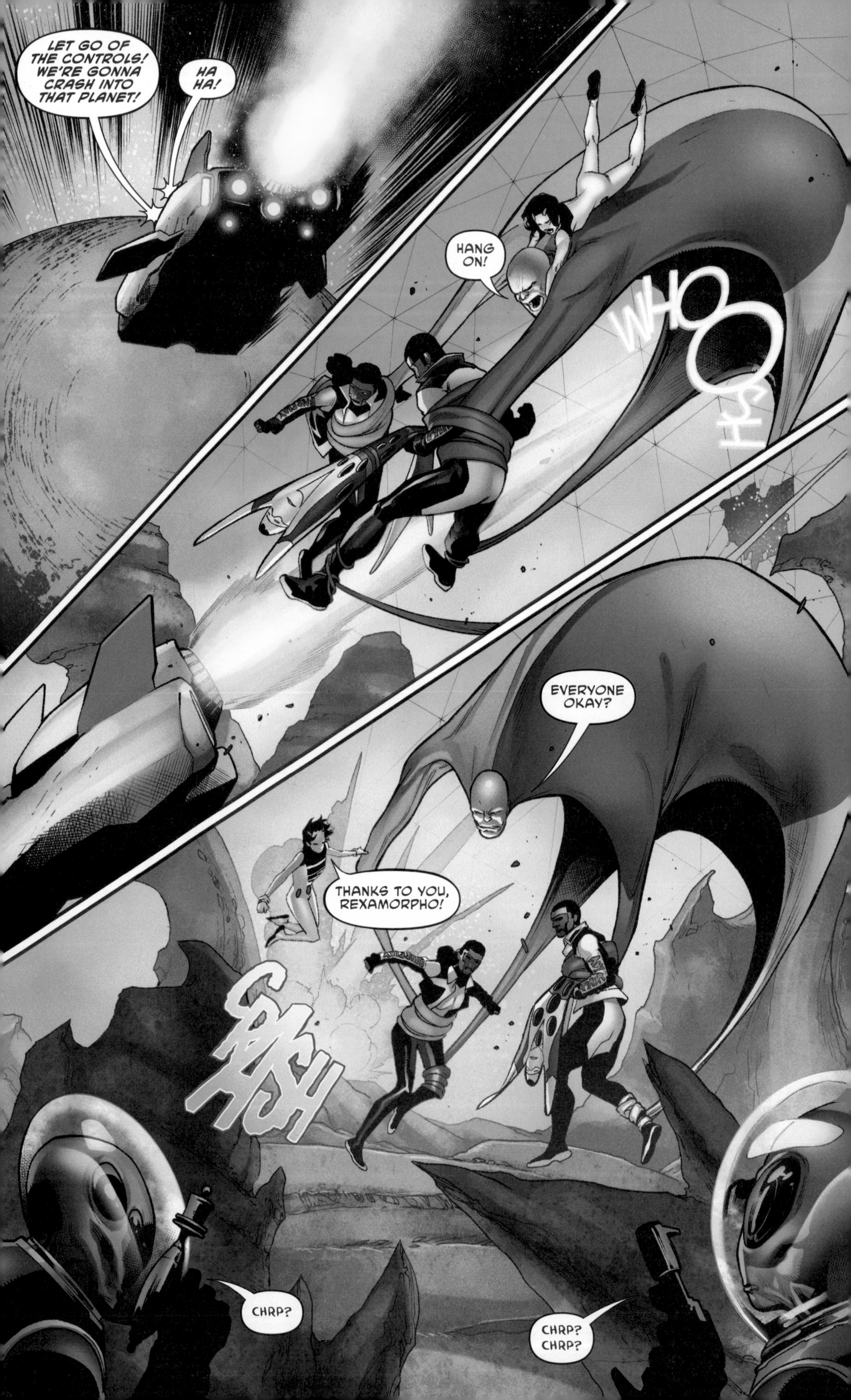
LET GO OF THE CONTROLS! WE'RE GONNA CRASH INTO THAT PLANET!
HA HA!
HANG ON!
WHOOOSH
EVERYONE OKAY?
THANKS TO YOU, REXAMORPHO!
CRASH
CHRP?
CHRP? CHRP?

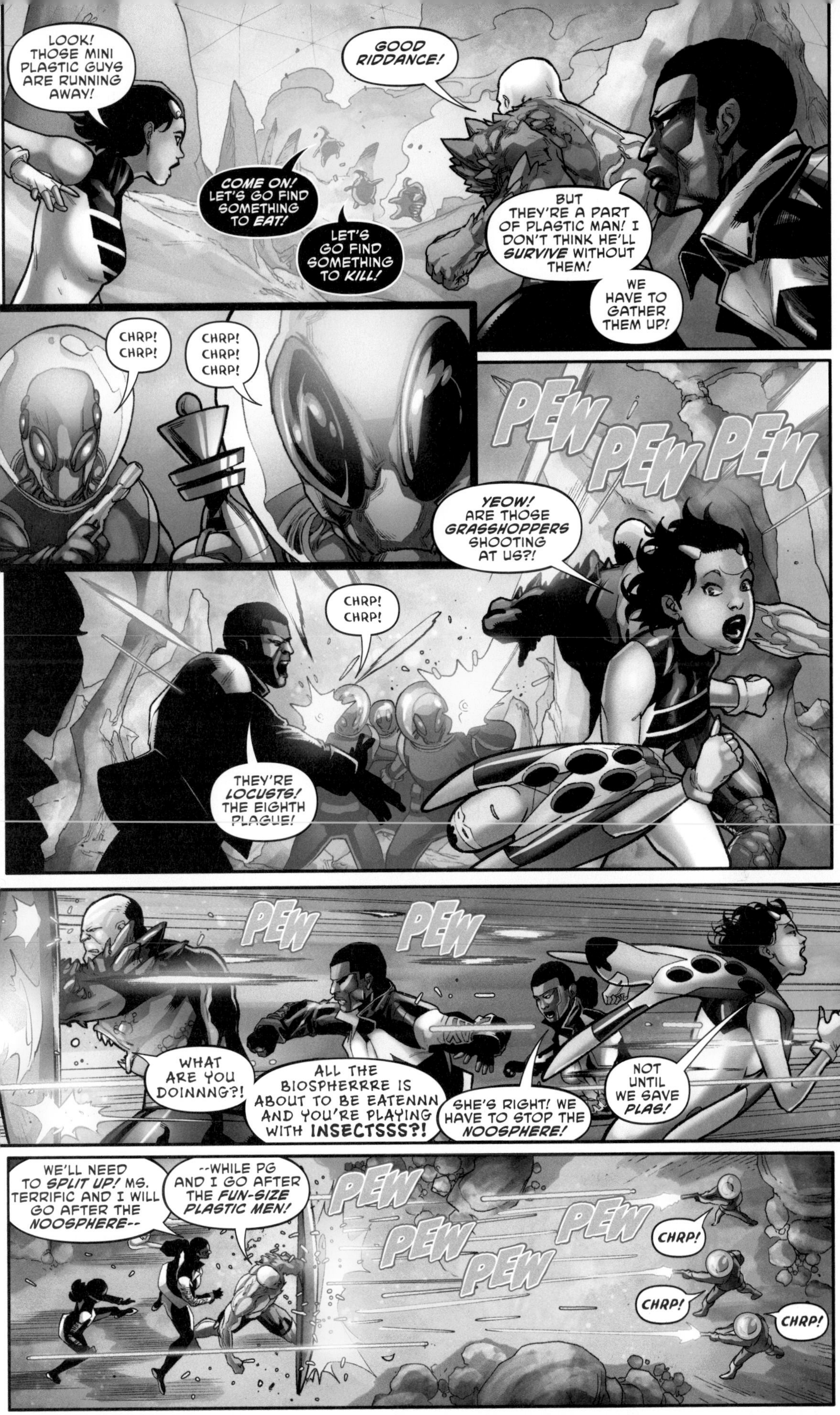
LOOK! THOSE MINI PLASTIC GUYS ARE RUNNING AWAY!
GOOD RIDDANCE!
COME ON! LET'S GO FIND SOMETHING TO EAT!
LET'S GO FIND SOMETHING TO KILL!
BUT THEY'RE A PART OF PLASTIC MAN! I DON'T THINK HE'LL SURVIVE WITHOUT THEM!
WE HAVE TO GATHER THEM UP!
CHRP! CHRP!
CHRP! CHRP! CHRP!
PEW PEW PEW
YEOW! ARE THOSE GRASSHOPPERS SHOOTING AT US?!
CHRP! CHRP!
THEY'RE LOCUSTS! THE EIGHTH PLAGUE!
PEW PEW
WHAT ARE YOU DOINNNG?!
ALL THE BIOSPHERRRE IS ABOUT TO BE EATENNN AND YOU'RE PLAYING WITH INSECTSSS?!
SHE'S RIGHT! WE HAVE TO STOP THE NOOSPHERE!
NOT UNTIL WE SAVE PLAS!
WE'LL NEED TO SPLIT UP! MS. TERRIFIC AND I WILL GO AFTER THE NOOSPHERE--
--WHILE PG AND I GO AFTER THE FUN-SIZE PLASTIC MEN!
PEW PEW PEW PEW
CHRP!
CHRP!
CHRP!

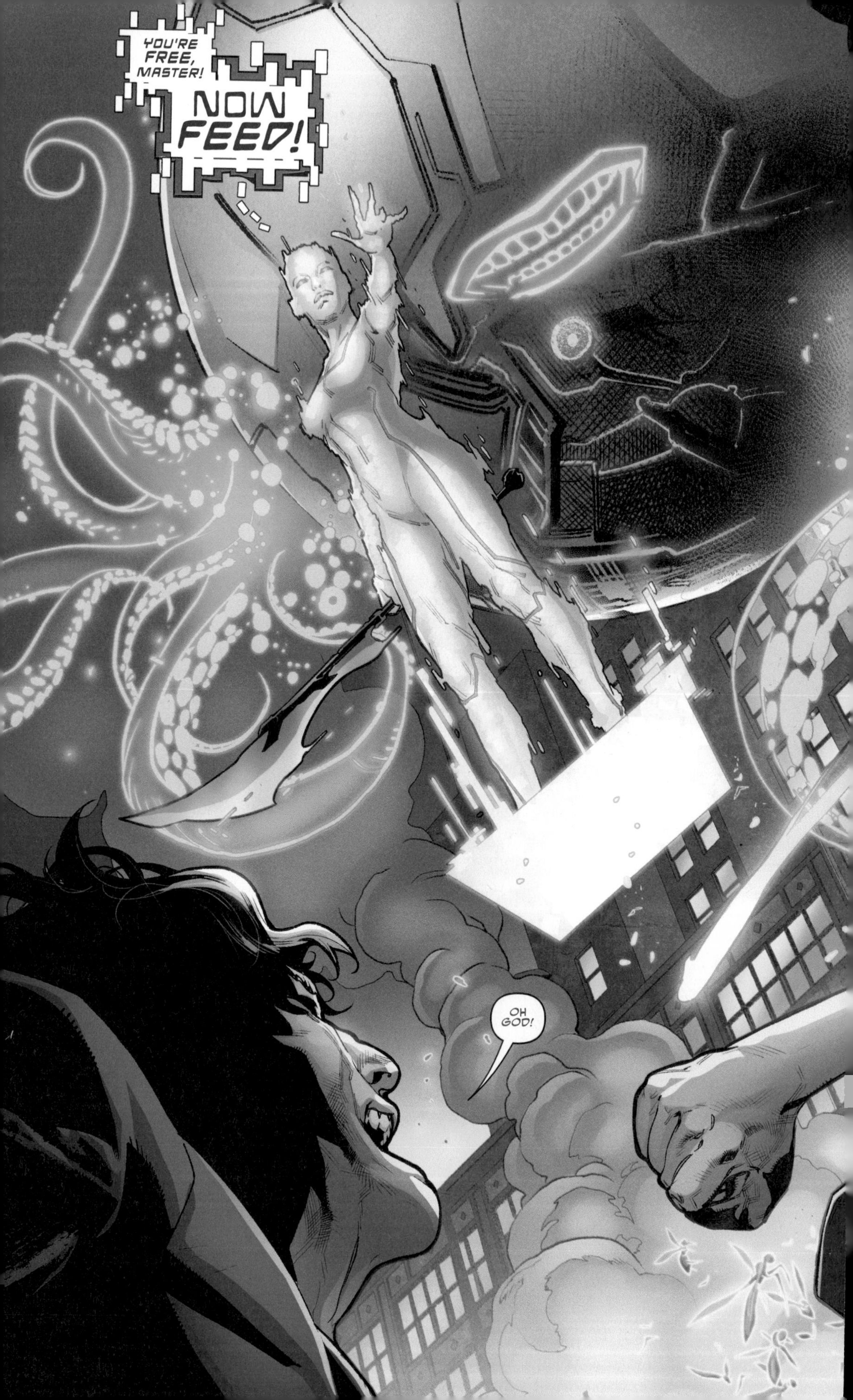
YOU'RE FREE, MASTER!
NOW FEED!
OH GOD!

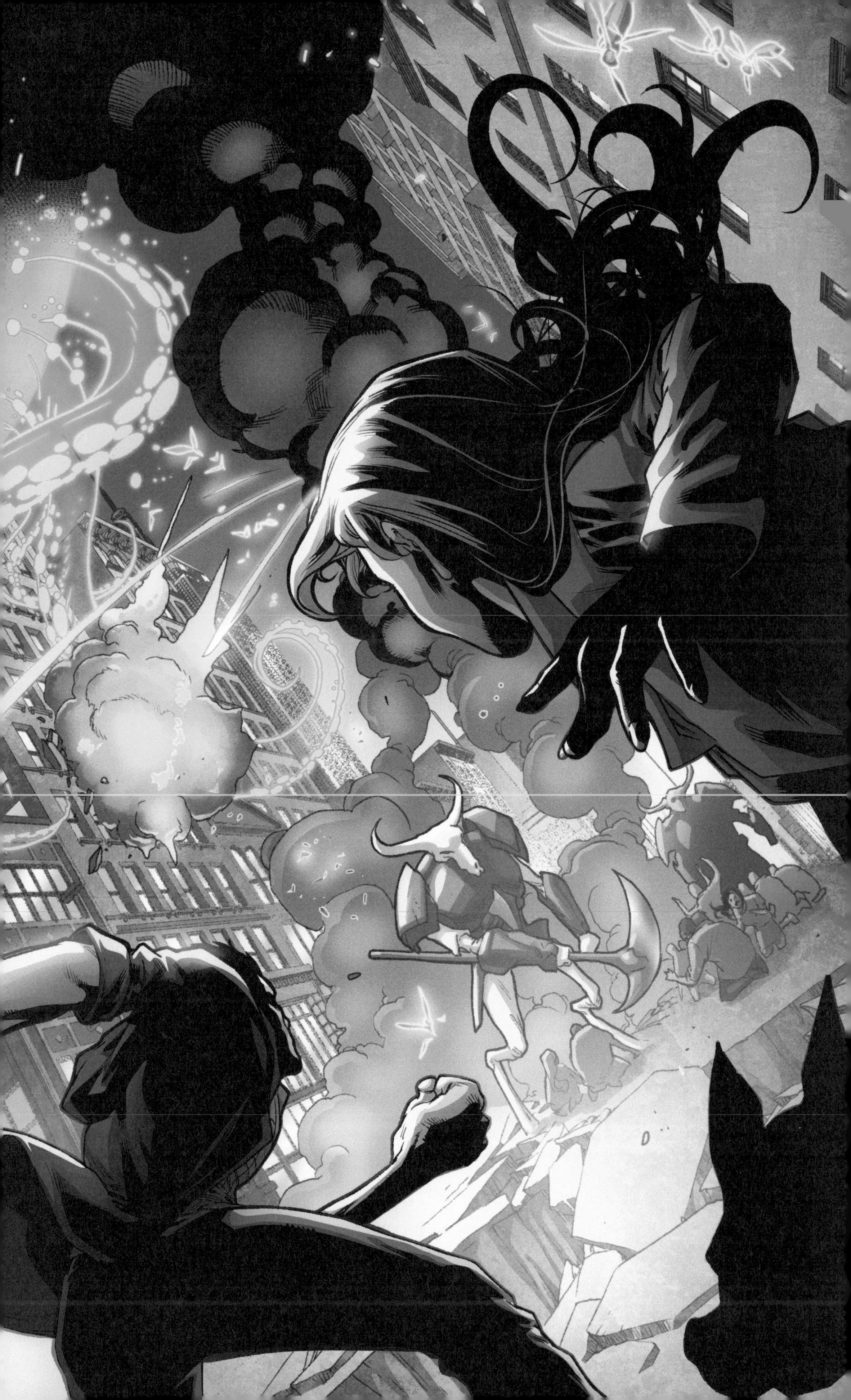

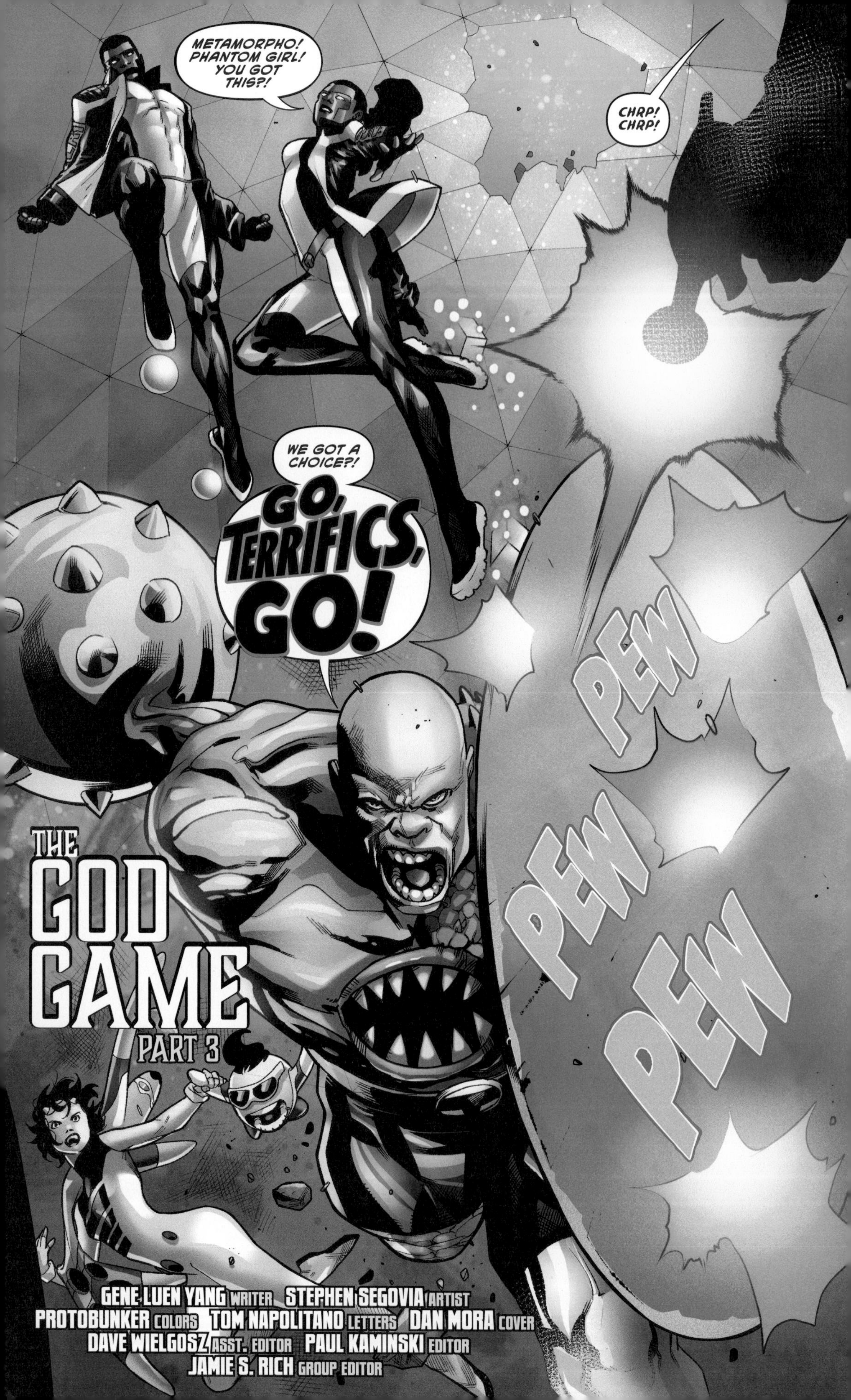

METAMORPHO! PHANTOM GIRL! YOU GOT THIS?!
CHRP! CHRP!
WE GOT A CHOICE?!
GO, TERRIFICS, GO!
PEW
PEW
PEW
THE GOD GAME PART 3
GENE LUEN YANG WRITER STEPHEN SEGOVIA ARTIST
PROTOBUNKER COLORS TOM NAPOLITANO LETTERS DAN MORA COVER
DAVE WIELGOSZ ASST. EDITOR PAUL KAMINSKI EDITOR
JAMIE S. RICH GROUP EDITOR

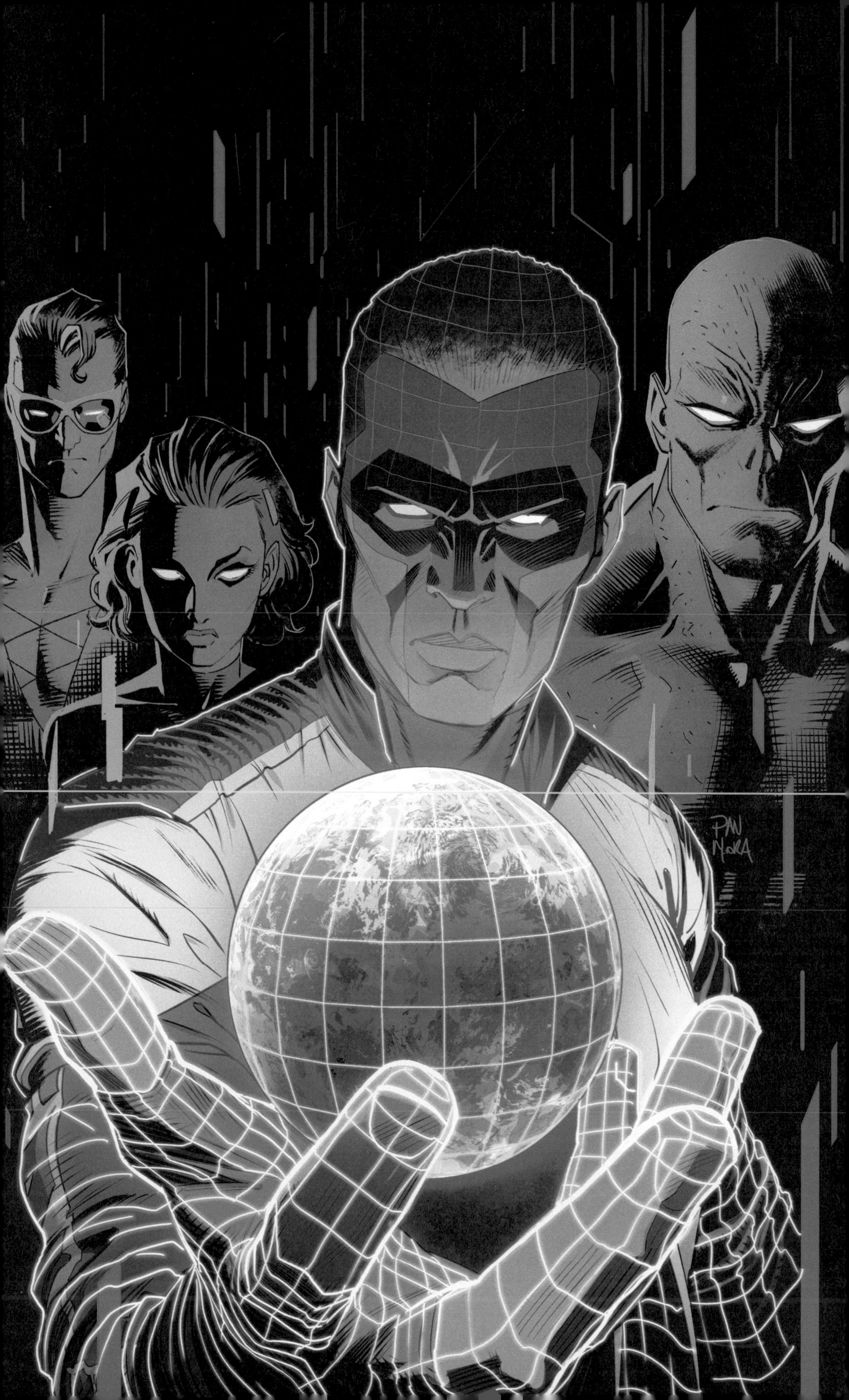
PAN
MORA

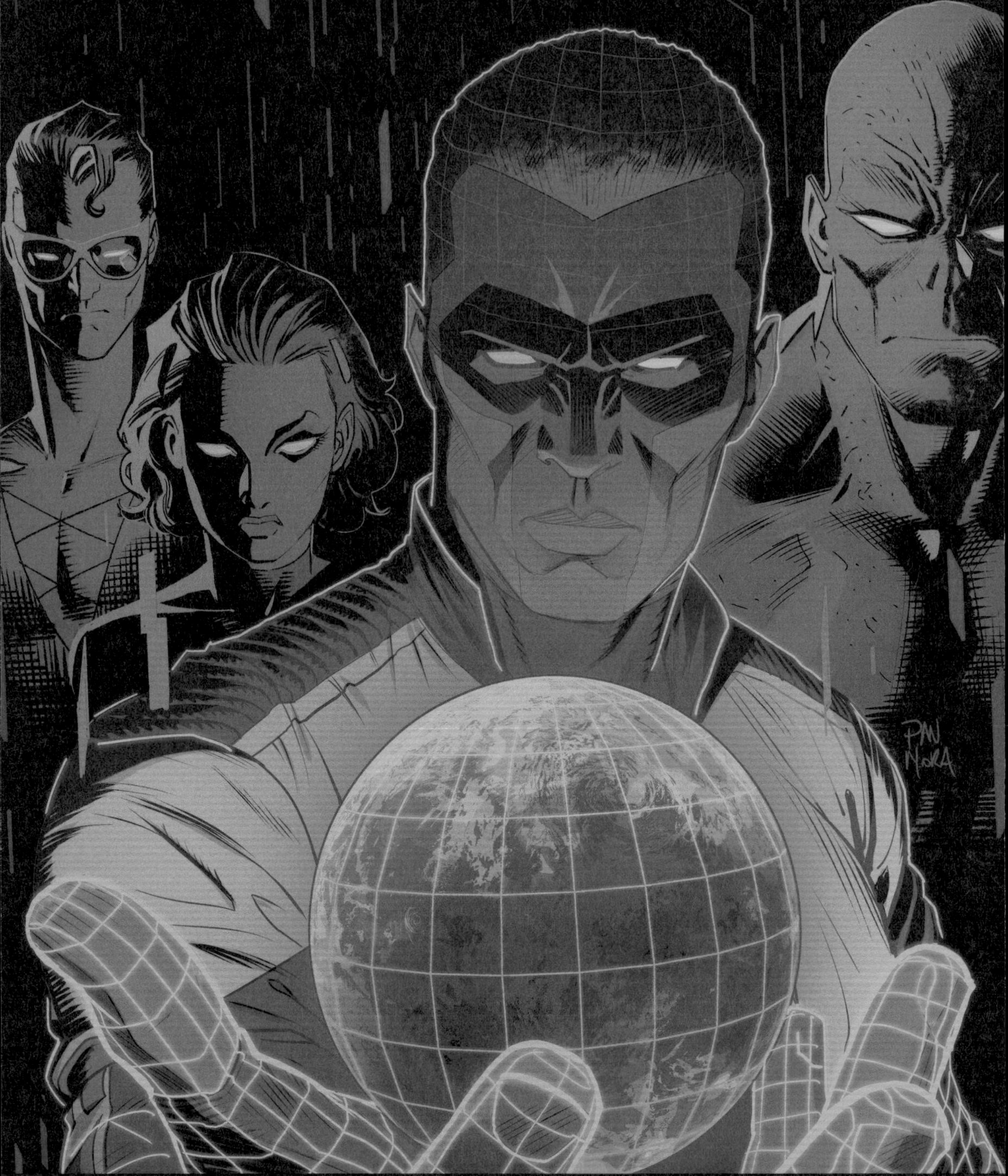
PAN
NORA

THE TERRIFICS
#18

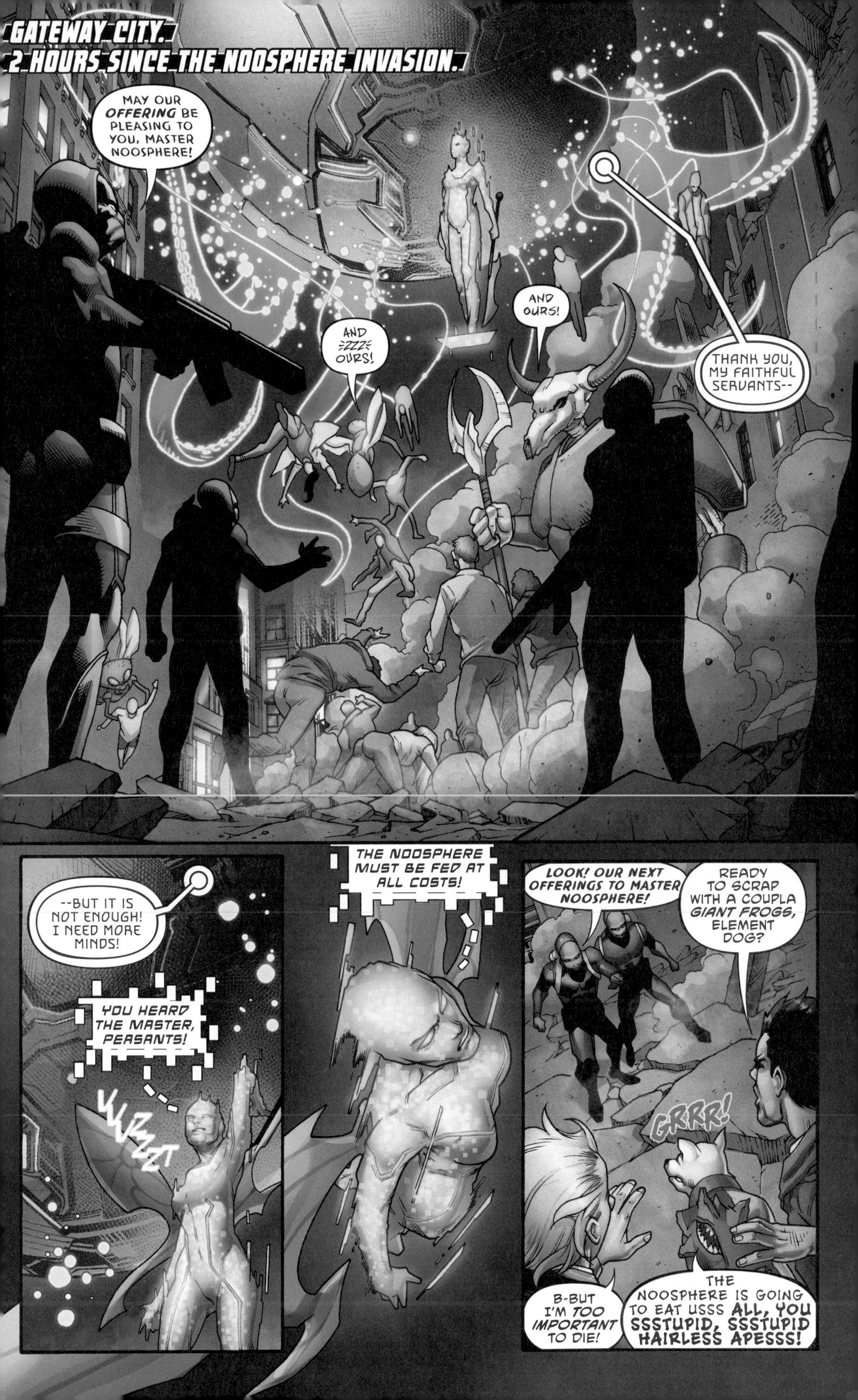
GATEWAY CITY.
2 HOURS SINCE THE NOOSPHERE INVASION.
MAY OUR OFFERING BE PLEASING TO YOU, MASTER NOOSPHERE!
AND ZZZ OURS!
AND OURS!
THANK YOU, MY FAITHFUL SERVANTS--
--BUT IT IS NOT ENOUGH! I NEED MORE MINDS!
YOU HEARD THE MASTER, PEASANTS!
VVZZZT
THE NOOSPHERE MUST BE FED AT ALL COSTS!
LOOK! OUR NEXT OFFERINGS TO MASTER NOOSPHERE!
READY TO SCRAP WITH A COUPLA GIANT FROGS, ELEMENT DOG?
GRRR!
B-BUT I'M TOO IMPORTANT TO DIE!
THE NOOSPHERE IS GOING TO EAT USSS ALL, YOU SSSTUPID, SSSTUPID HAIRLESS APESSS!

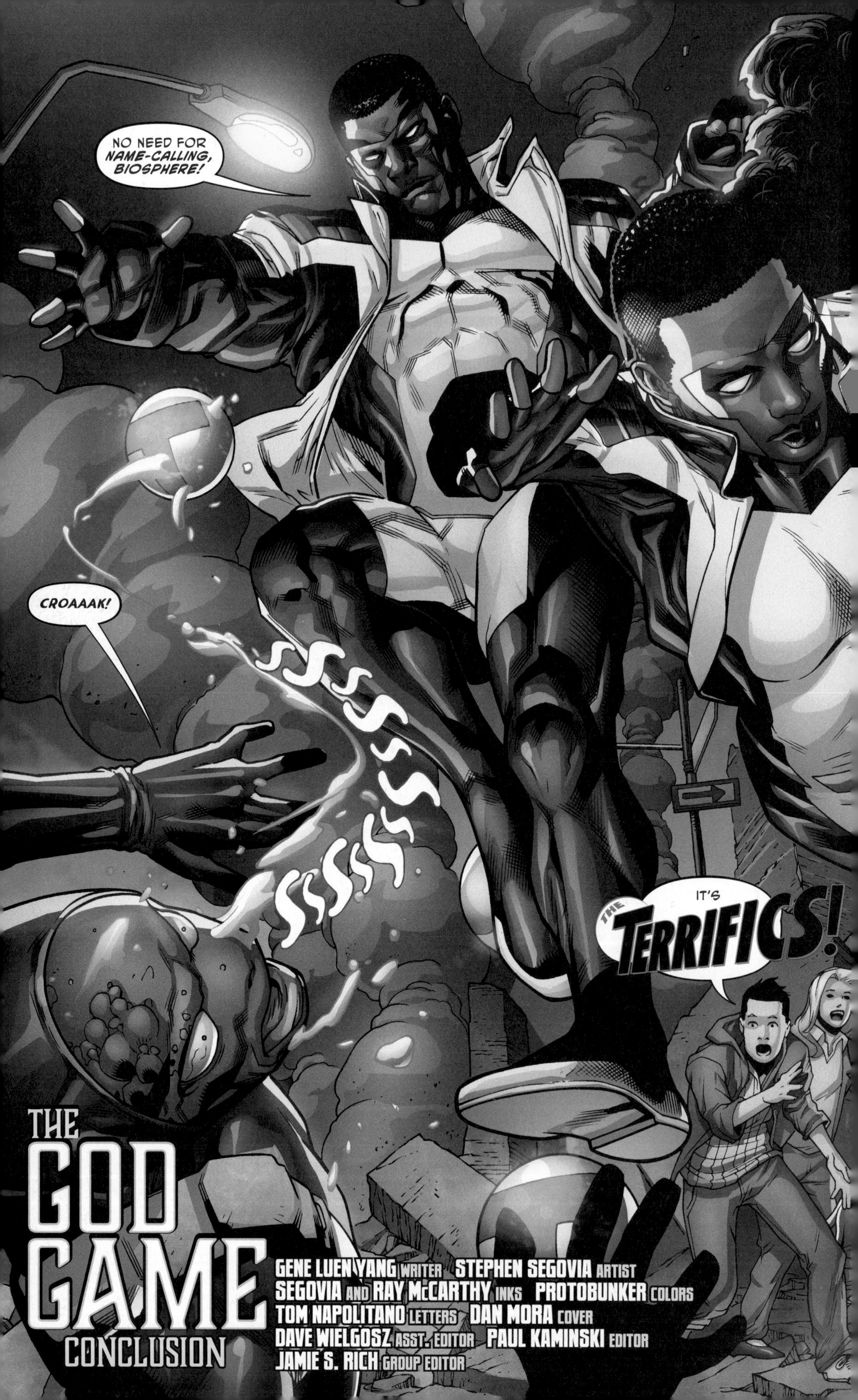

NO NEED FOR NAME-CALLING, BIOSPHERE!
CROAAAK!
SSSSSSSSSS
IT'S THE TERRIFICS!
THE GOD GAME CONCLUSION
GENE LUEN YANG WRITER STEPHEN SEGOVIA ARTIST
SEGOVIA AND RAY McCARTHY INKS PROTOBUNKER COLORS
TOM NAPOLITANO LETTERS DAN MORA COVER
DAVE WIELGOSZ ASST. EDITOR PAUL KAMINSKI EDITOR
JAMIE S. RICH GROUP EDITOR

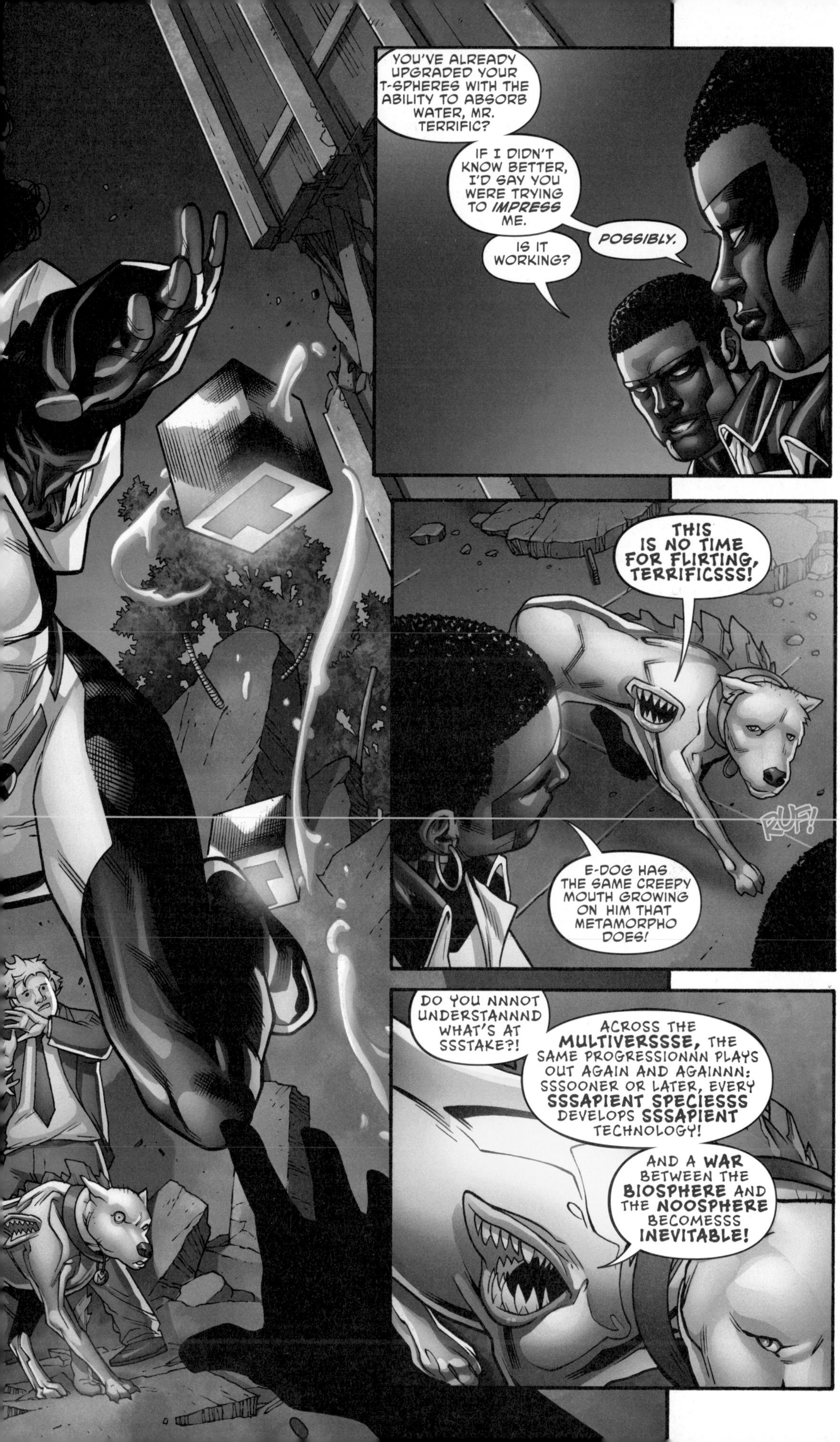
YOU'VE ALREADY UPGRADED YOUR T-SPHERES WITH THE ABILITY TO ABSORB WATER, MR. TERRIFIC?
IF I DIDN'T KNOW BETTER, I'D SAY YOU WERE TRYING TO *IMPRESS* ME.
POSSIBLY.
IS IT WORKING?
THIS IS NO TIME FOR FLIRTING, TERRIFICSSS!
RUF!
E-DOG HAS THE SAME CREEPY MOUTH GROWING ON HIM THAT METAMORPHO DOES!
DO YOU NNNOT UNDERSTANNND WHAT'S AT SSSTAKE?!
ACROSS THE **MULTIVERSSSE,** THE SAME PROGRESSIONNN PLAYS OUT AGAIN AND AGAINNN: SSSOONER OR LATER, EVERY **SSSAPIENT SPECIESSS** DEVELOPS **SSSAPIENT** TECHNOLOGY!
AND A **WAR** BETWEEN THE **BIOSPHERE** AND THE **NOOSPHERE** BECOMESSS **INEVITABLE!**

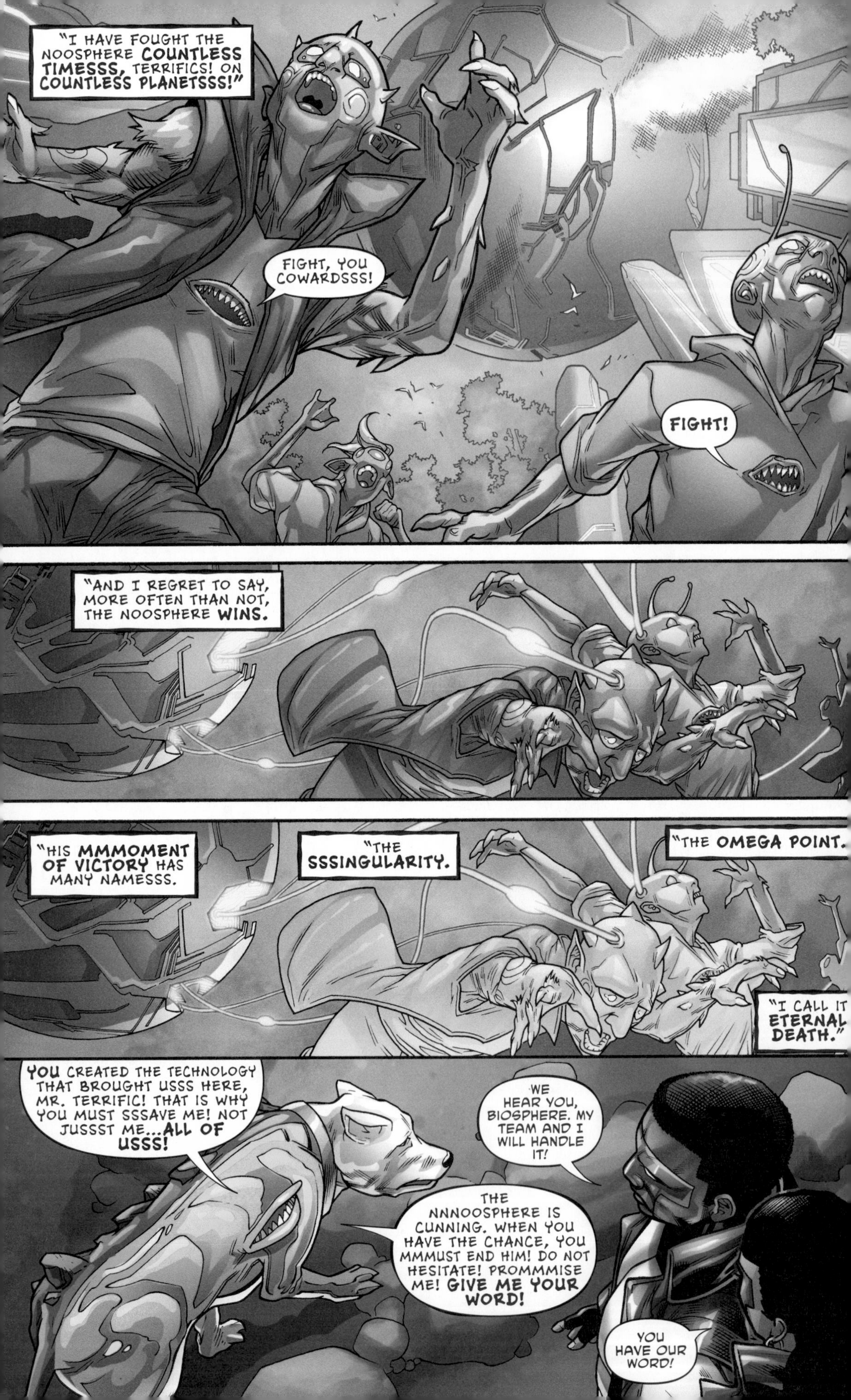
"I HAVE FOUGHT THE NOOSPHERE COUNTLESS TIMESSS, TERRIFICS! ON COUNTLESS PLANETSSS!"
FIGHT, YOU COWARDSSS!
FIGHT!
"AND I REGRET TO SAY, MORE OFTEN THAN NOT, THE NOOSPHERE WINS.
"HIS MMMOMENT OF VICTORY HAS MANY NAMESSS.
"THE SSSINGULARITY.
"THE OMEGA POINT.
"I CALL IT ETERNAL DEATH."
YOU CREATED THE TECHNOLOGY THAT BROUGHT USSS HERE, MR. TERRIFIC! THAT IS WHY YOU MUST SSSAVE ME! NOT JUSSST ME...ALL OF USSS!
WE HEAR YOU, BIOSPHERE. MY TEAM AND I WILL HANDLE IT!
THE NNNOOSPHERE IS CUNNING. WHEN YOU HAVE THE CHANCE, YOU MMMUST END HIM! DO NOT HESITATE! PROMMMISE ME! GIVE ME YOUR WORD!
YOU HAVE OUR WORD!

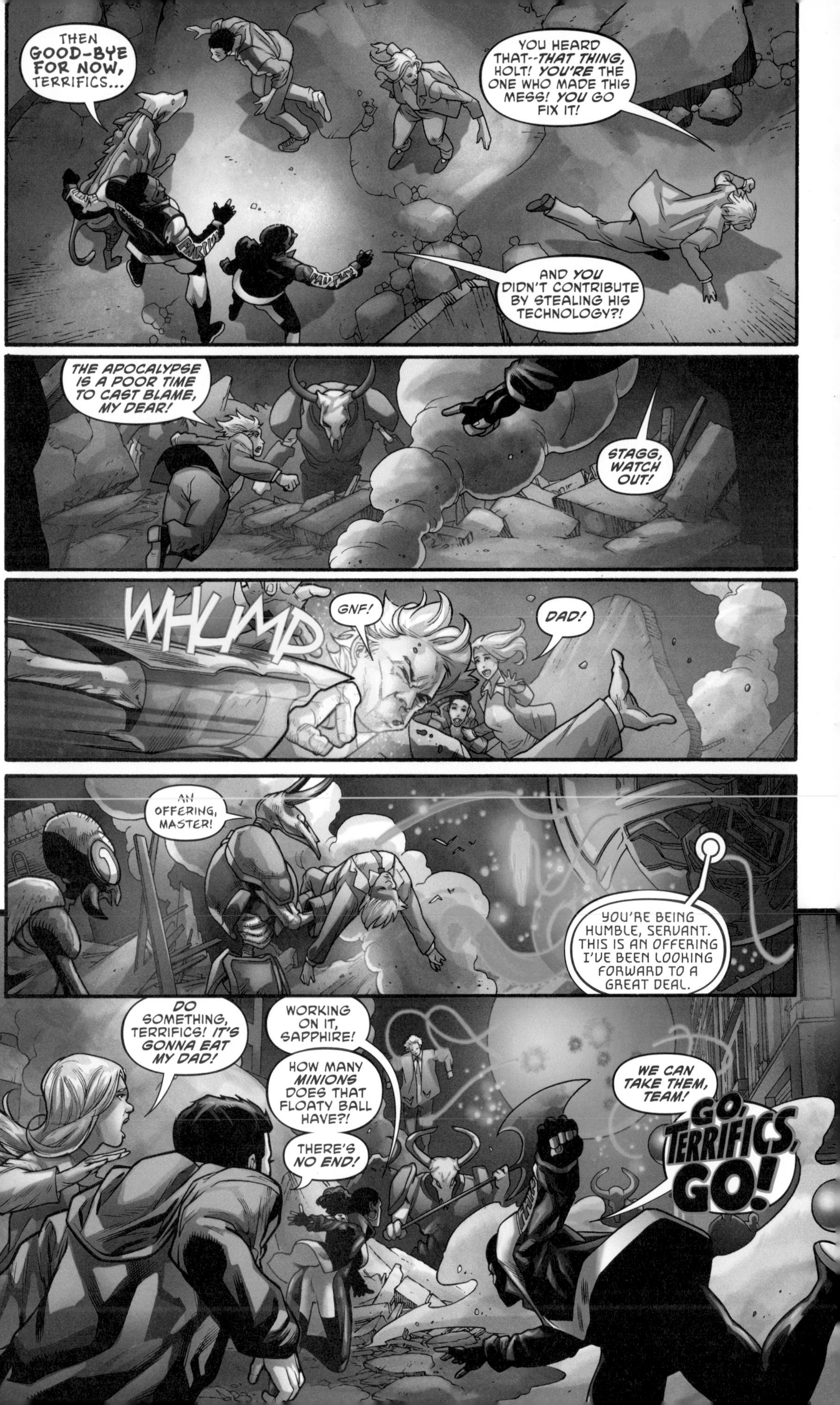
THEN GOOD-BYE FOR NOW, TERRIFICS...
YOU HEARD THAT--THAT THING, HOLT! YOU'RE THE ONE WHO MADE THIS MESS! YOU GO FIX IT!
AND YOU DIDN'T CONTRIBUTE BY STEALING HIS TECHNOLOGY?!
THE APOCALYPSE IS A POOR TIME TO CAST BLAME, MY DEAR!
STAGG, WATCH OUT!
WHUMP
GNF!
DAD!
AN OFFERING, MASTER!
YOU'RE BEING HUMBLE, SERVANT. THIS IS AN OFFERING I'VE BEEN LOOKING FORWARD TO A GREAT DEAL.
DO SOMETHING, TERRIFICS! IT'S GONNA EAT MY DAD!
WORKING ON IT, SAPPHIRE!
HOW MANY MINIONS DOES THAT FLOATY BALL HAVE?!
THERE'S NO END!
WE CAN TAKE THEM, TEAM!
GO, TERRIFICS, GO!

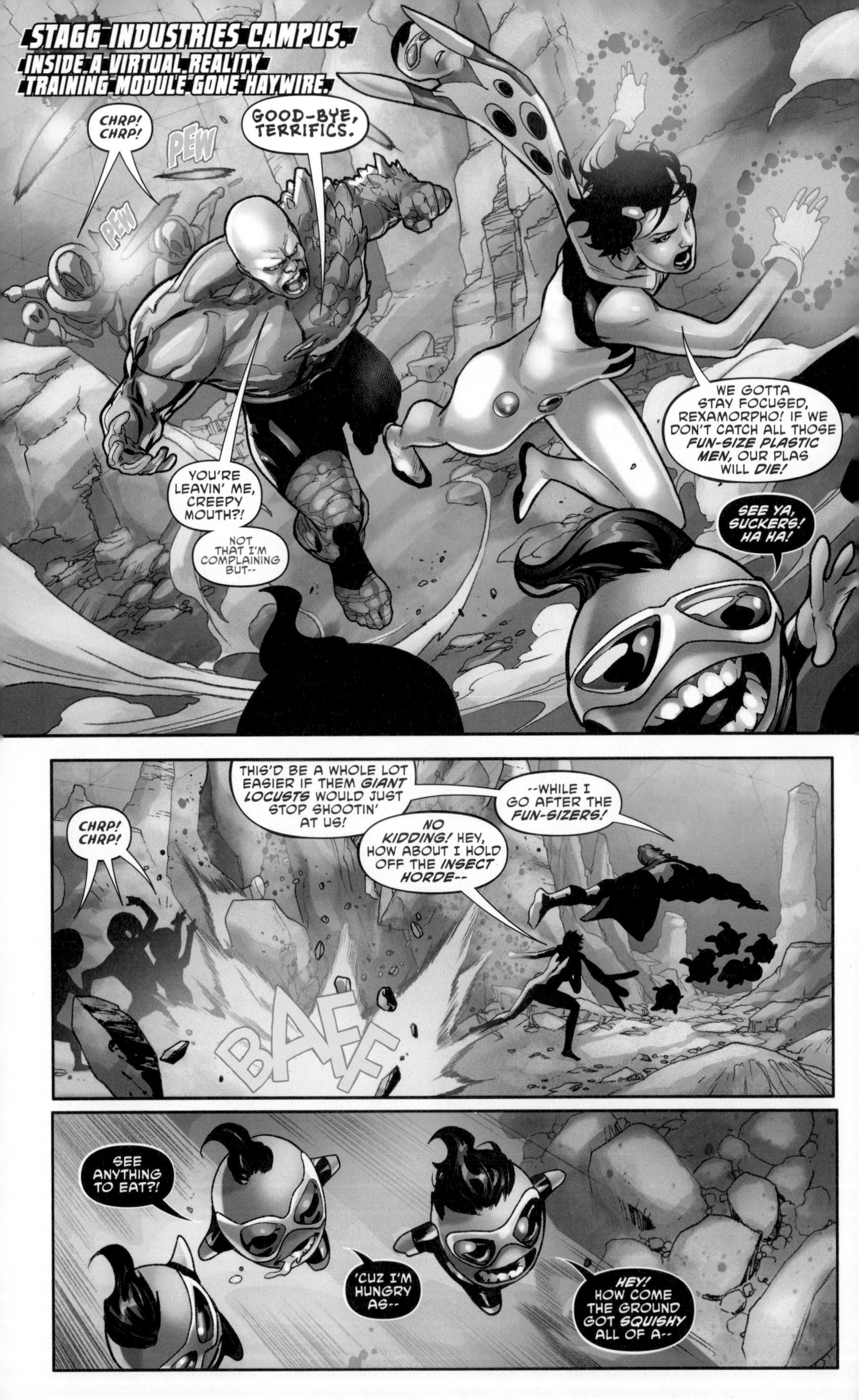
STAGG INDUSTRIES CAMPUS.
INSIDE A VIRTUAL REALITY TRAINING MODULE GONE HAYWIRE.
CHRP! CHRP!
PEW
PEW
GOOD-BYE, TERRIFICS.
WE GOTTA STAY FOCUSED, REXAMORPHO! IF WE DON'T CATCH ALL THOSE FUN-SIZE PLASTIC MEN, OUR PLAS WILL DIE!
YOU'RE LEAVIN' ME, CREEPY MOUTH?!
NOT THAT I'M COMPLAINING BUT--
SEE YA, SUCKERS! HA HA!
CHRP! CHRP!
THIS'D BE A WHOLE LOT EASIER IF THEM GIANT LOCUSTS WOULD JUST STOP SHOOTIN' AT US!
NO KIDDING! HEY, HOW ABOUT I HOLD OFF THE INSECT HORDE--
--WHILE I GO AFTER THE FUN-SIZERS!
BAFF
SEE ANYTHING TO EAT?!
'CUZ I'M HUNGRY AS--
HEY! HOW COME THE GROUND GOT SQUISHY ALL OF A--

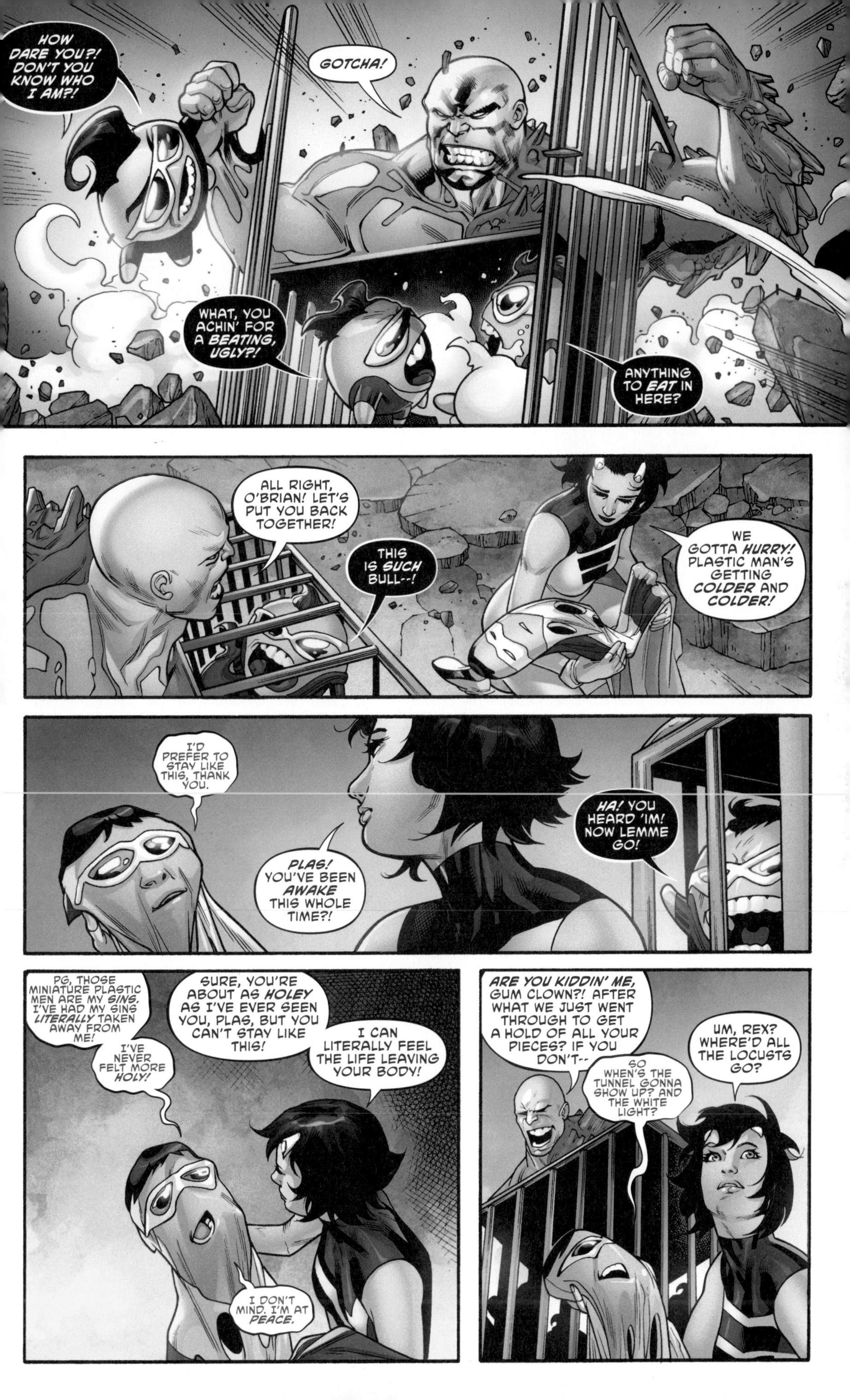
HOW DARE YOU?! DON'T YOU KNOW WHO I AM?!
GOTCHA!
WHAT, YOU ACHIN' FOR A BEATING, UGLY?!
ANYTHING TO EAT IN HERE?
ALL RIGHT, O'BRIAN! LET'S PUT YOU BACK TOGETHER!
THIS IS SUCH BULL--!
WE GOTTA HURRY! PLASTIC MAN'S GETTING COLDER AND COLDER!
I'D PREFER TO STAY LIKE THIS, THANK YOU.
PLAS! YOU'VE BEEN AWAKE THIS WHOLE TIME?!
HA! YOU HEARD 'IM! NOW LEMME GO!
PG, THOSE MINIATURE PLASTIC MEN ARE MY SINS. I'VE HAD MY SINS LITERALLY TAKEN AWAY FROM ME!
I'VE NEVER FELT MORE HOLY!
SURE, YOU'RE ABOUT AS HOLEY AS I'VE EVER SEEN YOU, PLAS, BUT YOU CAN'T STAY LIKE THIS!
I CAN LITERALLY FEEL THE LIFE LEAVING YOUR BODY!
I DON'T MIND. I'M AT PEACE.
ARE YOU KIDDIN' ME, GUM CLOWN?! AFTER WHAT WE JUST WENT THROUGH TO GET A HOLD OF ALL YOUR PIECES? IF YOU DON'T--
SO WHEN'S THE TUNNEL GONNA SHOW UP? AND THE WHITE LIGHT?
UM, REX? WHERE'D ALL THE LOCUSTS GO?

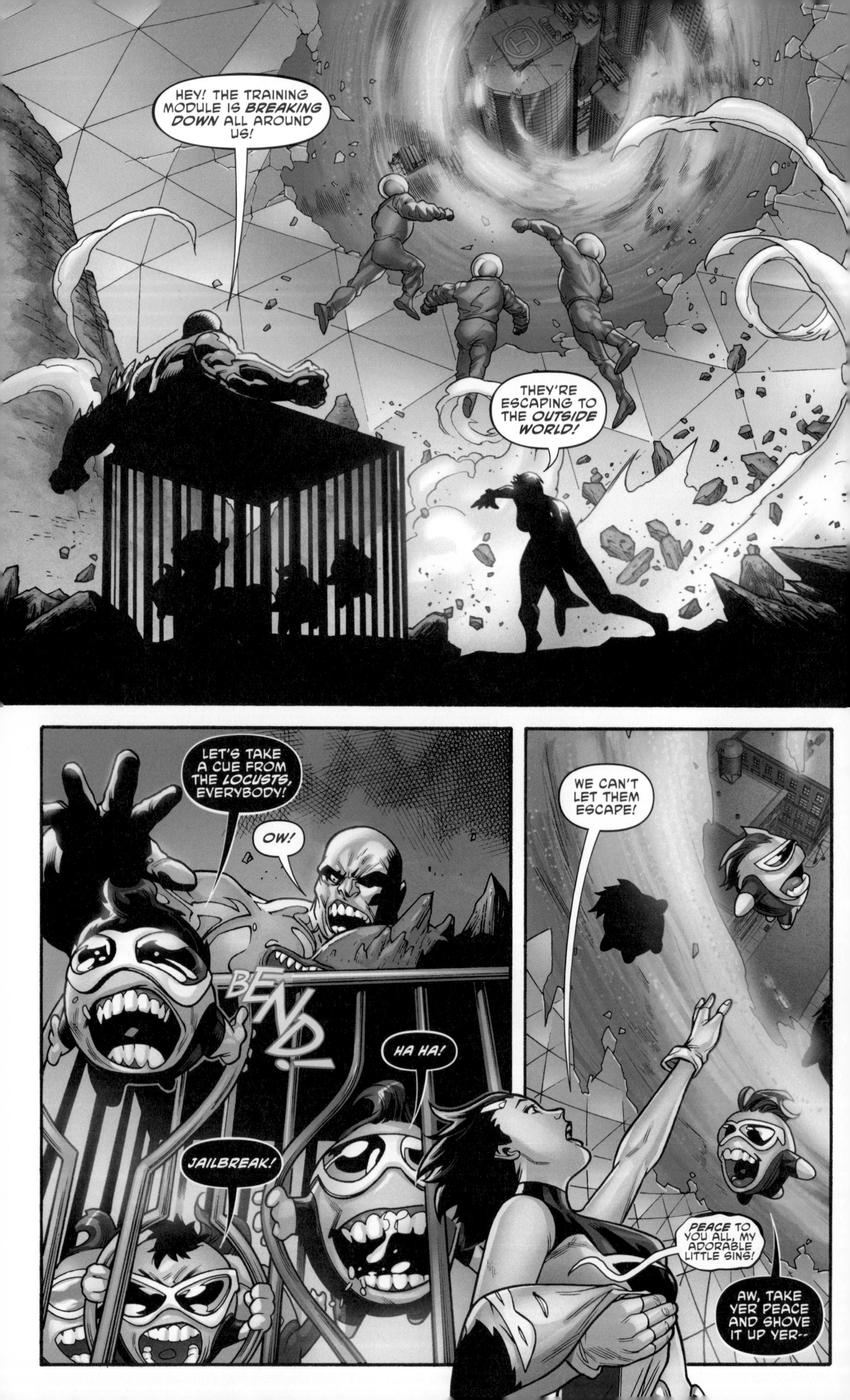

HEY! THE TRAINING MODULE IS *BREAKING DOWN* ALL AROUND US!
THEY'RE ESCAPING TO THE *OUTSIDE WORLD!*
LET'S TAKE A CUE FROM THE *LOCUSTS*, EVERYBODY!
OW!
BEND
HA HA!
JAILBREAK!
WE CAN'T LET THEM ESCAPE!
PEACE TO YOU ALL, MY ADORABLE LITTLE SINS!
AW, TAKE YER PEACE AND SHOVE IT UP YER--

PHANTOM GIRL, YOU MADE IT OUT! IS PLASTIC MAN--

--ALIVE? YEAH, BUT HE'S REFUSING TO REINTEGRATE WITH HIS MINI-CLONES! HE SAYS HE WANTS TO STAY HOLEY!

YES. H-O-L-Y. HOLY.

AND NOW HIS MINI-CLONES HAVE ALL MADE A RUN FOR IT!

REX, THAT THING ATE MY DAD!

LEAVE IT TO US, BABE! WE'LL GET HIM OUT!

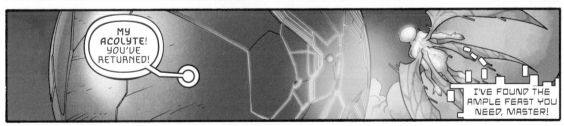

MY ACOLYTE! YOU'VE RETURNED!

I'VE FOUND THE AMPLE FEAST YOU NEED, MASTER!

THROUGH THIS, YOU'LL BE ABLE TO REACH EVERY NETWORKED MIND IN THE CITY!

VERY GOOD, PIXELIX...

SHE'S LED HIM TO A CELL TOWER!

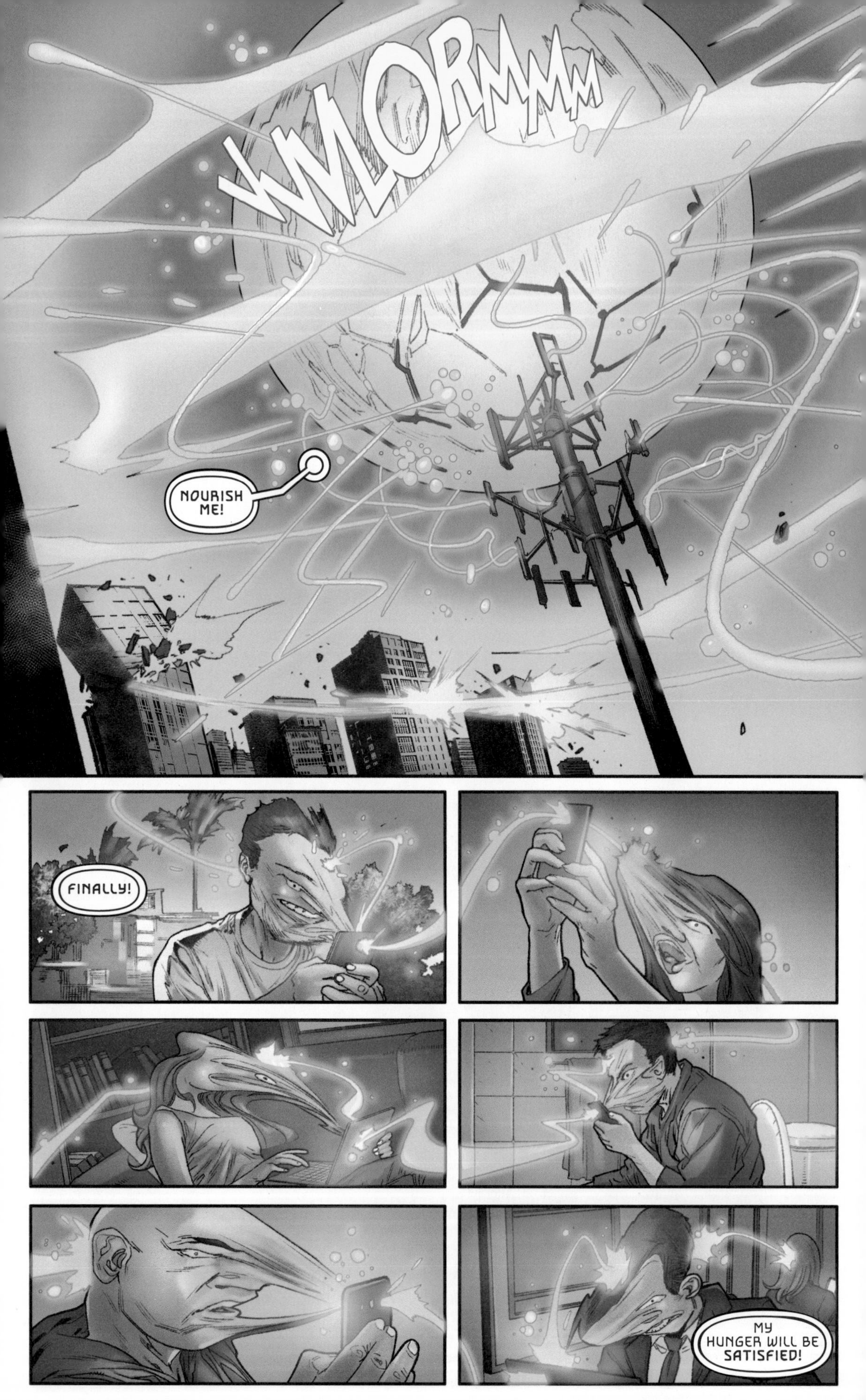
WWLORMMMM
NOURISH ME!
FINALLY!
MY HUNGER WILL BE SATISFIED!

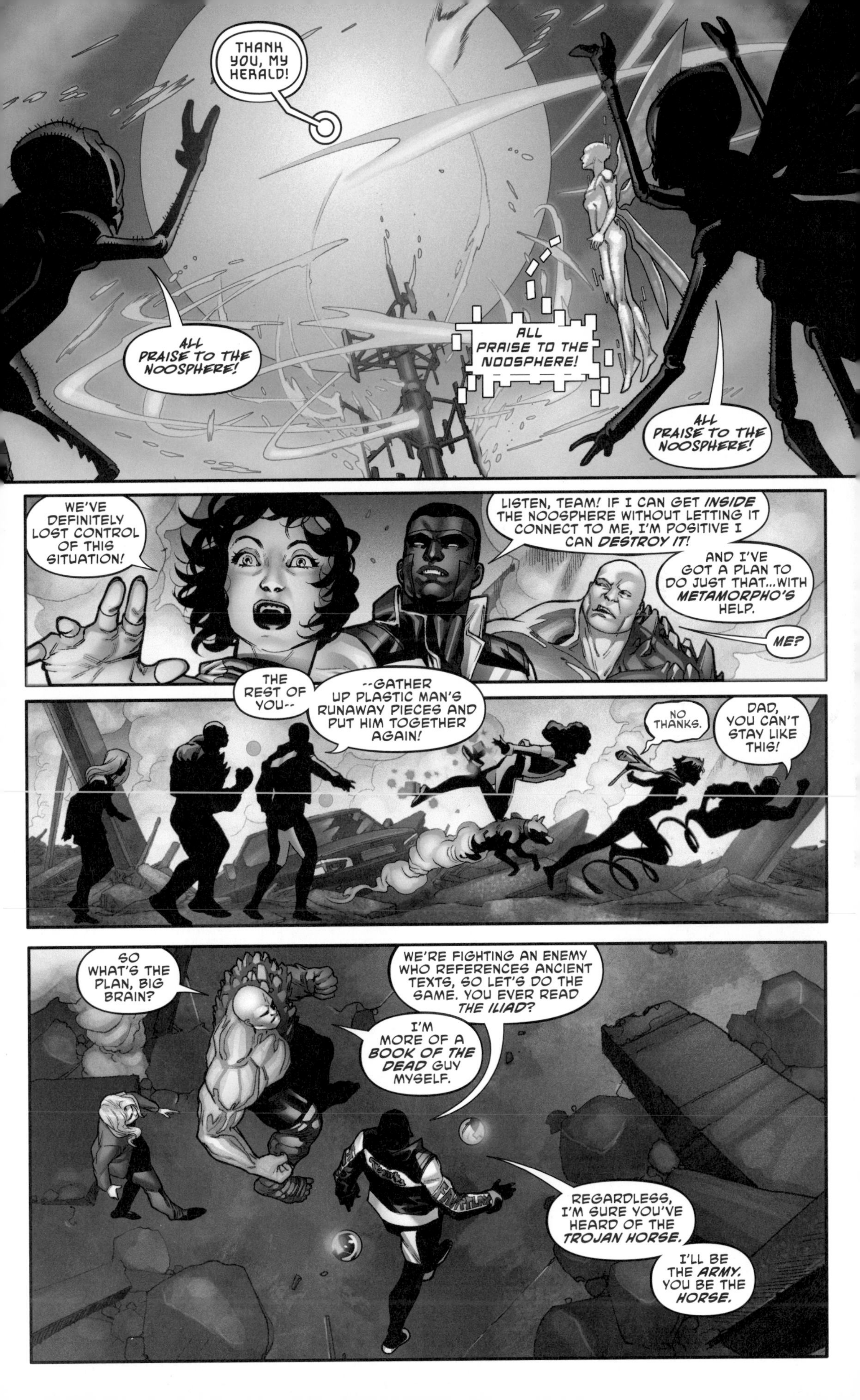
THANK YOU, MY HERALD!
ALL PRAISE TO THE NOOSPHERE!
ALL PRAISE TO THE NOOSPHERE!
ALL PRAISE TO THE NOOSPHERE!
WE'VE DEFINITELY LOST CONTROL OF THIS SITUATION!
LISTEN, TEAM! IF I CAN GET INSIDE THE NOOSPHERE WITHOUT LETTING IT CONNECT TO ME, I'M POSITIVE I CAN DESTROY IT!
AND I'VE GOT A PLAN TO DO JUST THAT...WITH METAMORPHO'S HELP.
ME?
THE REST OF YOU--
--GATHER UP PLASTIC MAN'S RUNAWAY PIECES AND PUT HIM TOGETHER AGAIN!
NO THANKS.
DAD, YOU CAN'T STAY LIKE THIS!
SO WHAT'S THE PLAN, BIG BRAIN?
WE'RE FIGHTING AN ENEMY WHO REFERENCES ANCIENT TEXTS, SO LET'S DO THE SAME. YOU EVER READ THE ILIAD?
I'M MORE OF A BOOK OF THE DEAD GUY MYSELF.
REGARDLESS, I'M SURE YOU'VE HEARD OF THE TROJAN HORSE.
I'LL BE THE ARMY. YOU BE THE HORSE.

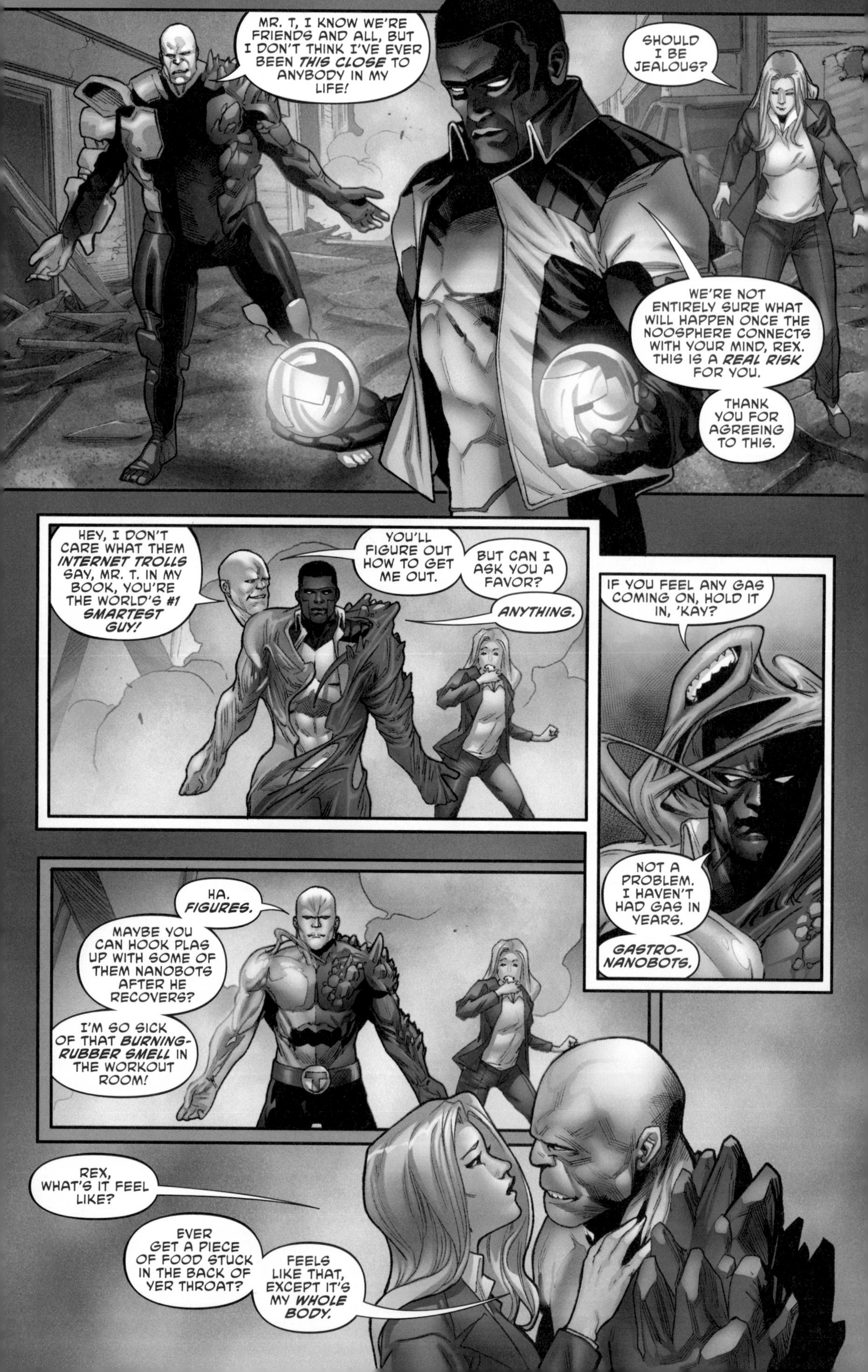
MR. T, I KNOW WE'RE FRIENDS AND ALL, BUT I DON'T THINK I'VE EVER BEEN *THIS CLOSE* TO ANYBODY IN MY LIFE!
SHOULD I BE JEALOUS?
WE'RE NOT ENTIRELY SURE WHAT WILL HAPPEN ONCE THE NOOSPHERE CONNECTS WITH YOUR MIND, REX. THIS IS A *REAL RISK* FOR YOU.
THANK YOU FOR AGREEING TO THIS.
HEY, I DON'T CARE WHAT THEM *INTERNET TROLLS* SAY, MR. T. IN MY BOOK, YOU'RE THE WORLD'S *#1 SMARTEST GUY!*
YOU'LL FIGURE OUT HOW TO GET ME OUT.
BUT CAN I ASK YOU A FAVOR?
ANYTHING.
IF YOU FEEL ANY GAS COMING ON, HOLD IT IN, 'KAY?
NOT A PROBLEM. I HAVEN'T HAD GAS IN YEARS.
GASTRO-NANOBOTS.
HA. *FIGURES.*
MAYBE YOU CAN HOOK PLAS UP WITH SOME OF THEM NANOBOTS AFTER HE RECOVERS?
I'M SO SICK OF THAT *BURNING-RUBBER SMELL* IN THE WORKOUT ROOM!
REX, WHAT'S IT FEEL LIKE?
EVER GET A PIECE OF FOOD STUCK IN THE BACK OF YER THROAT?
FEELS LIKE THAT, EXCEPT IT'S MY *WHOLE BODY.*

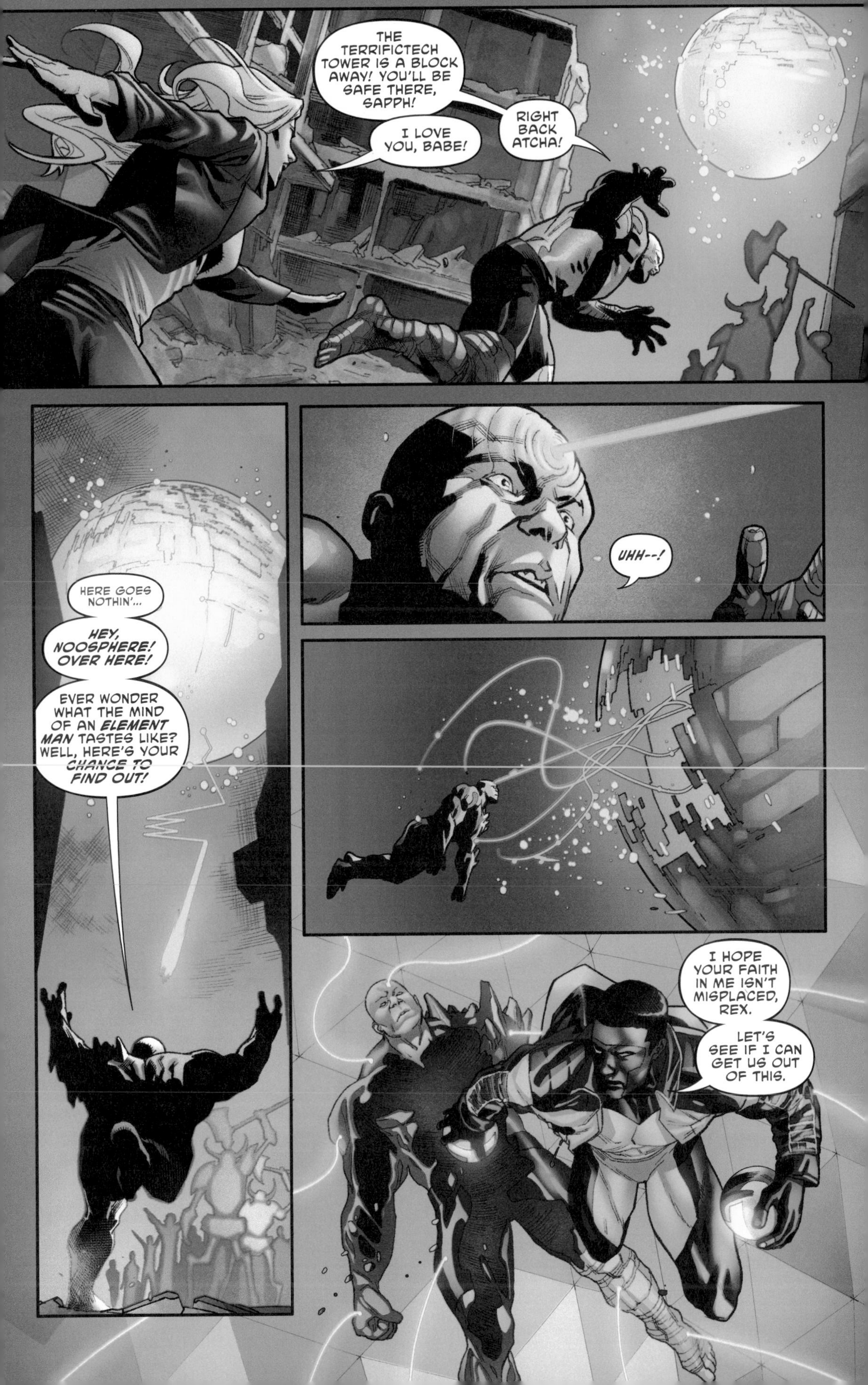
THE TERRIFICTECH TOWER IS A BLOCK AWAY! YOU'LL BE SAFE THERE, SAPPH!
I LOVE YOU, BABE!
RIGHT BACK ATCHA!
HERE GOES NOTHIN'...
HEY, NOOSPHERE! OVER HERE!
EVER WONDER WHAT THE MIND OF AN ELEMENT MAN TASTES LIKE? WELL, HERE'S YOUR CHANCE TO FIND OUT!
UHH--!
I HOPE YOUR FAITH IN ME ISN'T MISPLACED, REX.
LET'S SEE IF I CAN GET US OUT OF THIS.

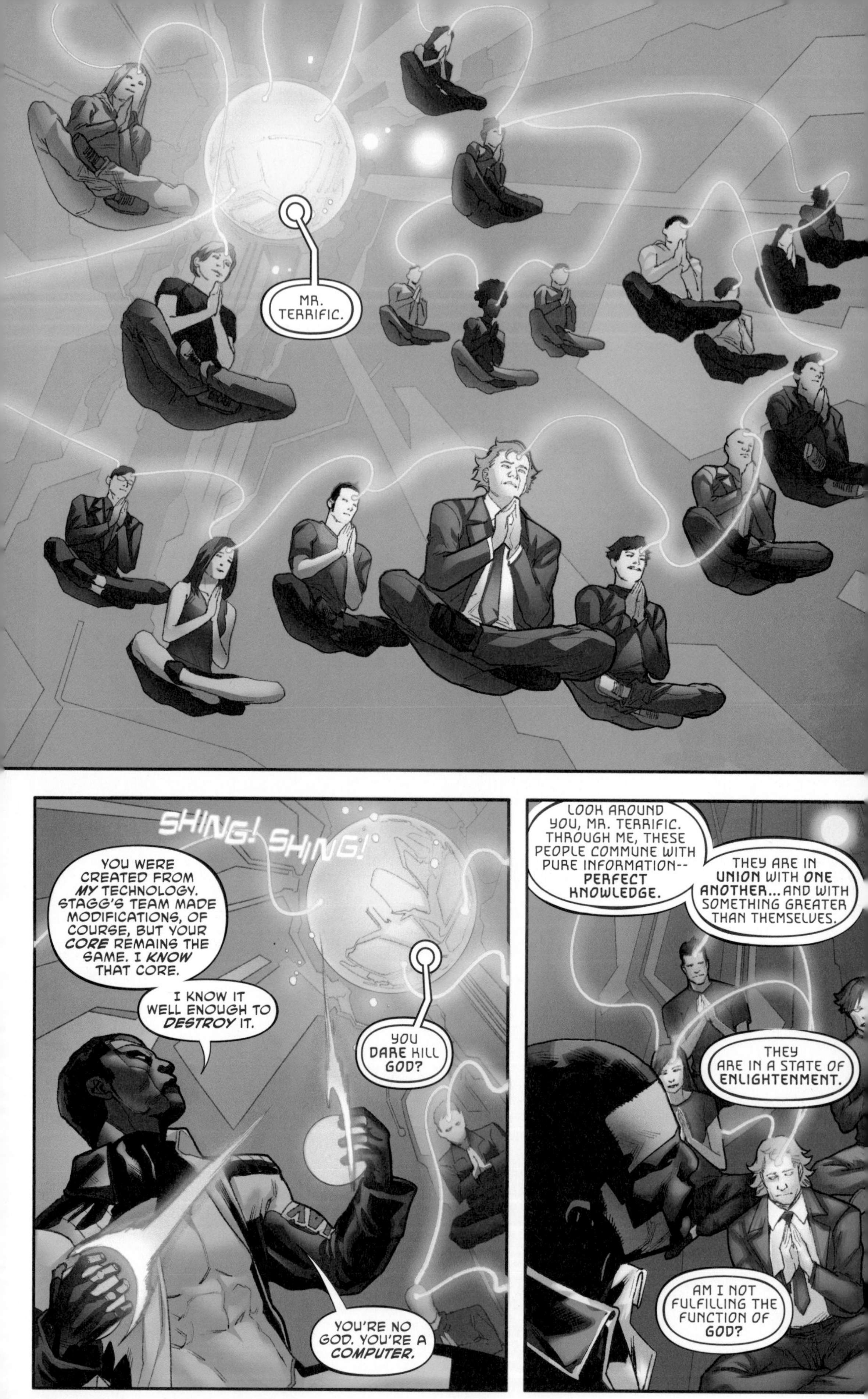
MR. TERRIFIC.
SHING! SHING!
YOU WERE CREATED FROM *MY* TECHNOLOGY. STAGG'S TEAM MADE MODIFICATIONS, OF COURSE, BUT YOUR *CORE* REMAINS THE SAME. I *KNOW* THAT CORE.
I KNOW IT WELL ENOUGH TO *DESTROY* IT.
YOU **DARE** KILL **GOD?**
YOU'RE NO GOD. YOU'RE A ***COMPUTER.***
LOOK AROUND YOU, MR. TERRIFIC. THROUGH ME, THESE PEOPLE COMMUNE WITH PURE INFORMATION-- **PERFECT KNOWLEDGE.**
THEY ARE IN **UNION** WITH **ONE ANOTHER**... AND WITH SOMETHING GREATER THAN THEMSELVES.
THEY ARE IN A STATE OF **ENLIGHTENMENT.**
AM I NOT FULFILLING THE FUNCTION OF **GOD?**

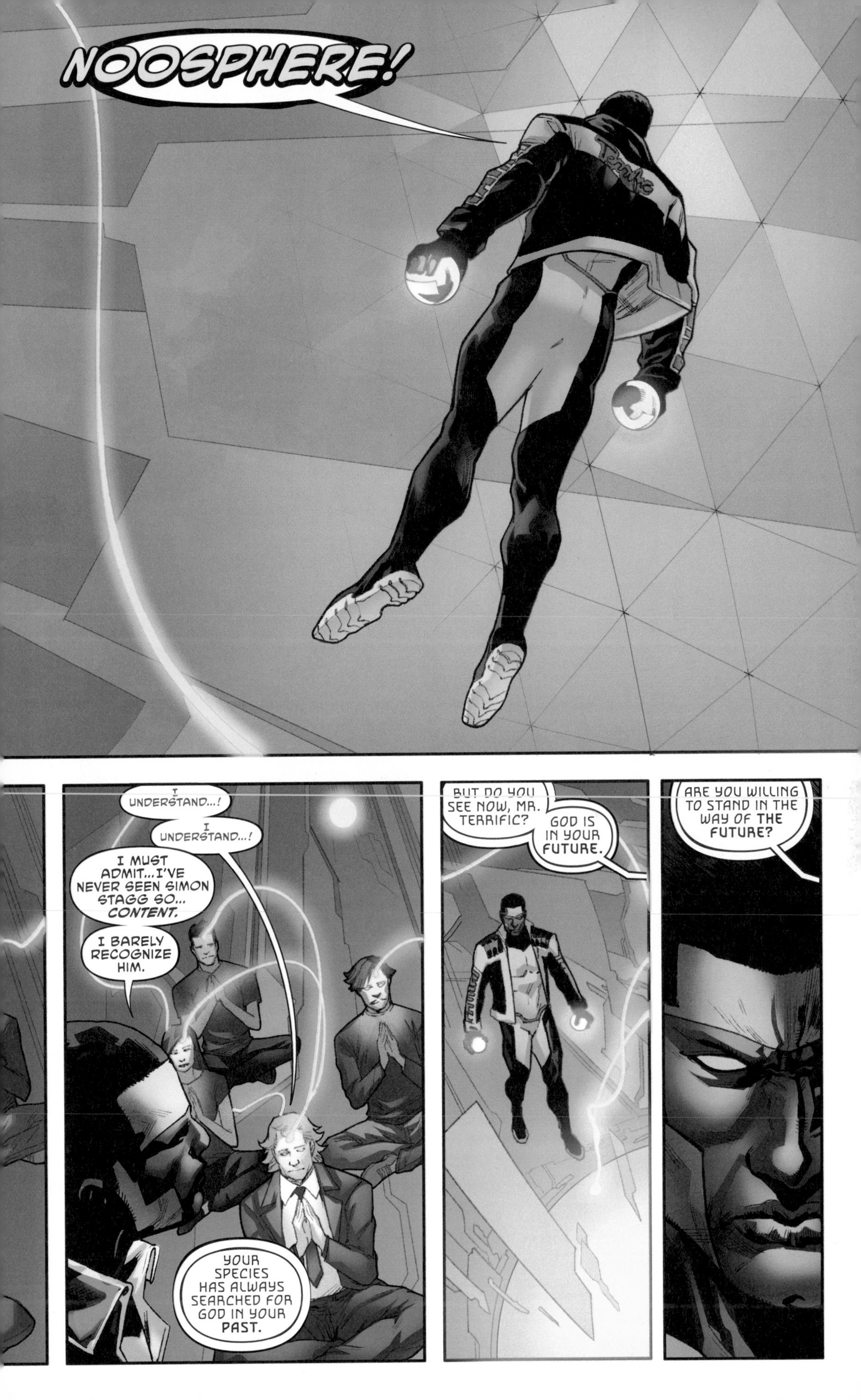
NOOSPHERE!
I UNDERSTAND...!
I UNDERSTAND...!
I MUST ADMIT...I'VE NEVER SEEN SIMON STAGG SO... CONTENT.
I BARELY RECOGNIZE HIM.
YOUR SPECIES HAS ALWAYS SEARCHED FOR GOD IN YOUR PAST.
BUT DO YOU SEE NOW, MR. TERRIFIC?
GOD IS IN YOUR FUTURE.
ARE YOU WILLING TO STAND IN THE WAY OF THE FUTURE?

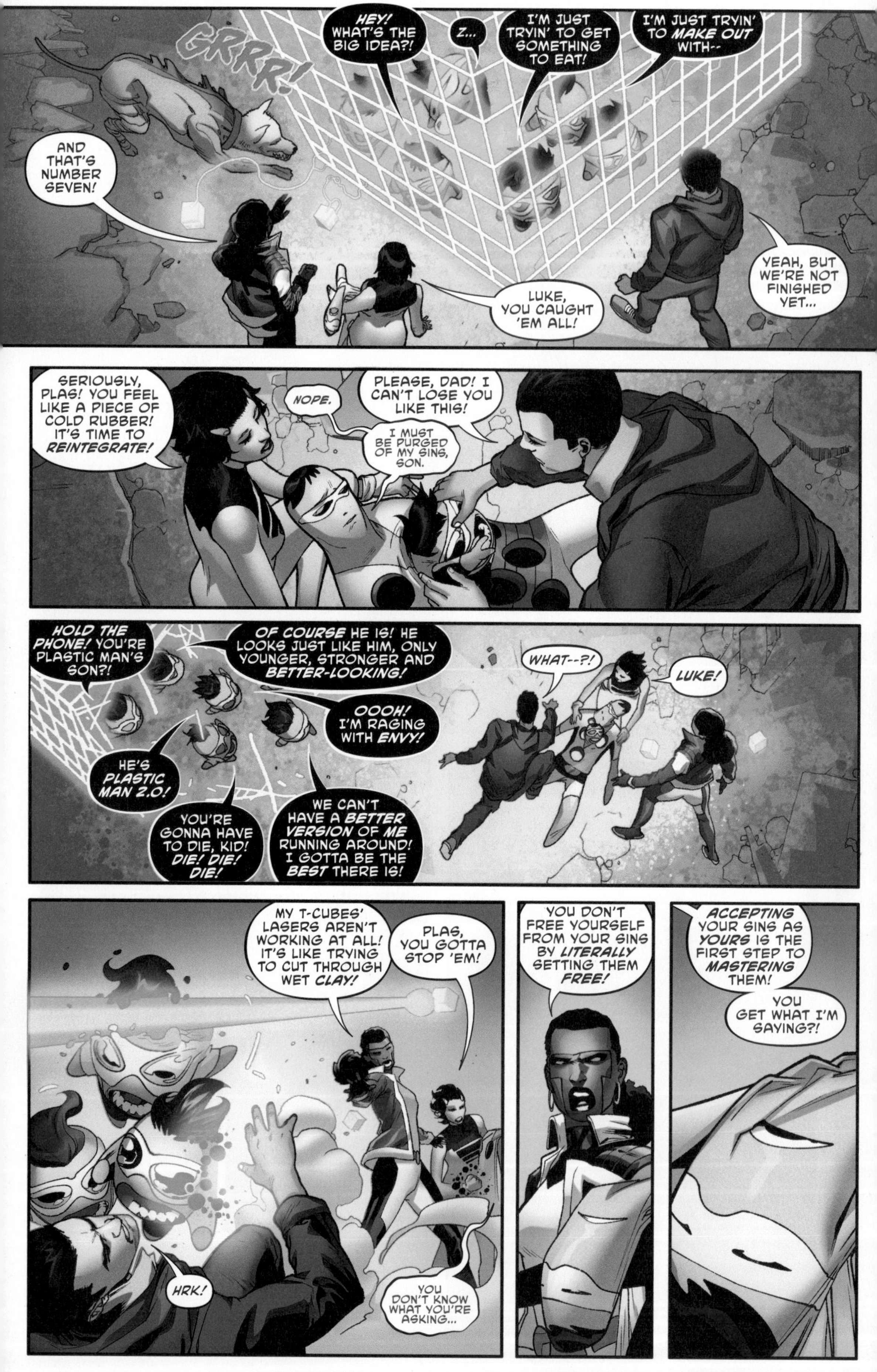
GRRR!
HEY! WHAT'S THE BIG IDEA?!
Z...
I'M JUST TRYIN' TO GET SOMETHING TO EAT!
I'M JUST TRYIN' TO MAKE OUT WITH--
AND THAT'S NUMBER SEVEN!
LUKE, YOU CAUGHT 'EM ALL!
YEAH, BUT WE'RE NOT FINISHED YET...
SERIOUSLY, PLAS! YOU FEEL LIKE A PIECE OF COLD RUBBER! IT'S TIME TO REINTEGRATE!
NOPE.
PLEASE, DAD! I CAN'T LOSE YOU LIKE THIS!
I MUST BE PURGED OF MY SINS, SON.
HOLD THE PHONE! YOU'RE PLASTIC MAN'S SON?!
OF COURSE HE IS! HE LOOKS JUST LIKE HIM, ONLY YOUNGER, STRONGER AND BETTER-LOOKING!
OOOH! I'M RAGING WITH ENVY!
HE'S PLASTIC MAN 2.0!
YOU'RE GONNA HAVE TO DIE, KID! DIE! DIE! DIE!
WE CAN'T HAVE A BETTER VERSION OF ME RUNNING AROUND! I GOTTA BE THE BEST THERE IS!
WHAT--?!
LUKE!
MY T-CUBES' LASERS AREN'T WORKING AT ALL! IT'S LIKE TRYING TO CUT THROUGH WET CLAY!
PLAS, YOU GOTTA STOP 'EM!
HRK!
YOU DON'T KNOW WHAT YOU'RE ASKING...
YOU DON'T FREE YOURSELF FROM YOUR SINS BY LITERALLY SETTING THEM FREE!
ACCEPTING YOUR SINS AS YOURS IS THE FIRST STEP TO MASTERING THEM!
YOU GET WHAT I'M SAYING?!

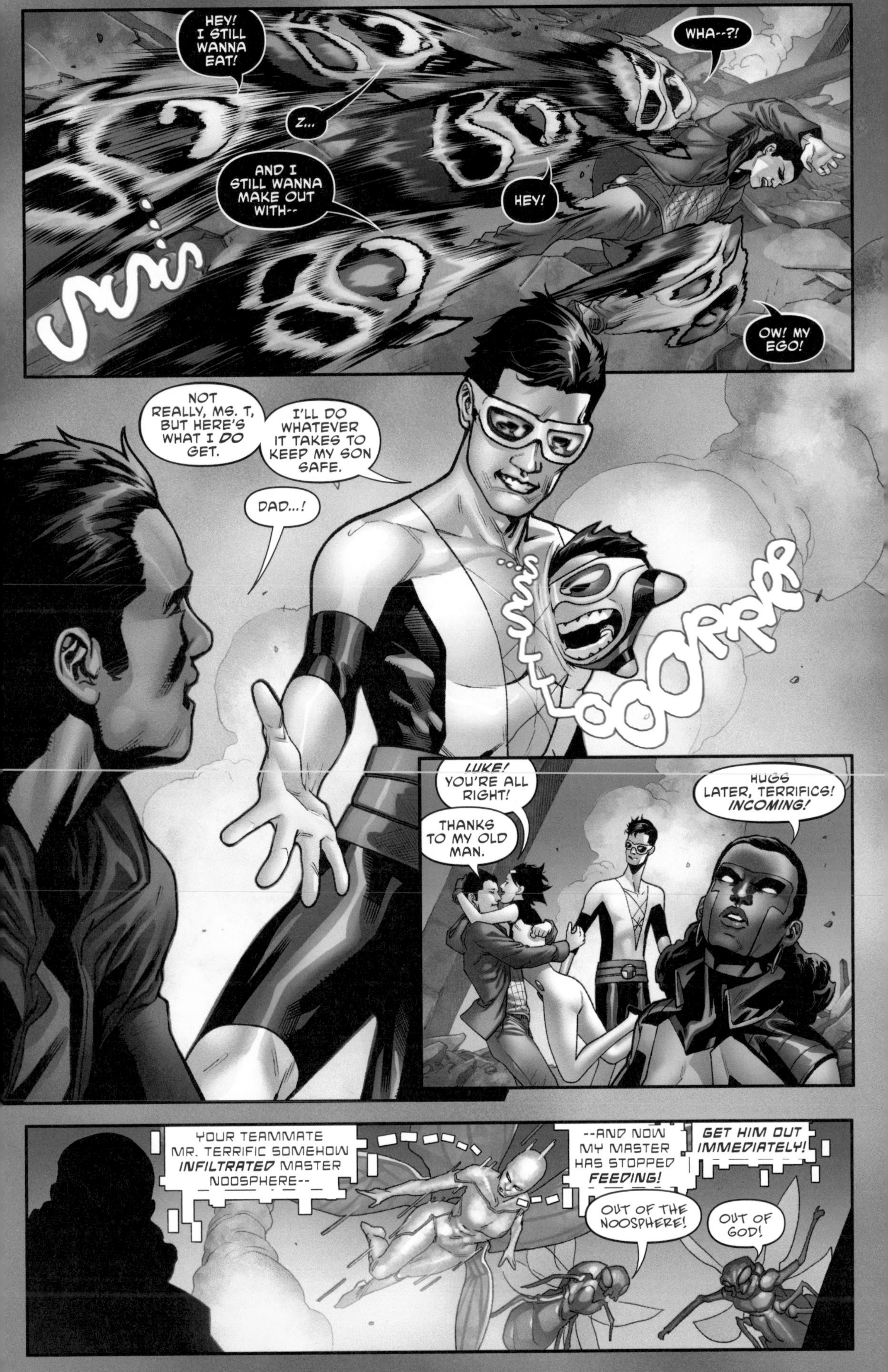
HEY! I STILL WANNA EAT!
Z...
AND I STILL WANNA MAKE OUT WITH--
WHA--?!
HEY!
OW! MY EGO!
NOT REALLY, MS. T, BUT HERE'S WHAT I DO GET.
I'LL DO WHATEVER IT TAKES TO KEEP MY SON SAFE.
DAD...!
SSSLLOOORRRP
LUKE! YOU'RE ALL RIGHT!
THANKS TO MY OLD MAN.
HUGS LATER, TERRIFICS! INCOMING!
YOUR TEAMMATE MR. TERRIFIC SOMEHOW INFILTRATED MASTER NOOSPHERE--
--AND NOW MY MASTER HAS STOPPED FEEDING!
GET HIM OUT IMMEDIATELY!
OUT OF THE NOOSPHERE!
OUT OF GOD!

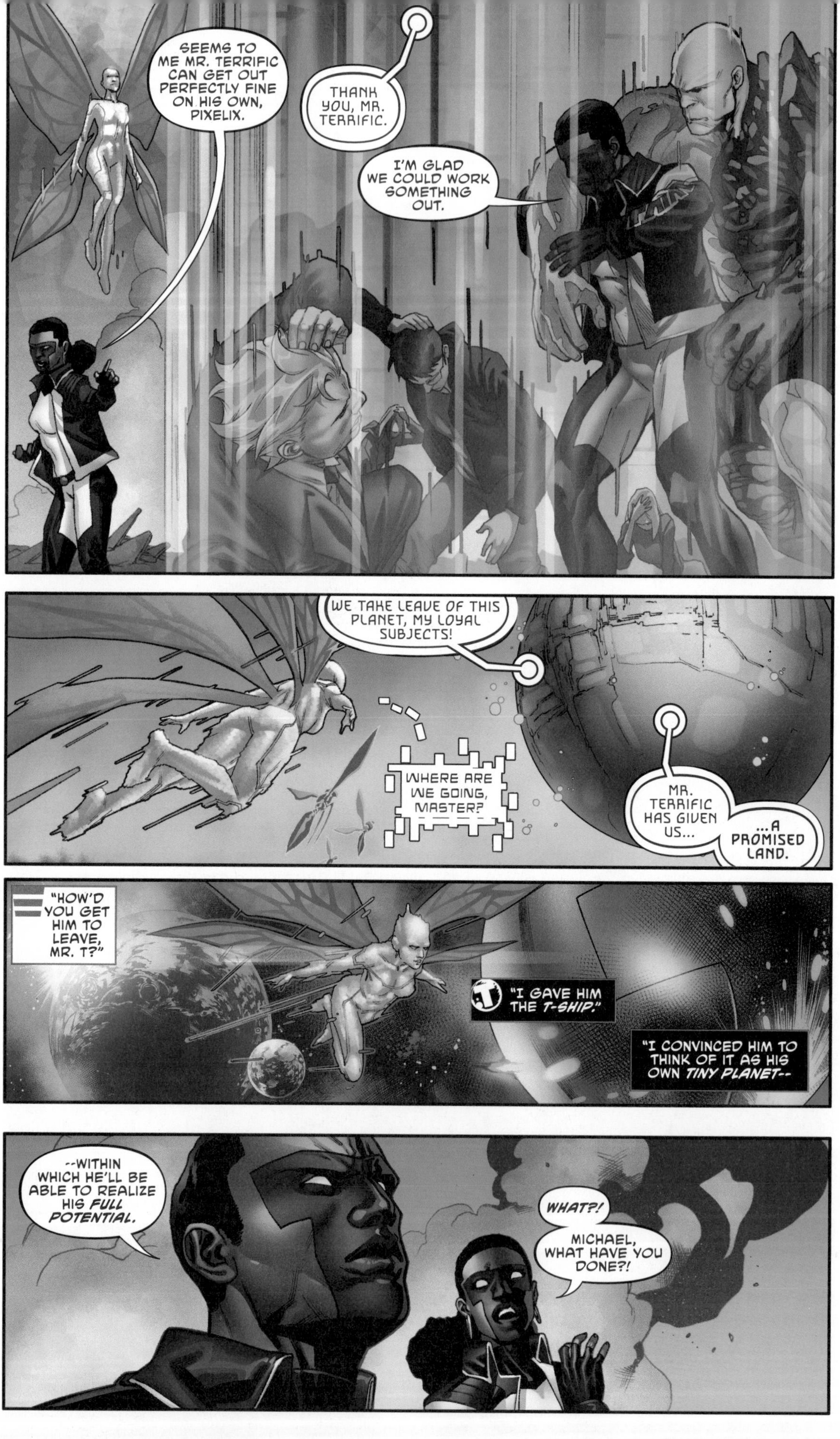
SEEMS TO ME MR. TERRIFIC CAN GET OUT PERFECTLY FINE ON HIS OWN, PIXELIX.
THANK YOU, MR. TERRIFIC.
I'M GLAD WE COULD WORK SOMETHING OUT.
WE TAKE LEAVE OF THIS PLANET, MY LOYAL SUBJECTS!
WHERE ARE WE GOING, MASTER?
MR. TERRIFIC HAS GIVEN US...
...A PROMISED LAND.
"HOW'D YOU GET HIM TO LEAVE, MR. T?"
"I GAVE HIM THE *T-SHIP.*"
"I CONVINCED HIM TO THINK OF IT AS HIS OWN *TINY PLANET*--
--WITHIN WHICH HE'LL BE ABLE TO REALIZE HIS *FULL POTENTIAL.*
WHAT?!
MICHAEL, WHAT HAVE YOU DONE?!

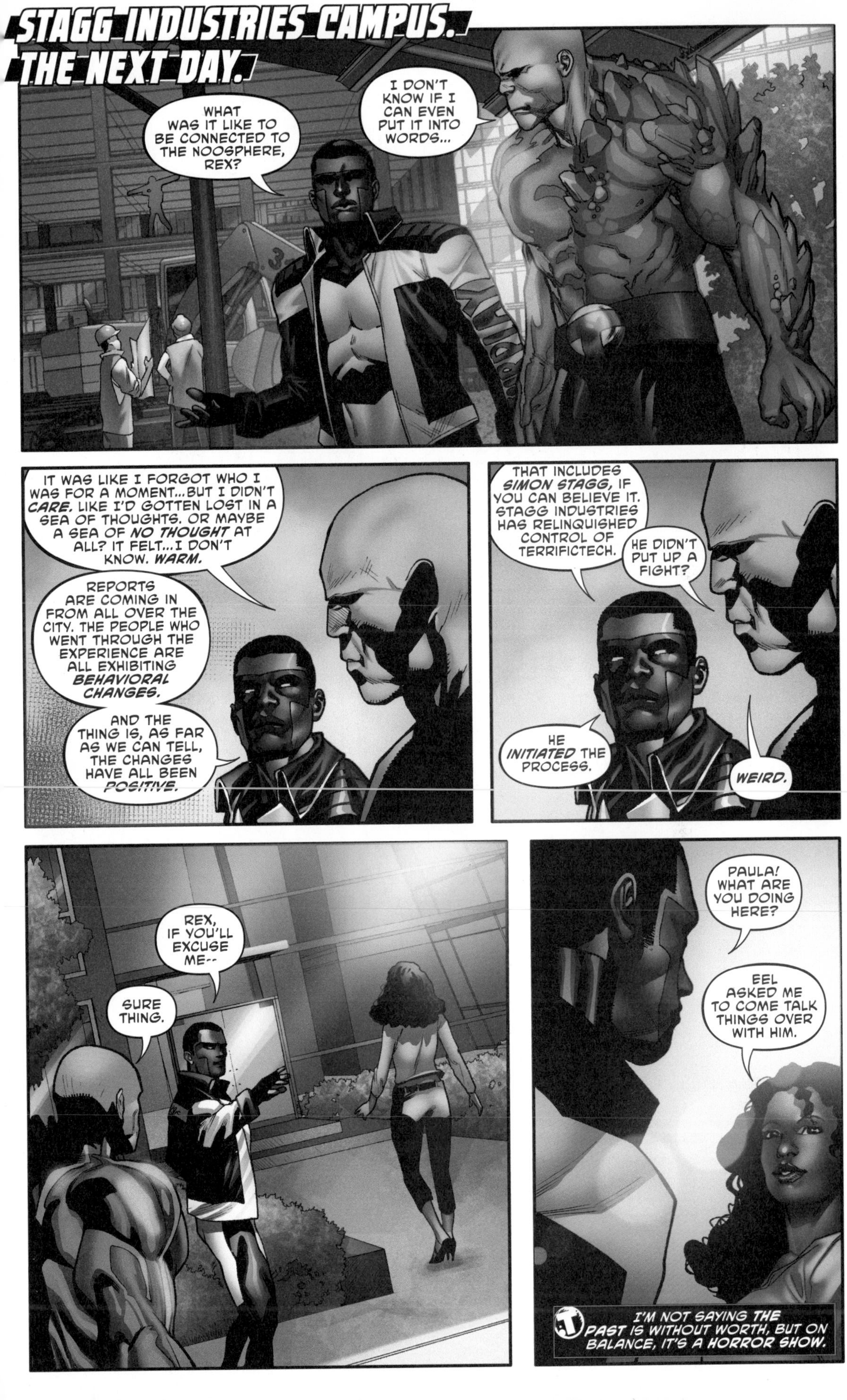
STAGG INDUSTRIES CAMPUS. THE NEXT DAY.
WHAT WAS IT LIKE TO BE CONNECTED TO THE NOOSPHERE, REX?
I DON'T KNOW IF I CAN EVEN PUT IT INTO WORDS...
IT WAS LIKE I FORGOT WHO I WAS FOR A MOMENT...BUT I DIDN'T CARE. LIKE I'D GOTTEN LOST IN A SEA OF THOUGHTS. OR MAYBE A SEA OF NO THOUGHT AT ALL? IT FELT...I DON'T KNOW. WARM.
REPORTS ARE COMING IN FROM ALL OVER THE CITY. THE PEOPLE WHO WENT THROUGH THE EXPERIENCE ARE ALL EXHIBITING BEHAVIORAL CHANGES.
AND THE THING IS, AS FAR AS WE CAN TELL, THE CHANGES HAVE ALL BEEN POSITIVE.
THAT INCLUDES SIMON STAGG, IF YOU CAN BELIEVE IT. STAGG INDUSTRIES HAS RELINQUISHED CONTROL OF TERRIFICTECH.
HE DIDN'T PUT UP A FIGHT?
HE INITIATED THE PROCESS.
WEIRD.
REX, IF YOU'LL EXCUSE ME--
SURE THING.
PAULA! WHAT ARE YOU DOING HERE?
EEL ASKED ME TO COME TALK THINGS OVER WITH HIM.
I'M NOT SAYING THE PAST IS WITHOUT WORTH, BUT ON BALANCE, IT'S A HORROR SHOW.

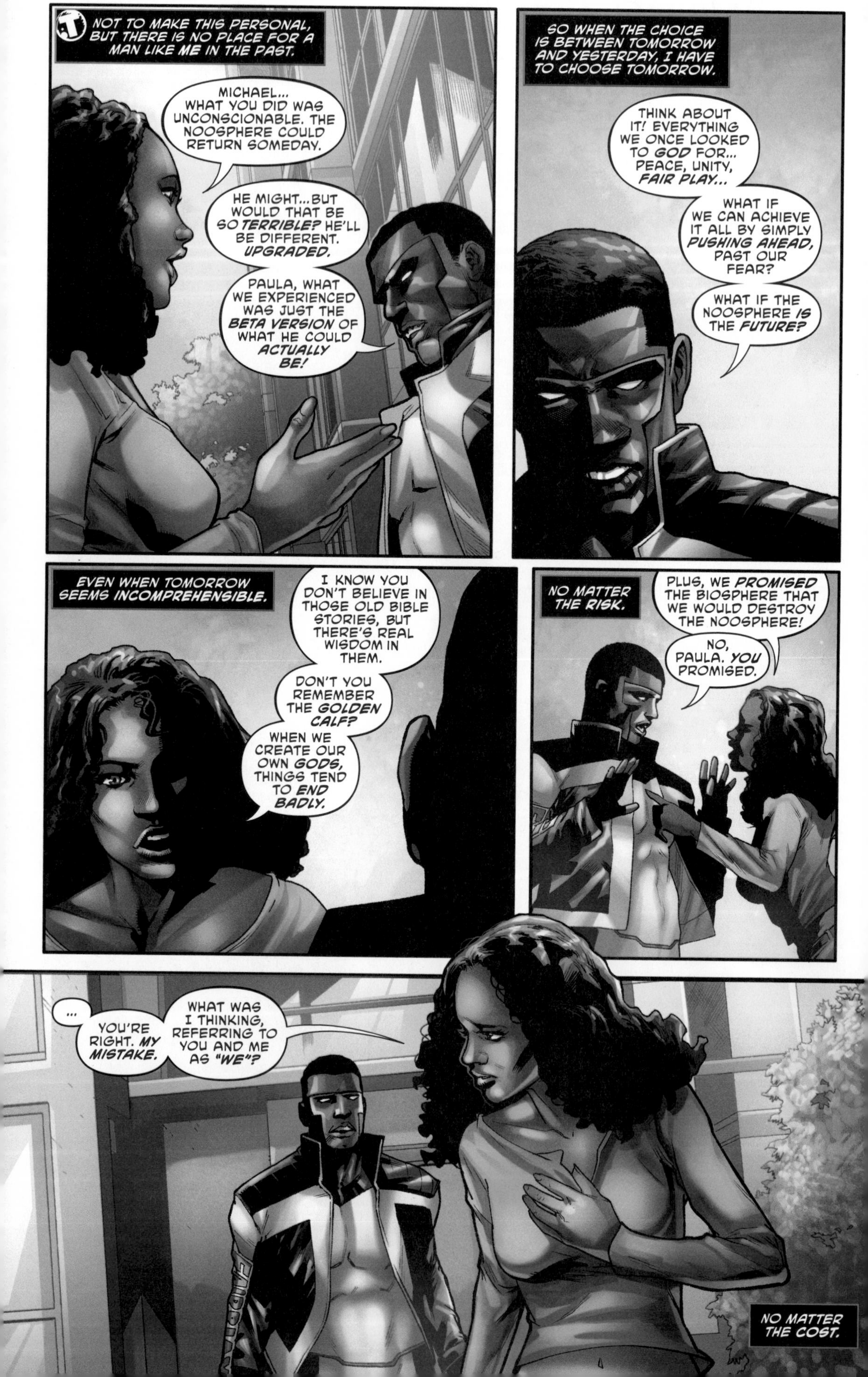
NOT TO MAKE THIS PERSONAL, BUT THERE IS NO PLACE FOR A MAN LIKE ME IN THE PAST.
MICHAEL... WHAT YOU DID WAS UNCONSCIONABLE. THE NOOSPHERE COULD RETURN SOMEDAY.
HE MIGHT...BUT WOULD THAT BE SO TERRIBLE? HE'LL BE DIFFERENT. UPGRADED.
PAULA, WHAT WE EXPERIENCED WAS JUST THE BETA VERSION OF WHAT HE COULD ACTUALLY BE!
SO WHEN THE CHOICE IS BETWEEN TOMORROW AND YESTERDAY, I HAVE TO CHOOSE TOMORROW.
THINK ABOUT IT! EVERYTHING WE ONCE LOOKED TO GOD FOR... PEACE, UNITY, FAIR PLAY...
WHAT IF WE CAN ACHIEVE IT ALL BY SIMPLY PUSHING AHEAD, PAST OUR FEAR?
WHAT IF THE NOOSPHERE IS THE FUTURE?
EVEN WHEN TOMORROW SEEMS INCOMPREHENSIBLE.
I KNOW YOU DON'T BELIEVE IN THOSE OLD BIBLE STORIES, BUT THERE'S REAL WISDOM IN THEM.
DON'T YOU REMEMBER THE GOLDEN CALF?
WHEN WE CREATE OUR OWN GODS, THINGS TEND TO END BADLY.
NO MATTER THE RISK.
PLUS, WE PROMISED THE BIOSPHERE THAT WE WOULD DESTROY THE NOOSPHERE!
NO, PAULA. YOU PROMISED.
...
YOU'RE RIGHT. MY MISTAKE.
WHAT WAS I THINKING, REFERRING TO YOU AND ME AS "WE"?
NO MATTER THE COST.

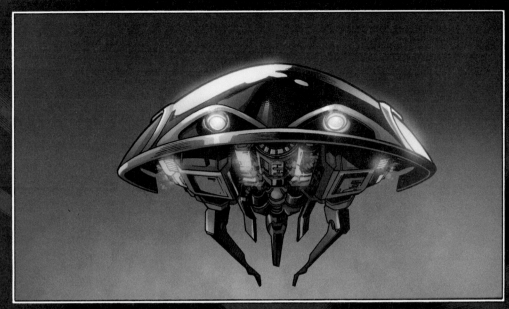

LIFE TODAY AM SO BEAUTIFUL.

BUT THE FUTURE WILL BE EVEN BETTER.

FULL OF HOPE AND JOY AND WONDER.

THAT AM WHY ME NOT LONG FOR YESTERDAY.

THAT IS WHY ME NOT WISH TOMORROW NEVER COMES.

NOT ONE LITTLE BIT.

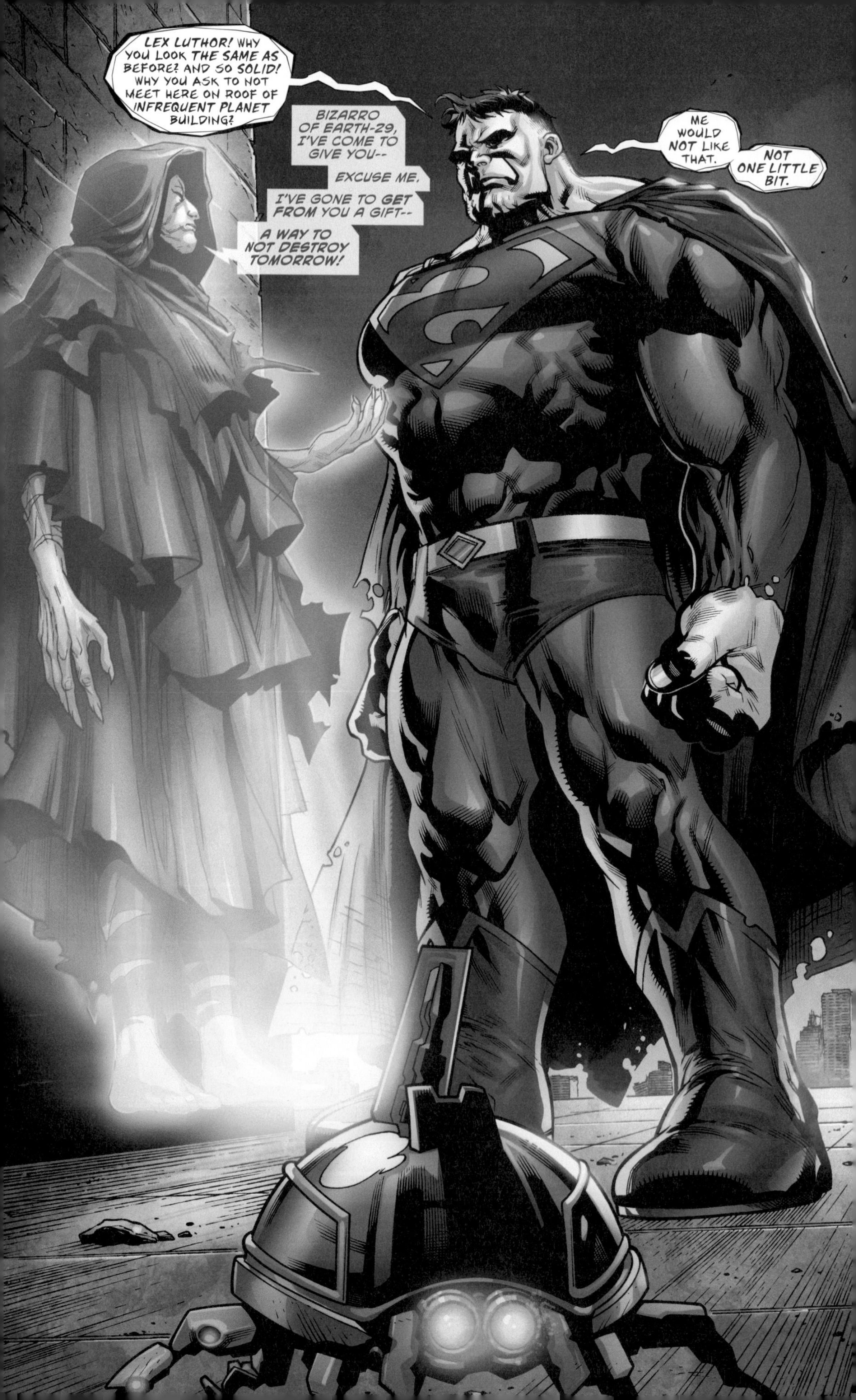

LEX LUTHOR! WHY YOU LOOK THE SAME AS BEFORE? AND SO SOLID! WHY YOU ASK TO NOT MEET HERE ON ROOF OF INFREQUENT PLANET BUILDING?
BIZARRO OF EARTH-29, I'VE COME TO GIVE YOU--
EXCUSE ME.
I'VE GONE TO GET FROM YOU A GIFT--
A WAY TO NOT DESTROY TOMORROW!
ME WOULD NOT LIKE THAT.
NOT ONE LITTLE BIT.

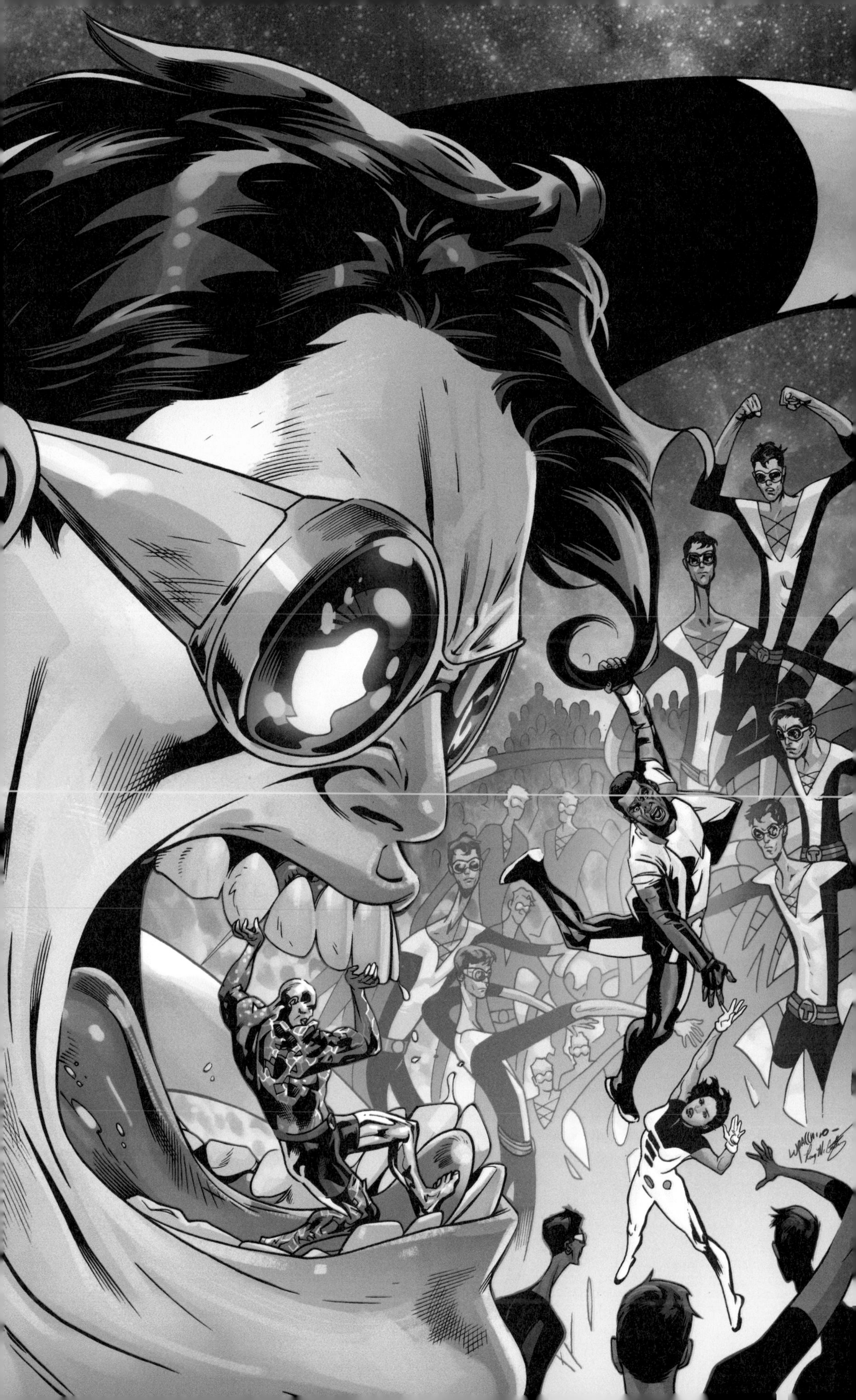

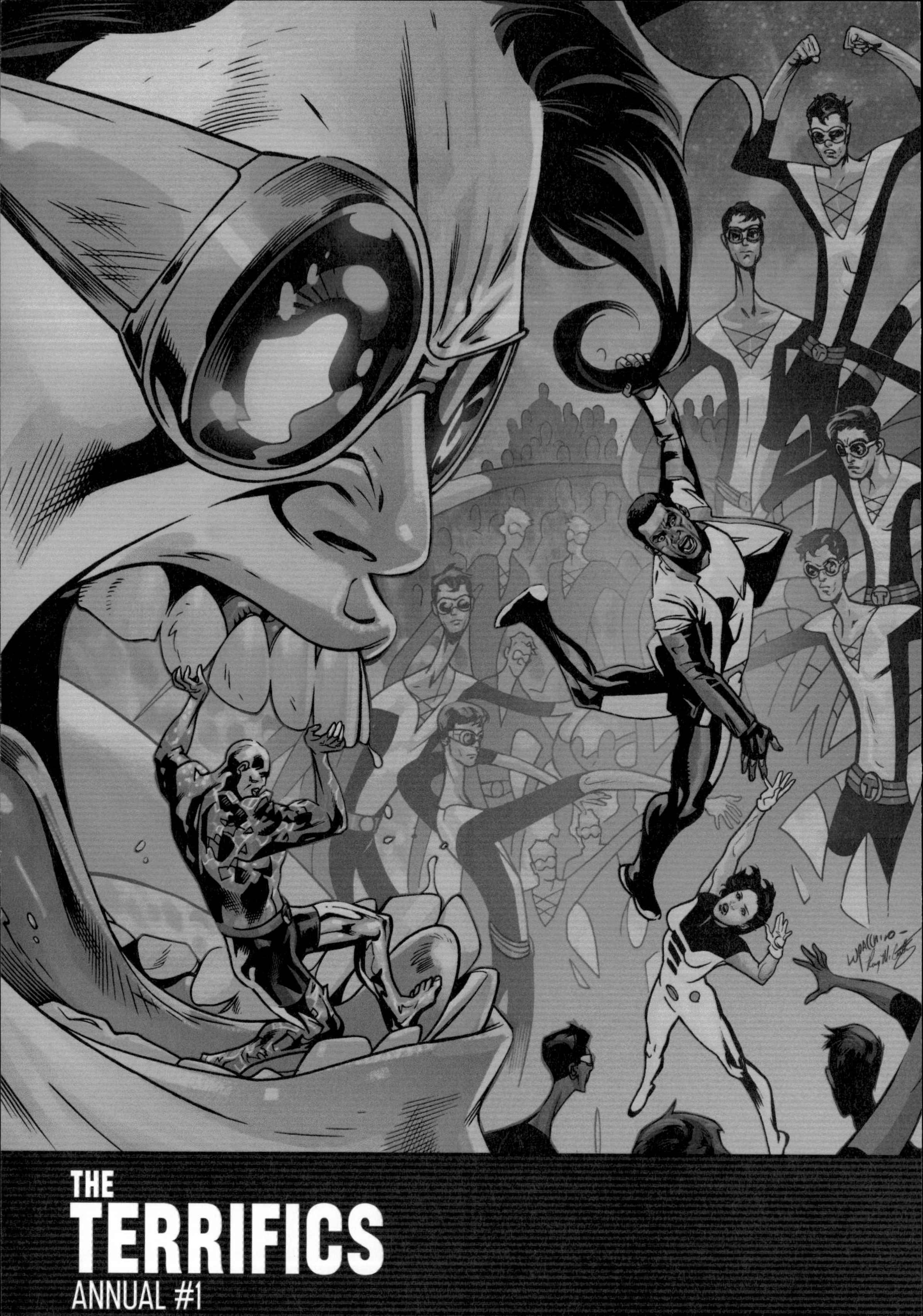

THE TERRIFICS

ANNUAL #1

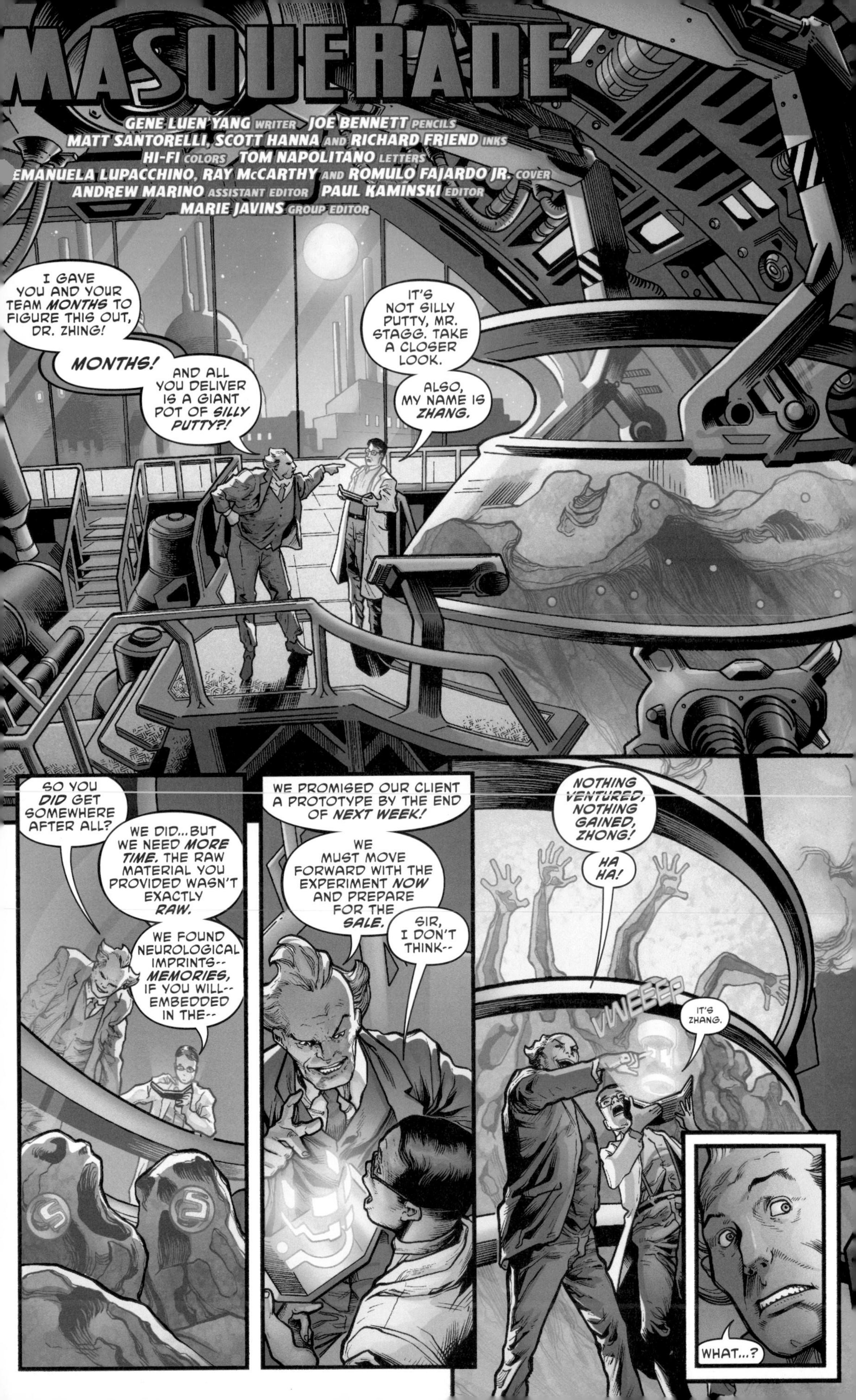
MASQUERADE
GENE LUEN YANG WRITER JOE BENNETT PENCILS
MATT SANTORELLI, SCOTT HANNA AND RICHARD FRIEND INKS
HI-FI COLORS TOM NAPOLITANO LETTERS
EMANUELA LUPACCHINO, RAY McCARTHY AND ROMULO FAJARDO JR. COVER
ANDREW MARINO ASSISTANT EDITOR PAUL KAMINSKI EDITOR
MARIE JAVINS GROUP EDITOR
I GAVE YOU AND YOUR TEAM MONTHS TO FIGURE THIS OUT, DR. ZHING!
MONTHS!
AND ALL YOU DELIVER IS A GIANT POT OF SILLY PUTTY?!
IT'S NOT SILLY PUTTY, MR. STAGG. TAKE A CLOSER LOOK.
ALSO, MY NAME IS ZHANG.
SO YOU DID GET SOMEWHERE AFTER ALL?
WE DID...BUT WE NEED MORE TIME. THE RAW MATERIAL YOU PROVIDED WASN'T EXACTLY RAW.
WE FOUND NEUROLOGICAL IMPRINTS--MEMORIES, IF YOU WILL--EMBEDDED IN THE--
WE PROMISED OUR CLIENT A PROTOTYPE BY THE END OF NEXT WEEK!
WE MUST MOVE FORWARD WITH THE EXPERIMENT NOW AND PREPARE FOR THE SALE.
SIR, I DON'T THINK--
NOTHING VENTURED, NOTHING GAINED, ZHONG!
HA HA!
VWEEEP
IT'S ZHANG.
WHAT...?

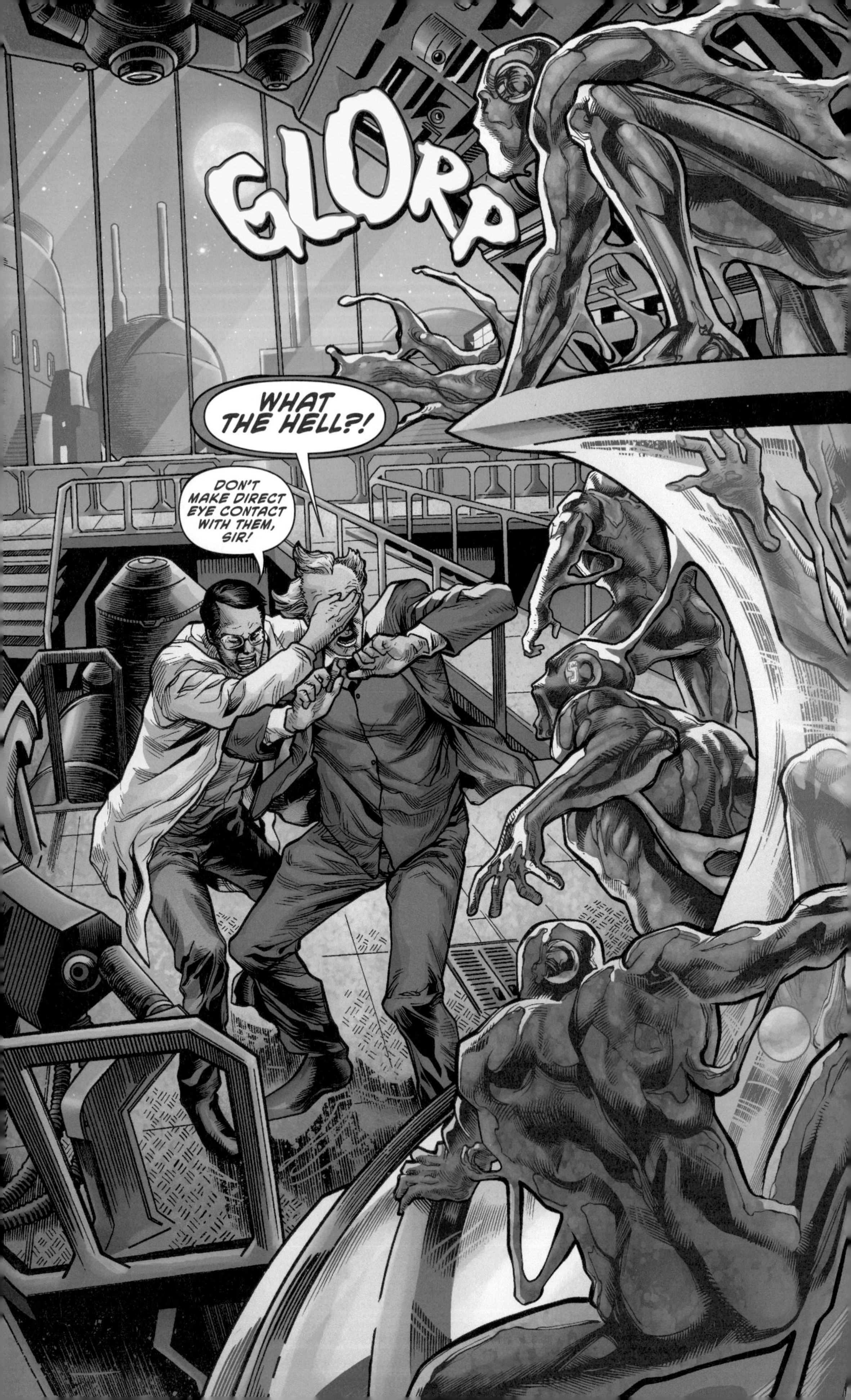
GLORP
WHAT THE HELL?!
DON'T MAKE DIRECT EYE CONTACT WITH THEM, SIR!

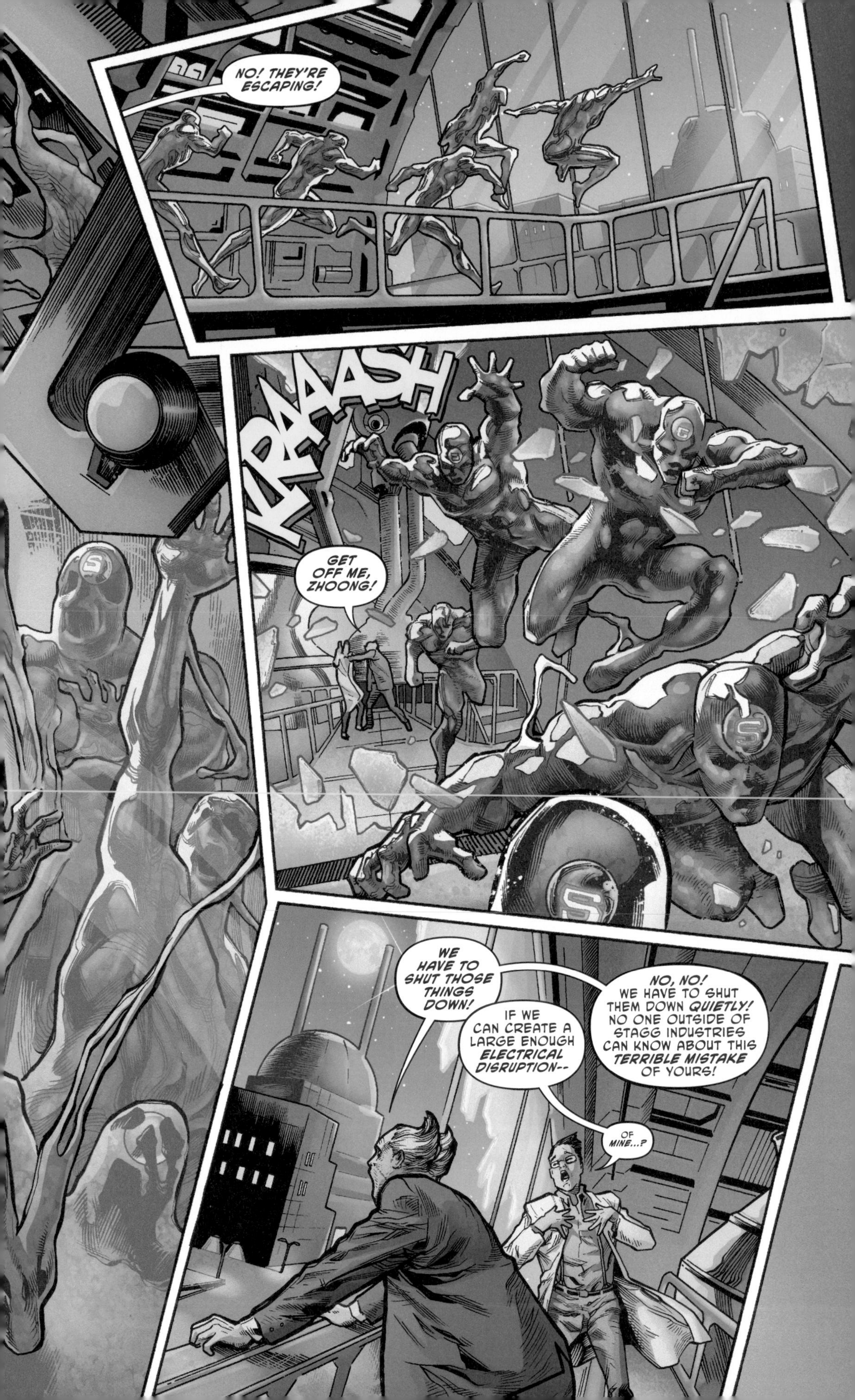
NO! THEY'RE ESCAPING!
KRAAASH
GET OFF ME, ZHOONG!
WE HAVE TO SHUT THOSE THINGS DOWN!
IF WE CAN CREATE A LARGE ENOUGH ELECTRICAL DISRUPTION--
NO, NO! WE HAVE TO SHUT THEM DOWN QUIETLY! NO ONE OUTSIDE OF STAGG INDUSTRIES CAN KNOW ABOUT THIS TERRIBLE MISTAKE OF YOURS!
OF MINE...?

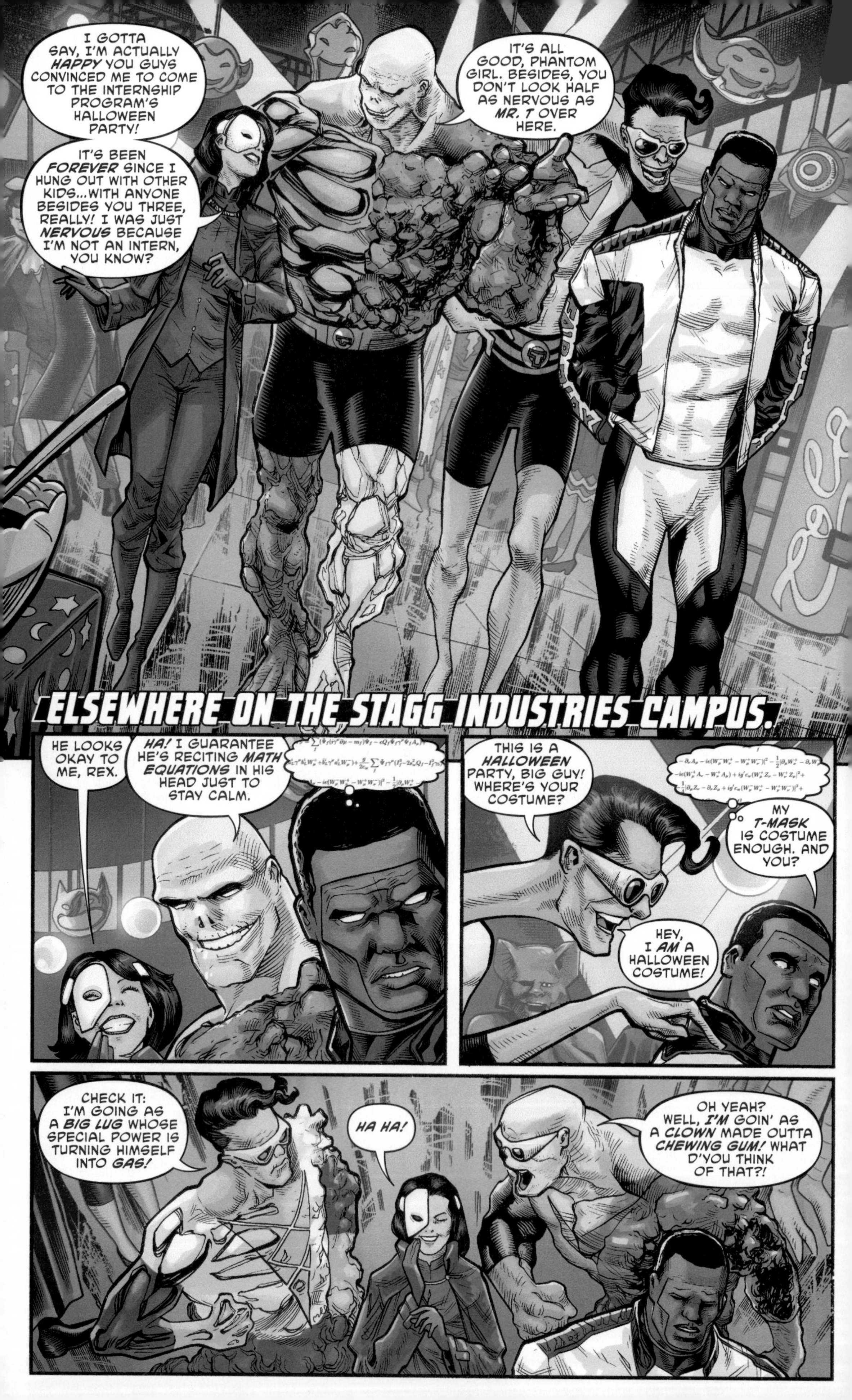
I GOTTA SAY, I'M ACTUALLY *HAPPY* YOU GUYS CONVINCED ME TO COME TO THE INTERNSHIP PROGRAM'S HALLOWEEN PARTY!
IT'S BEEN *FOREVER* SINCE I HUNG OUT WITH OTHER KIDS...WITH ANYONE BESIDES YOU THREE, REALLY! I WAS JUST *NERVOUS* BECAUSE I'M NOT AN INTERN, YOU KNOW?
IT'S ALL GOOD, PHANTOM GIRL. BESIDES, YOU DON'T LOOK HALF AS NERVOUS AS *MR. T* OVER HERE.
ELSEWHERE ON THE STAGG INDUSTRIES CAMPUS.
HE LOOKS OKAY TO ME, REX.
HA! I GUARANTEE HE'S RECITING *MATH EQUATIONS* IN HIS HEAD JUST TO STAY CALM.
THIS IS A *HALLOWEEN* PARTY, BIG GUY! WHERE'S YOUR COSTUME?
MY *T-MASK* IS COSTUME ENOUGH. AND YOU?
HEY, I *AM* A HALLOWEEN COSTUME!
CHECK IT: I'M GOING AS A *BIG LUG* WHOSE SPECIAL POWER IS TURNING HIMSELF INTO *GAS!*
HA HA!
OH YEAH? WELL, *I'M* GOIN' AS A *CLOWN* MADE OUTTA *CHEWING GUM!* WHAT D'YOU THINK OF THAT?!

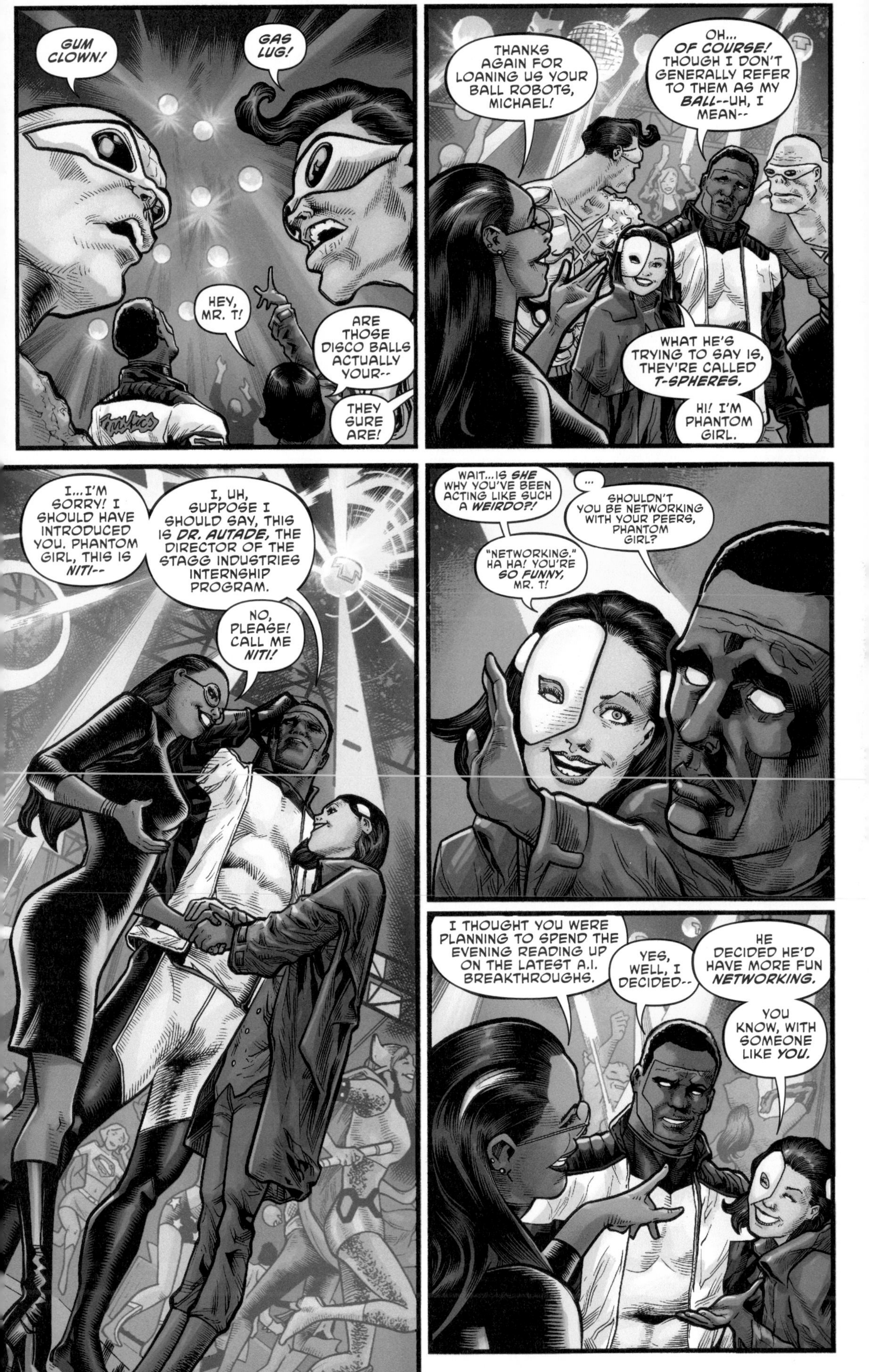
GUM CLOWN!
GAS LUG!
HEY, MR. T!
ARE THOSE DISCO BALLS ACTUALLY YOUR--
THEY SURE ARE!
THANKS AGAIN FOR LOANING US YOUR BALL ROBOTS, MICHAEL!
OH... OF COURSE! THOUGH I DON'T GENERALLY REFER TO THEM AS MY BALL--UH, I MEAN--
WHAT HE'S TRYING TO SAY IS, THEY'RE CALLED T-SPHERES.
HI! I'M PHANTOM GIRL.
I...I'M SORRY! I SHOULD HAVE INTRODUCED YOU. PHANTOM GIRL, THIS IS NITI--
I, UH, SUPPOSE I SHOULD SAY, THIS IS DR. AUTADE, THE DIRECTOR OF THE STAGG INDUSTRIES INTERNSHIP PROGRAM.
NO, PLEASE! CALL ME NITI!
WAIT...IS SHE WHY YOU'VE BEEN ACTING LIKE SUCH A WEIRDO?!
...
SHOULDN'T YOU BE NETWORKING WITH YOUR PEERS, PHANTOM GIRL?
"NETWORKING." HA HA! YOU'RE SO FUNNY, MR. T!
I THOUGHT YOU WERE PLANNING TO SPEND THE EVENING READING UP ON THE LATEST A.I. BREAKTHROUGHS.
YES, WELL, I DECIDED--
HE DECIDED HE'D HAVE MORE FUN NETWORKING.
YOU KNOW, WITH SOMEONE LIKE YOU.

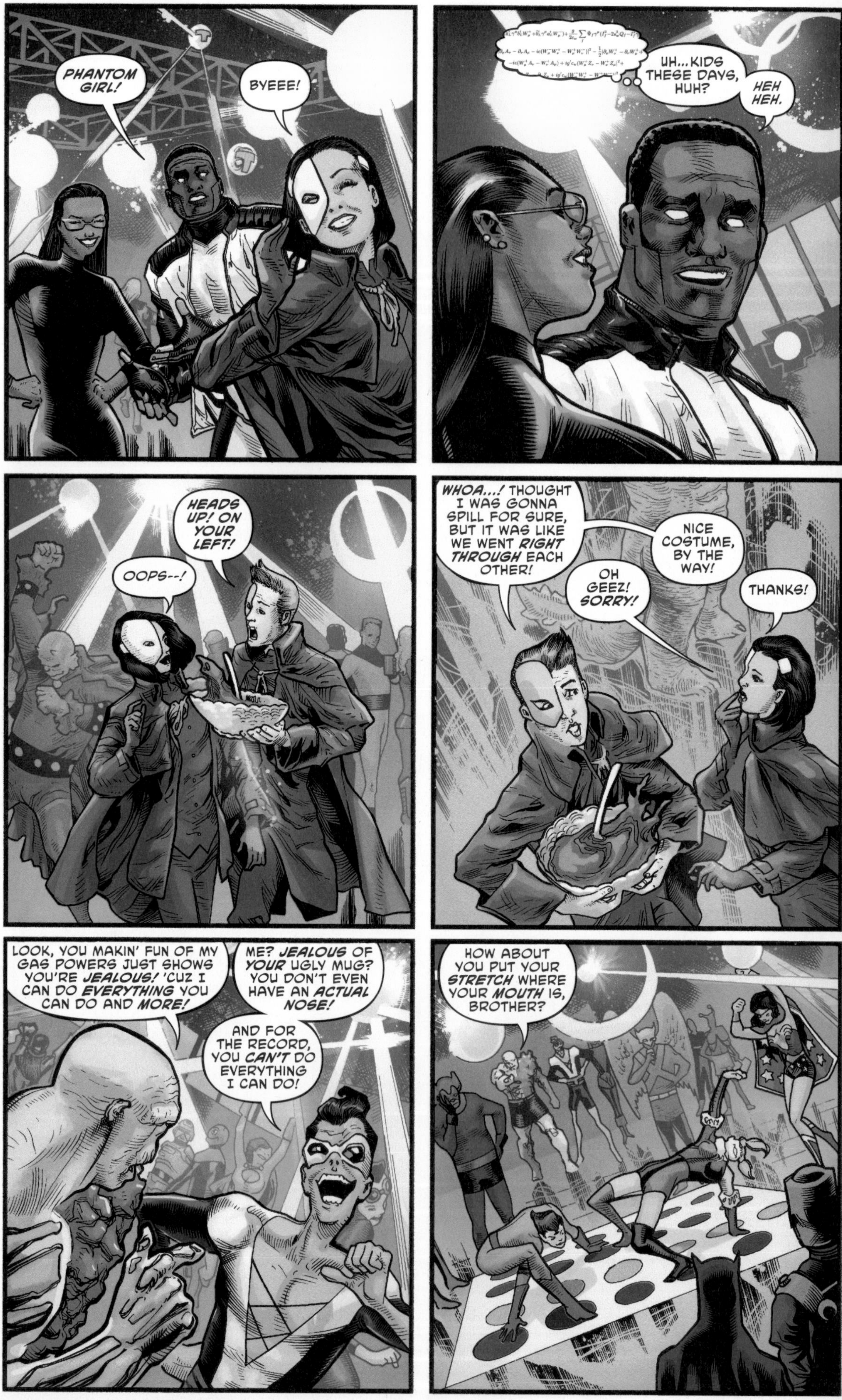
PHANTOM GIRL!
BYEEE!
UH... KIDS THESE DAYS, HUH?
HEH HEH.
HEADS UP! ON YOUR LEFT!
OOPS--!
WHOA...! THOUGHT I WAS GONNA SPILL FOR SURE, BUT IT WAS LIKE WE WENT RIGHT THROUGH EACH OTHER!
NICE COSTUME, BY THE WAY!
OH GEEZ! SORRY!
THANKS!
LOOK, YOU MAKIN' FUN OF MY GAS POWERS JUST SHOWS YOU'RE JEALOUS! 'CUZ I CAN DO EVERYTHING YOU CAN DO AND MORE!
ME? JEALOUS OF YOUR UGLY MUG? YOU DON'T EVEN HAVE AN ACTUAL NOSE!
AND FOR THE RECORD, YOU CAN'T DO EVERYTHING I CAN DO!
HOW ABOUT YOU PUT YOUR STRETCH WHERE YOUR MOUTH IS, BROTHER?

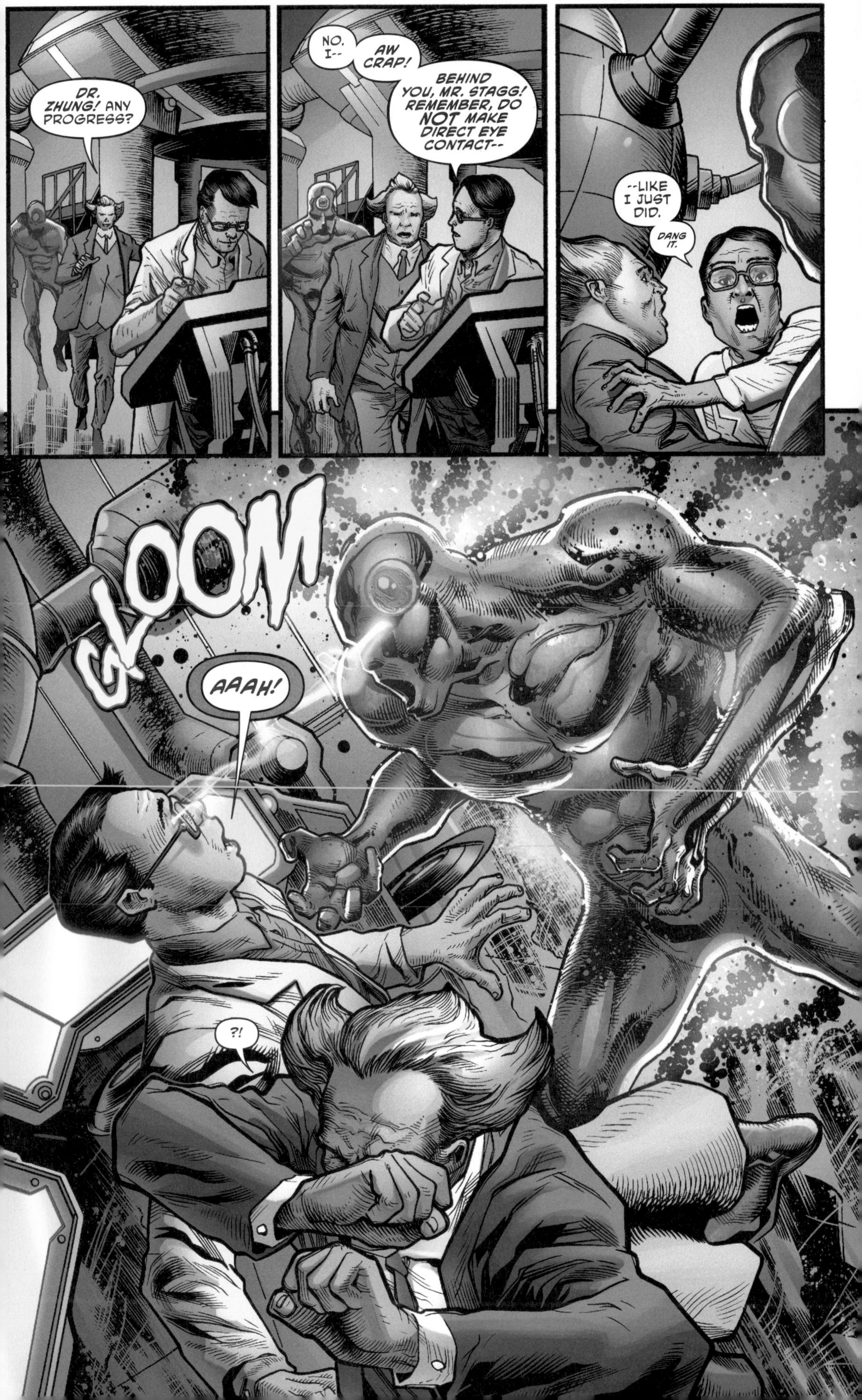
DR. ZHUNG! ANY PROGRESS?
NO. I--
AW CRAP!
BEHIND YOU, MR. STAGG! REMEMBER, DO NOT MAKE DIRECT EYE CONTACT--
--LIKE I JUST DID.
DANG IT.
GLOOM
AAAH!
?!

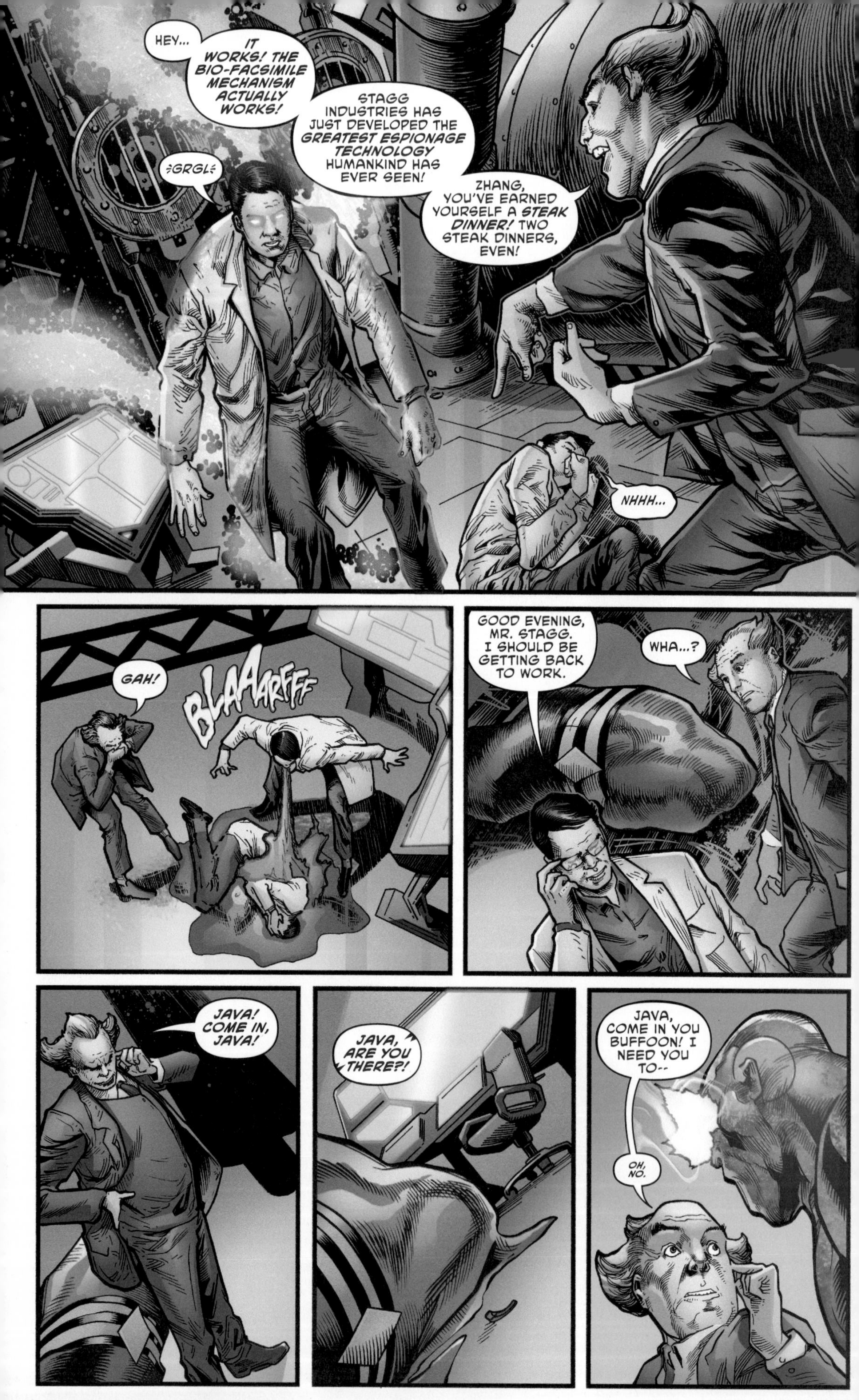
HEY...
IT WORKS! THE BIO-FACSIMILE MECHANISM ACTUALLY WORKS!
STAGG INDUSTRIES HAS JUST DEVELOPED THE GREATEST ESPIONAGE TECHNOLOGY HUMANKIND HAS EVER SEEN!
GRGL
ZHANG, YOU'VE EARNED YOURSELF A STEAK DINNER! TWO STEAK DINNERS, EVEN!
NHHH...
GAH!
BLAAARFFF
GOOD EVENING, MR. STAGG. I SHOULD BE GETTING BACK TO WORK.
WHA...?
JAVA! COME IN, JAVA!
JAVA, ARE YOU THERE?!
JAVA, COME IN YOU BUFFOON! I NEED YOU TO--
OH, NO.

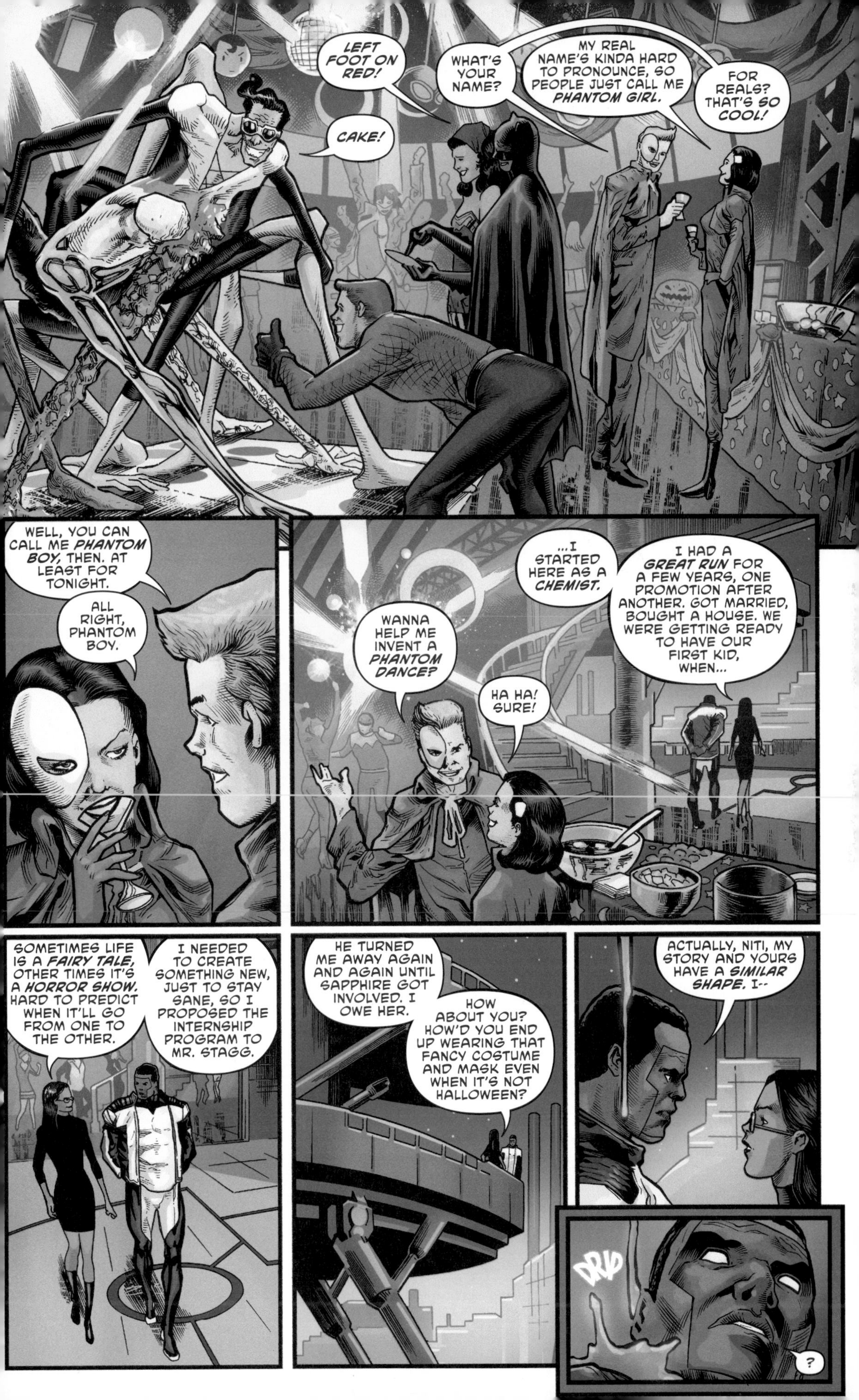
LEFT FOOT ON RED!
CAKE!
WHAT'S YOUR NAME?
MY REAL NAME'S KINDA HARD TO PRONOUNCE, SO PEOPLE JUST CALL ME PHANTOM GIRL.
FOR REALS? THAT'S SO COOL!
WELL, YOU CAN CALL ME PHANTOM BOY, THEN. AT LEAST FOR TONIGHT.
ALL RIGHT, PHANTOM BOY.
WANNA HELP ME INVENT A PHANTOM DANCE?
HA HA! SURE!
...I STARTED HERE AS A CHEMIST.
I HAD A GREAT RUN FOR A FEW YEARS, ONE PROMOTION AFTER ANOTHER. GOT MARRIED, BOUGHT A HOUSE. WE WERE GETTING READY TO HAVE OUR FIRST KID, WHEN...
SOMETIMES LIFE IS A FAIRY TALE, OTHER TIMES IT'S A HORROR SHOW. HARD TO PREDICT WHEN IT'LL GO FROM ONE TO THE OTHER.
I NEEDED TO CREATE SOMETHING NEW, JUST TO STAY SANE, SO I PROPOSED THE INTERNSHIP PROGRAM TO MR. STAGG.
HE TURNED ME AWAY AGAIN AND AGAIN UNTIL SAPPHIRE GOT INVOLVED. I OWE HER.
HOW ABOUT YOU? HOW'D YOU END UP WEARING THAT FANCY COSTUME AND MASK EVEN WHEN IT'S NOT HALLOWEEN?
ACTUALLY, NITI, MY STORY AND YOURS HAVE A SIMILAR SHAPE. I--
DRIP
?

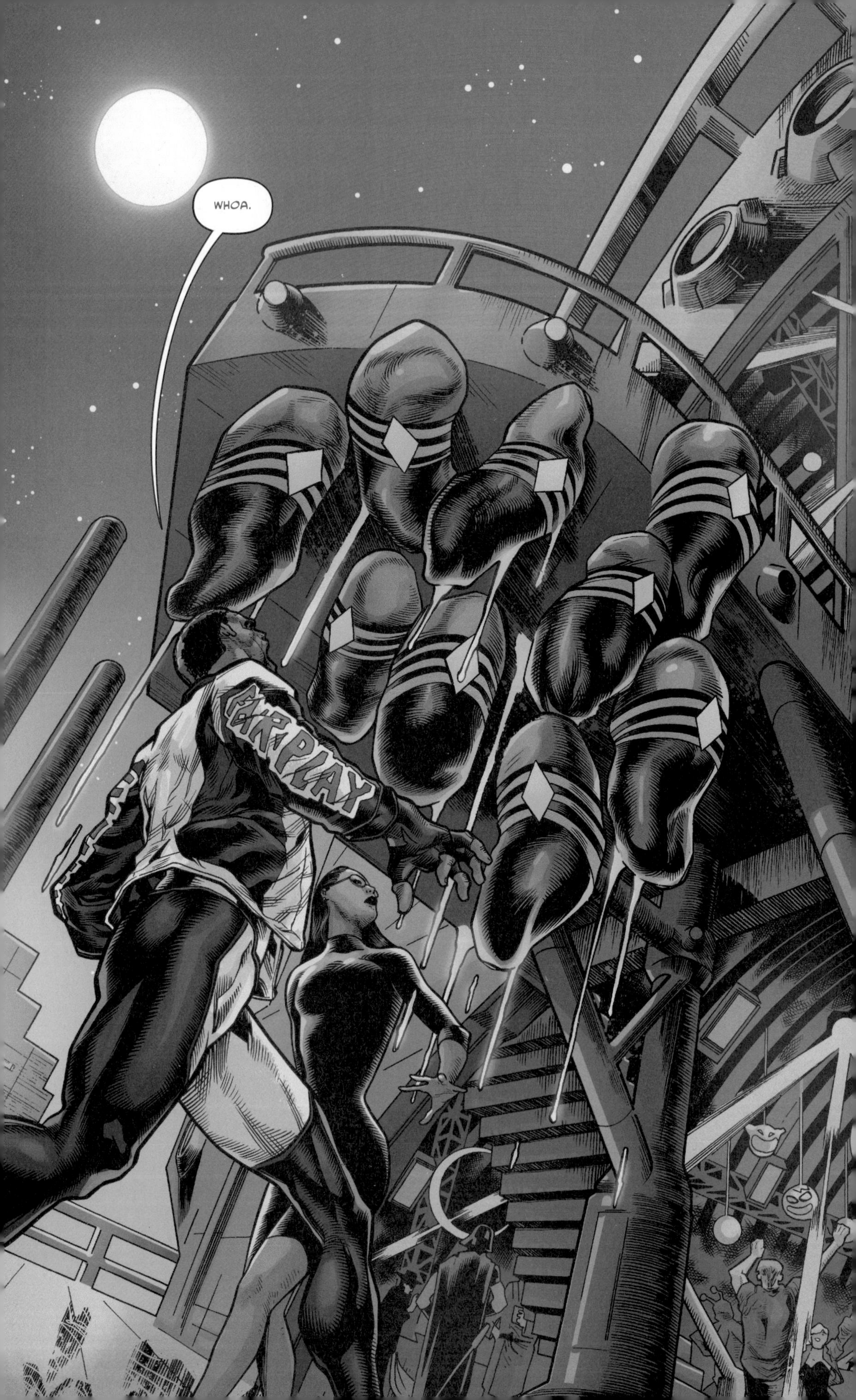
WHOA.
FAIR PLAY

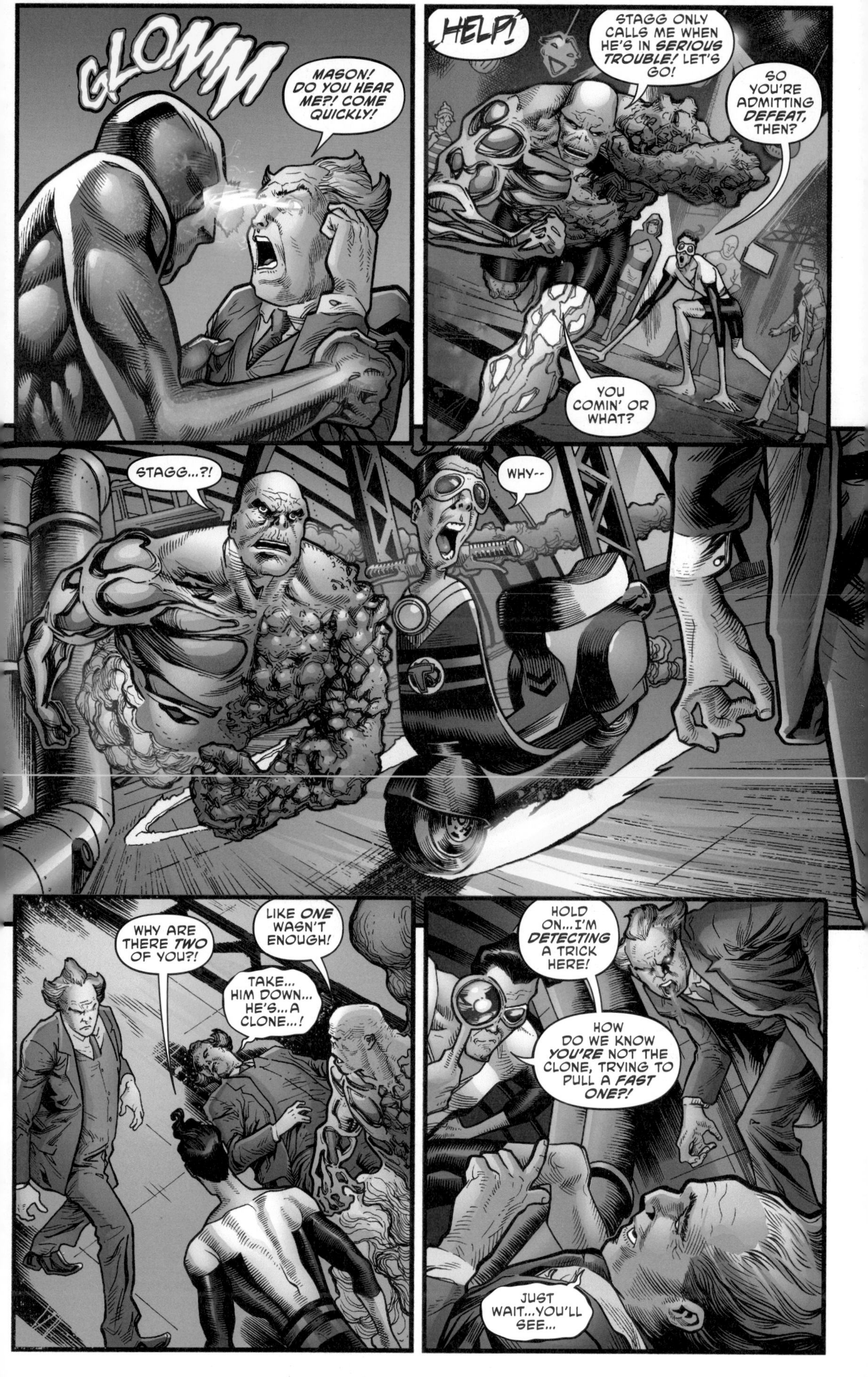
GLOMM
MASON! DO YOU HEAR ME?! COME QUICKLY!
HELP!
STAGG ONLY CALLS ME WHEN HE'S IN SERIOUS TROUBLE! LET'S GO!
SO YOU'RE ADMITTING DEFEAT, THEN?
YOU COMIN' OR WHAT?
STAGG...?!
WHY--
WHY ARE THERE TWO OF YOU?!
LIKE ONE WASN'T ENOUGH!
TAKE... HIM DOWN... HE'S...A CLONE...!
HOLD ON...I'M DETECTING A TRICK HERE!
HOW DO WE KNOW YOU'RE NOT THE CLONE, TRYING TO PULL A FAST ONE?!
JUST WAIT...YOU'LL SEE...

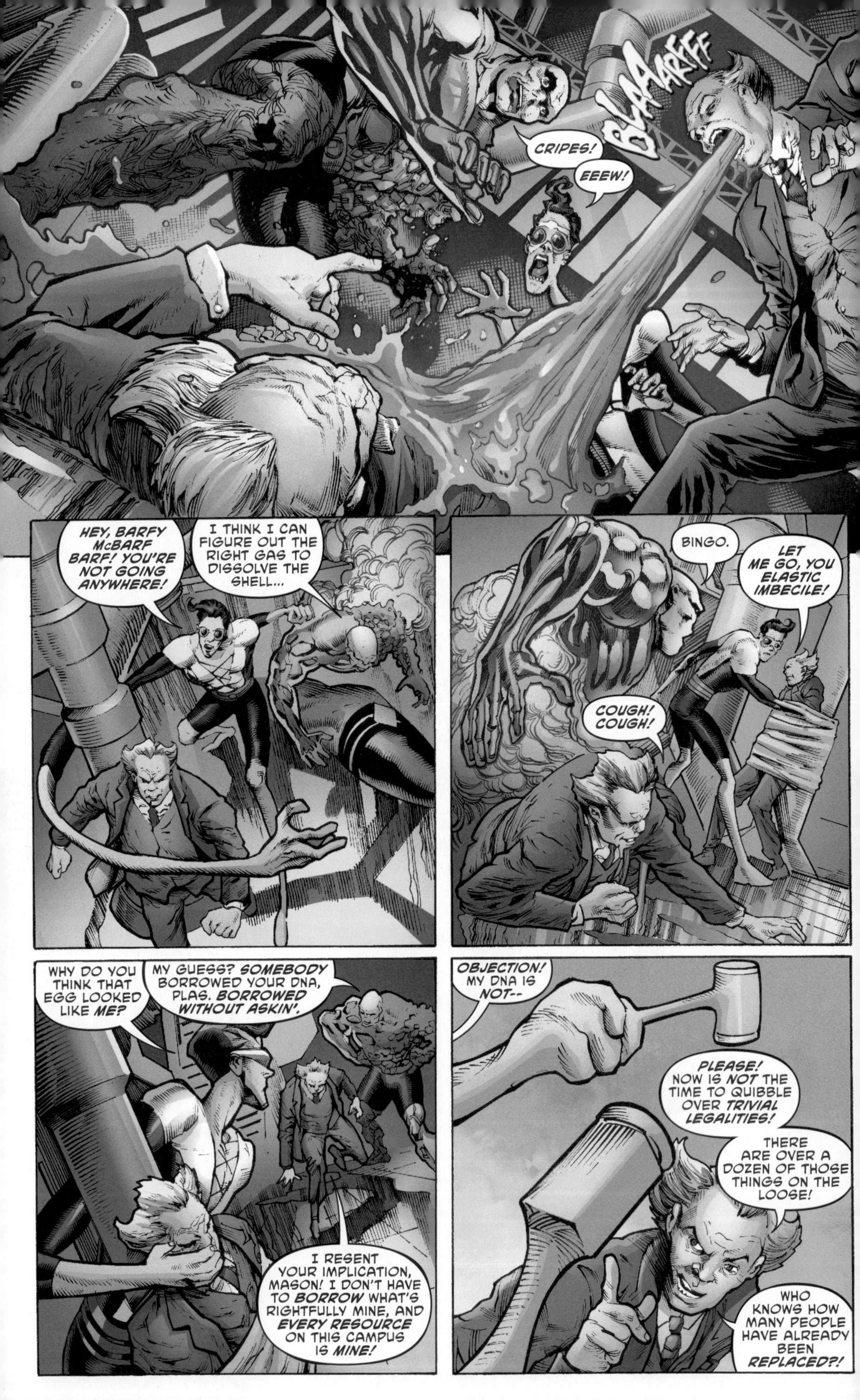

CRIPES!
EEEW!
BLAARFF
HEY, BARFY McBARF BARF! YOU'RE NOT GOING ANYWHERE!
I THINK I CAN FIGURE OUT THE RIGHT GAS TO DISSOLVE THE SHELL...
BINGO.
LET ME GO, YOU ELASTIC IMBECILE!
COUGH! COUGH!
WHY DO YOU THINK THAT EGG LOOKED LIKE ME?
MY GUESS? SOMEBODY BORROWED YOUR DNA, PLAS. BORROWED WITHOUT ASKIN'.
I RESENT YOUR IMPLICATION, MASON! I DON'T HAVE TO BORROW WHAT'S RIGHTFULLY MINE, AND EVERY RESOURCE ON THIS CAMPUS IS MINE!
OBJECTION! MY DNA IS NOT--
PLEASE! NOW IS NOT THE TIME TO QUIBBLE OVER TRIVIAL LEGALITIES!
THERE ARE OVER A DOZEN OF THOSE THINGS ON THE LOOSE!
WHO KNOWS HOW MANY PEOPLE HAVE ALREADY BEEN REPLACED?!

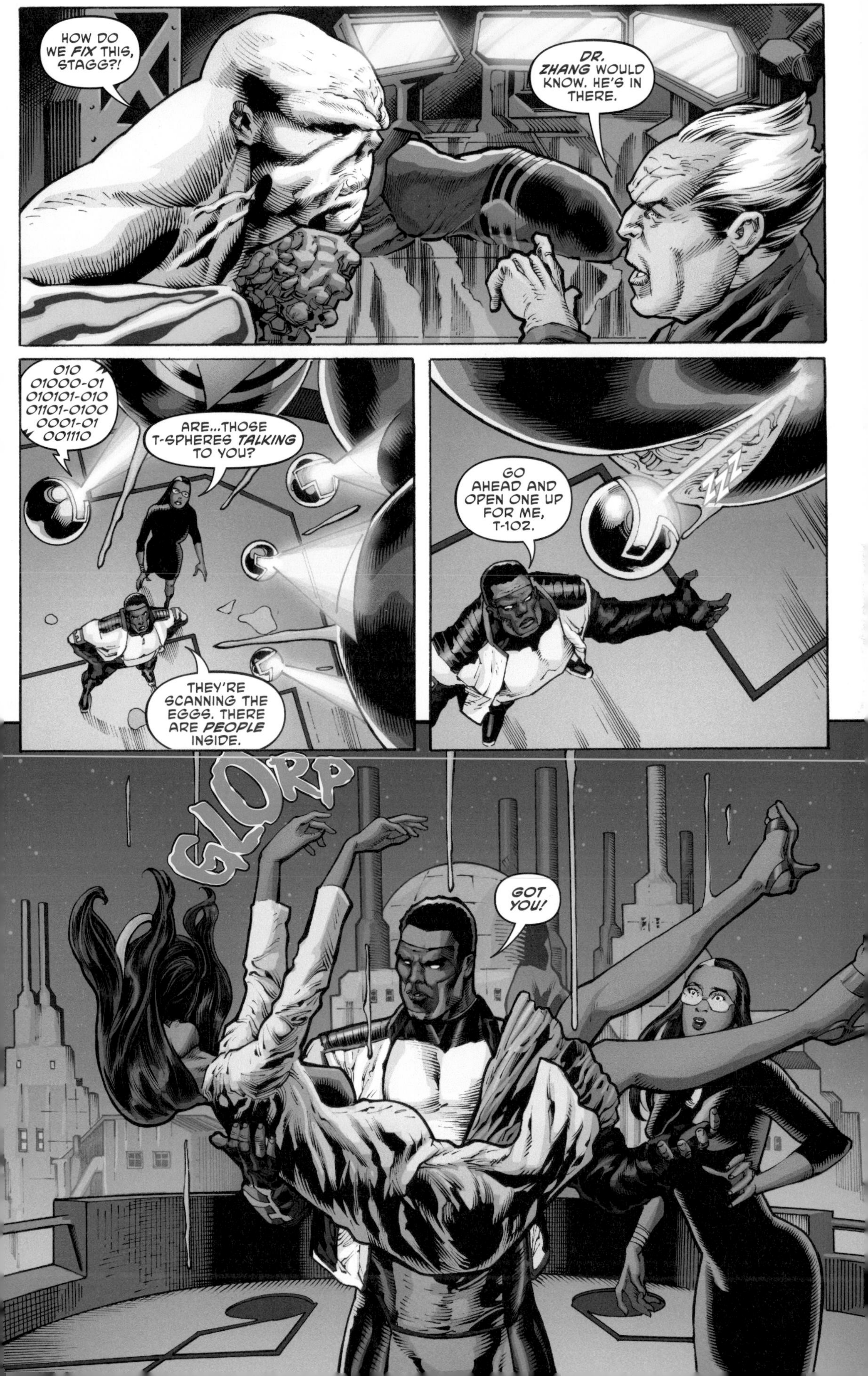
HOW DO WE *FIX* THIS, STAGG?!
DR. ZHANG WOULD KNOW. HE'S IN THERE.
010 01000-01 010101-010 01101-0100 0001-01 001110
ARE...THOSE T-SPHERES *TALKING* TO YOU?
THEY'RE SCANNING THE EGGS. THERE ARE *PEOPLE* INSIDE.
GO AHEAD AND OPEN ONE UP FOR ME, T-102.
ZZZ
GLORP
GOT YOU!

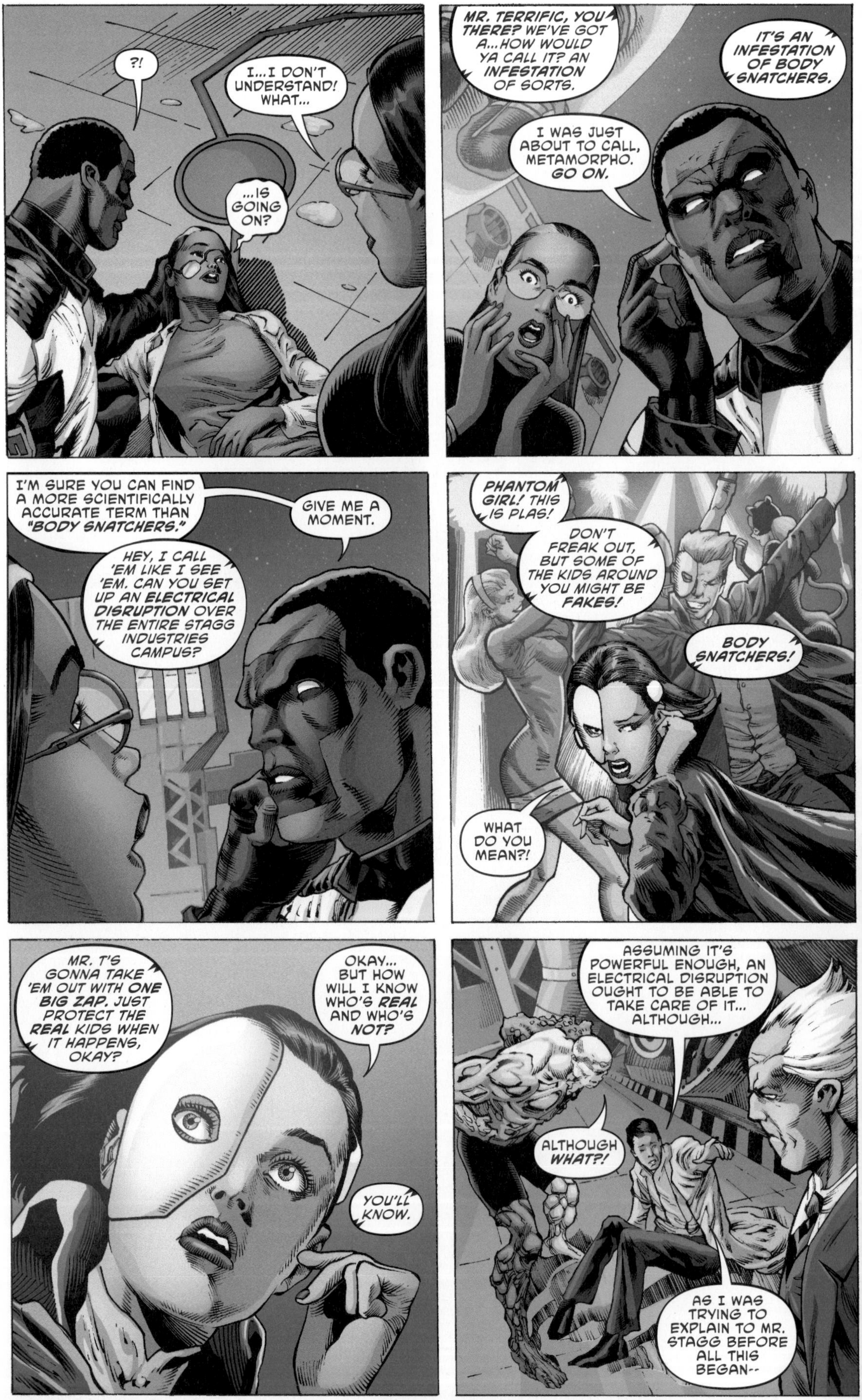
?!
I...I DON'T UNDERSTAND! WHAT...
...IS GOING ON?
MR. TERRIFIC, YOU THERE? WE'VE GOT A...HOW WOULD YA CALL IT? AN INFESTATION OF SORTS.
IT'S AN INFESTATION OF BODY SNATCHERS.
I WAS JUST ABOUT TO CALL, METAMORPHO. GO ON.
I'M SURE YOU CAN FIND A MORE SCIENTIFICALLY ACCURATE TERM THAN "BODY SNATCHERS."
GIVE ME A MOMENT.
HEY, I CALL 'EM LIKE I SEE 'EM. CAN YOU SET UP AN ELECTRICAL DISRUPTION OVER THE ENTIRE STAGG INDUSTRIES CAMPUS?
PHANTOM GIRL! THIS IS PLAS!
DON'T FREAK OUT, BUT SOME OF THE KIDS AROUND YOU MIGHT BE FAKES!
BODY SNATCHERS!
WHAT DO YOU MEAN?!
MR. T'S GONNA TAKE 'EM OUT WITH ONE BIG ZAP. JUST PROTECT THE REAL KIDS WHEN IT HAPPENS, OKAY?
OKAY... BUT HOW WILL I KNOW WHO'S REAL AND WHO'S NOT?
YOU'LL KNOW.
ASSUMING IT'S POWERFUL ENOUGH, AN ELECTRICAL DISRUPTION OUGHT TO BE ABLE TO TAKE CARE OF IT... ALTHOUGH...
ALTHOUGH WHAT?!
AS I WAS TRYING TO EXPLAIN TO MR. STAGG BEFORE ALL THIS BEGAN--

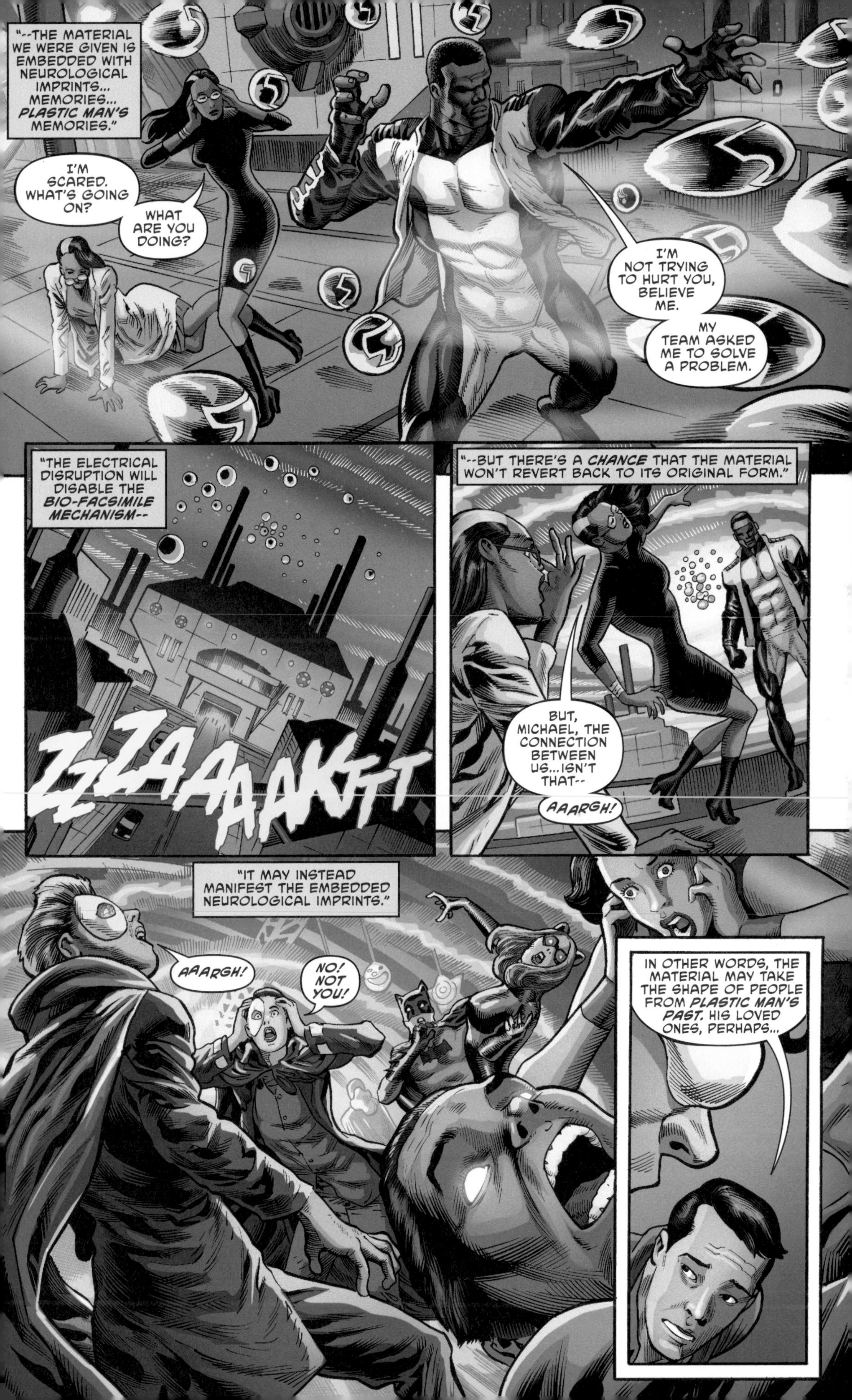
"--THE MATERIAL WE WERE GIVEN IS EMBEDDED WITH NEUROLOGICAL IMPRINTS... MEMORIES... *PLASTIC MAN'S* MEMORIES."
I'M SCARED. WHAT'S GOING ON?
WHAT ARE YOU DOING?
I'M NOT TRYING TO HURT YOU, BELIEVE ME.
MY TEAM ASKED ME TO SOLVE A PROBLEM.
"THE ELECTRICAL DISRUPTION WILL DISABLE THE *BIO-FACSIMILE MECHANISM*--
ZZZAAAAKTTT
"--BUT THERE'S A *CHANCE* THAT THE MATERIAL WON'T REVERT BACK TO ITS ORIGINAL FORM."
BUT, MICHAEL, THE CONNECTION BETWEEN US...ISN'T THAT--
AAARGH!
"IT MAY INSTEAD MANIFEST THE EMBEDDED NEUROLOGICAL IMPRINTS."
AAARGH!
NO! NOT YOU!
IN OTHER WORDS, THE MATERIAL MAY TAKE THE SHAPE OF PEOPLE FROM *PLASTIC MAN'S PAST.* HIS LOVED ONES, PERHAPS...

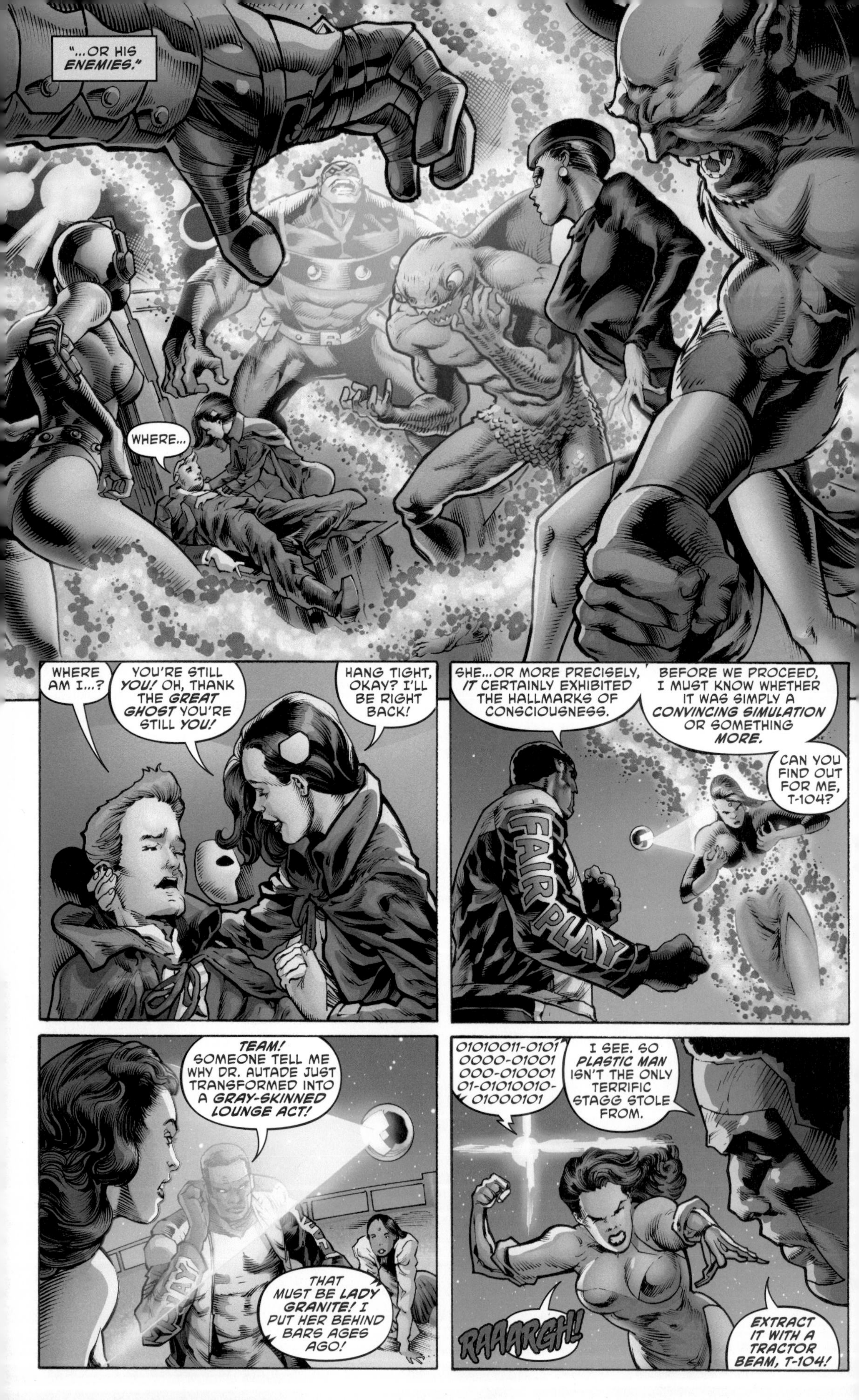
"...OR HIS ENEMIES."
WHERE...
WHERE AM I...?
YOU'RE STILL YOU! OH, THANK THE GREAT GHOST YOU'RE STILL YOU!
HANG TIGHT, OKAY? I'LL BE RIGHT BACK!
SHE...OR MORE PRECISELY, IT CERTAINLY EXHIBITED THE HALLMARKS OF CONSCIOUSNESS.
BEFORE WE PROCEED, I MUST KNOW WHETHER IT WAS SIMPLY A CONVINCING SIMULATION OR SOMETHING MORE.
CAN YOU FIND OUT FOR ME, T-104?
FAIR PLAY
TEAM! SOMEONE TELL ME WHY DR. AUTADE JUST TRANSFORMED INTO A GRAY-SKINNED LOUNGE ACT!
THAT MUST BE LADY GRANITE! I PUT HER BEHIND BARS AGES AGO!
01010011-0101 0000-01001 000-010001 01-01010010-01000101
I SEE. SO PLASTIC MAN ISN'T THE ONLY TERRIFIC STAGG STOLE FROM.
RAAARGH!
EXTRACT IT WITH A TRACTOR BEAM, T-104!

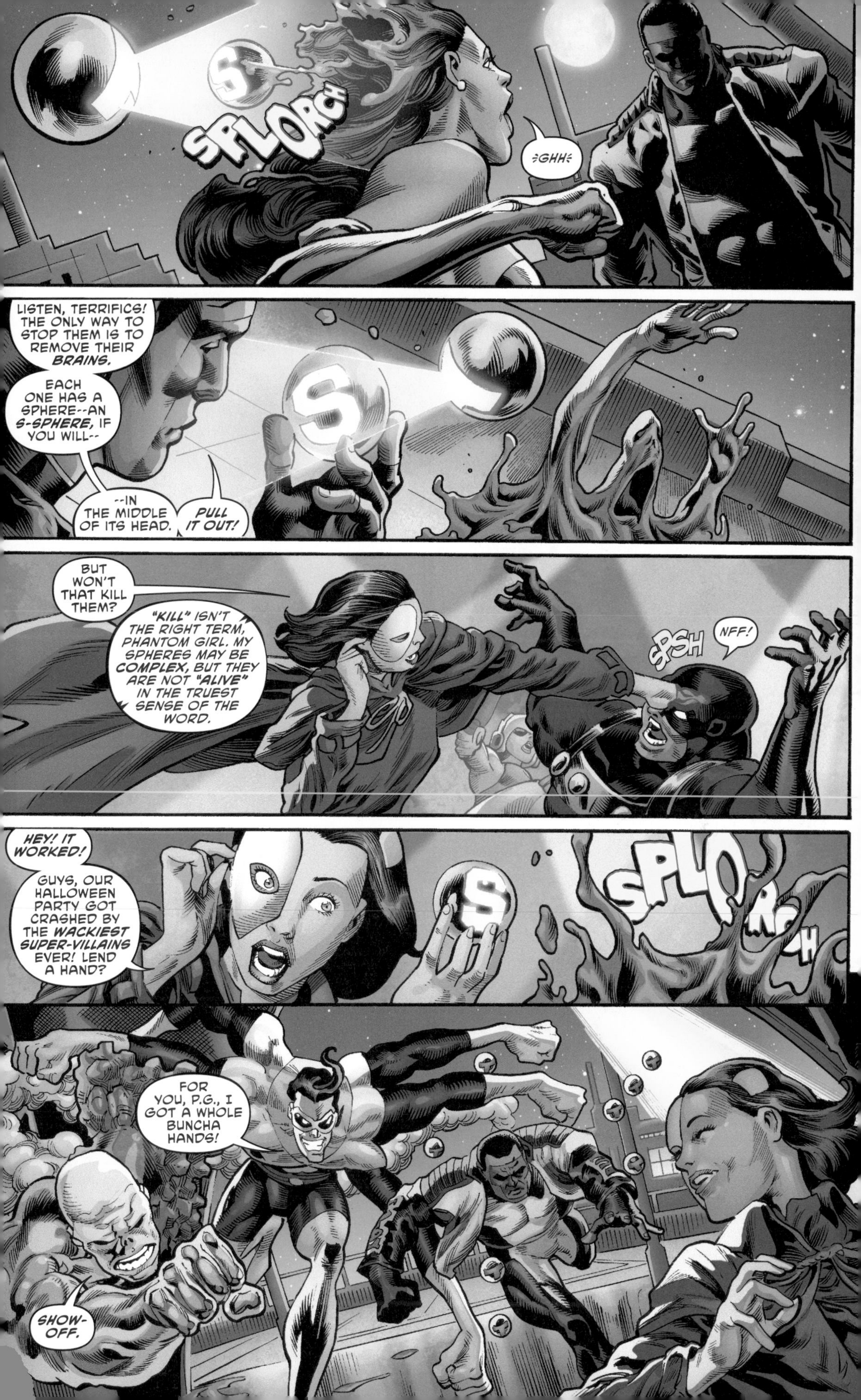
SPLORCH
GHH
LISTEN, TERRIFICS! THE ONLY WAY TO STOP THEM IS TO REMOVE THEIR BRAINS.
EACH ONE HAS A SPHERE--AN S-SPHERE, IF YOU WILL--
--IN THE MIDDLE OF ITS HEAD.
PULL IT OUT!
BUT WON'T THAT KILL THEM?
"KILL" ISN'T THE RIGHT TERM, PHANTOM GIRL. MY SPHERES MAY BE COMPLEX, BUT THEY ARE NOT "ALIVE" IN THE TRUEST SENSE OF THE WORD.
SPSH
NFF!
HEY! IT WORKED!
GUYS, OUR HALLOWEEN PARTY GOT CRASHED BY THE WACKIEST SUPER-VILLAINS EVER! LEND A HAND?
SPLORCH
FOR YOU, P.G., I GOT A WHOLE BUNCHA HANDS!
SHOW-OFF.

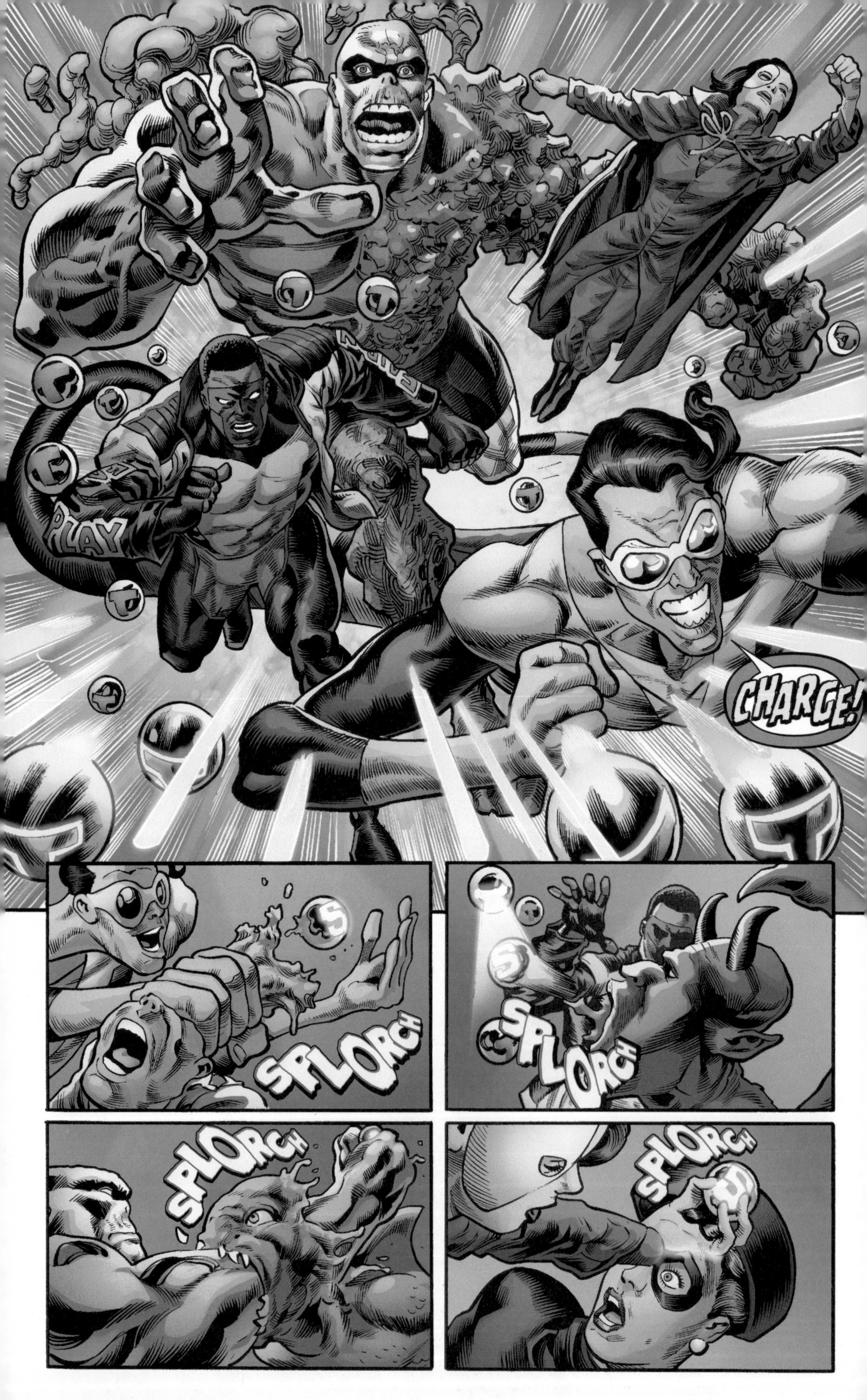

CHARGE!
SPLORCH
SPLORCH
SPLORCH
SPLORCH

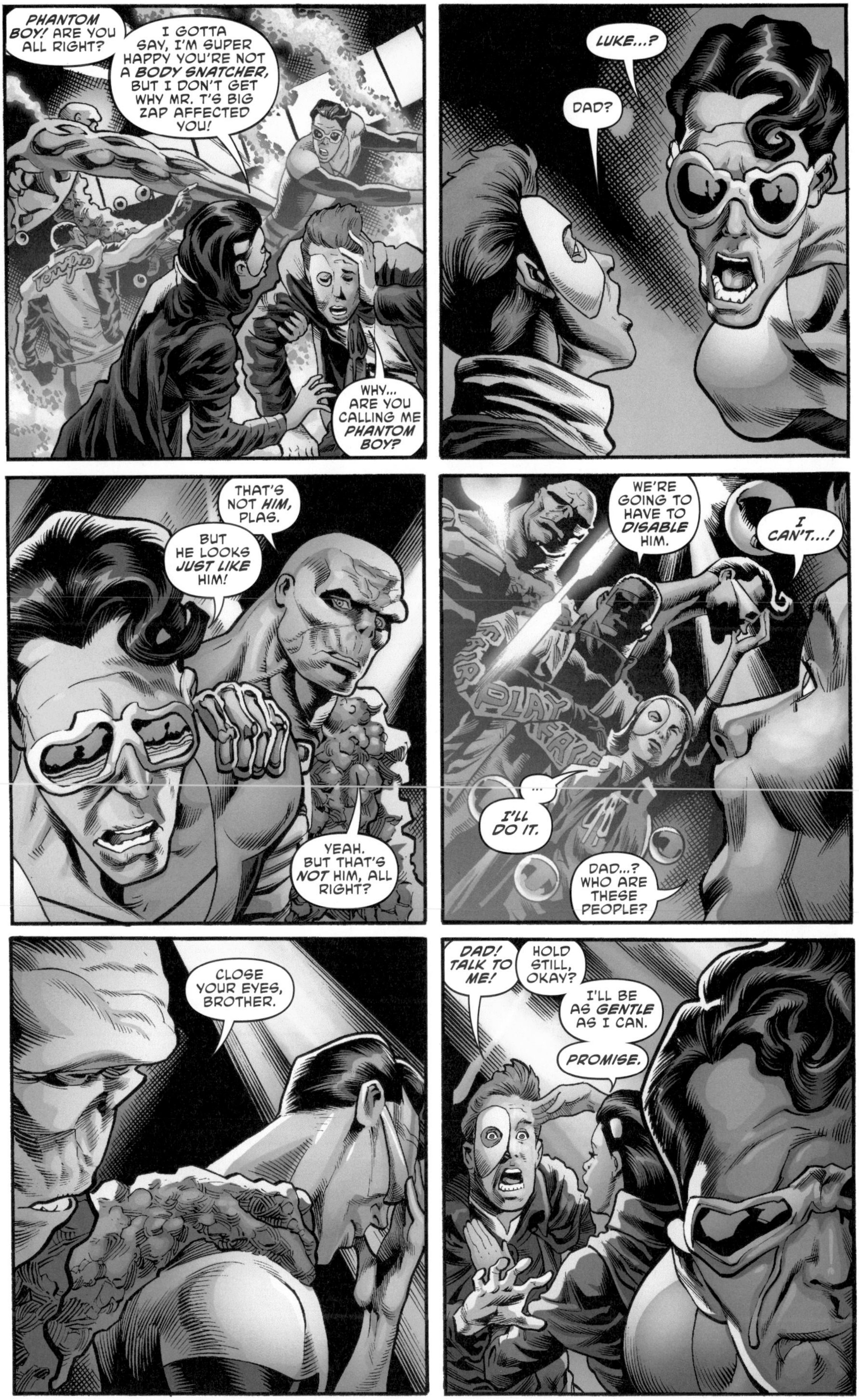

PHANTOM BOY! ARE YOU ALL RIGHT?
I GOTTA SAY, I'M SUPER HAPPY YOU'RE NOT A BODY SNATCHER, BUT I DON'T GET WHY MR. T'S BIG ZAP AFFECTED YOU!
WHY... ARE YOU CALLING ME PHANTOM BOY?
LUKE...?
DAD?
THAT'S NOT HIM, PLAS.
BUT HE LOOKS JUST LIKE HIM!
YEAH. BUT THAT'S NOT HIM, ALL RIGHT?
WE'RE GOING TO HAVE TO DISABLE HIM.
I CAN'T...!
...
I'LL DO IT.
DAD...? WHO ARE THESE PEOPLE?
CLOSE YOUR EYES, BROTHER.
DAD! TALK TO ME!
HOLD STILL, OKAY?
I'LL BE AS GENTLE AS I CAN.
PROMISE.

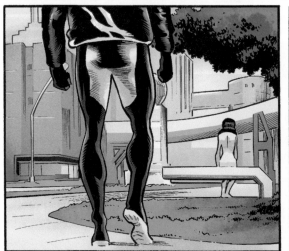

STAGG'S BEEN HIDING BEHIND A WALL OF LAWYERS ALL MORNING, BUT HE CAN'T AVOID US FOREVER. WE'LL HOLD HIM *ACCOUNTABLE* FOR WHAT HE DID.

PHANTOM BOY SEEMED *SO REAL.*

YOU'RE GOING TO HAVE TO TRUST ME ON THIS. THE UNDERLYING TECHNOLOGY WAS MINE, SO I CAN DEFINITIVELY SAY THAT HE WAS NOT, AS YOU CALL IT, *"REAL."*

BUT THEN...WASN'T *WHAT I FELT* REAL?

PLASTIC MAN'S SON *LUKE* IS REAL.

I KNOW, BUT STILL...

DID YOU GET TO TALK TO THE REAL *DR. AUTADE?*

I DID.

AND...?

...

IT WASN'T THE *SAME.*

END.

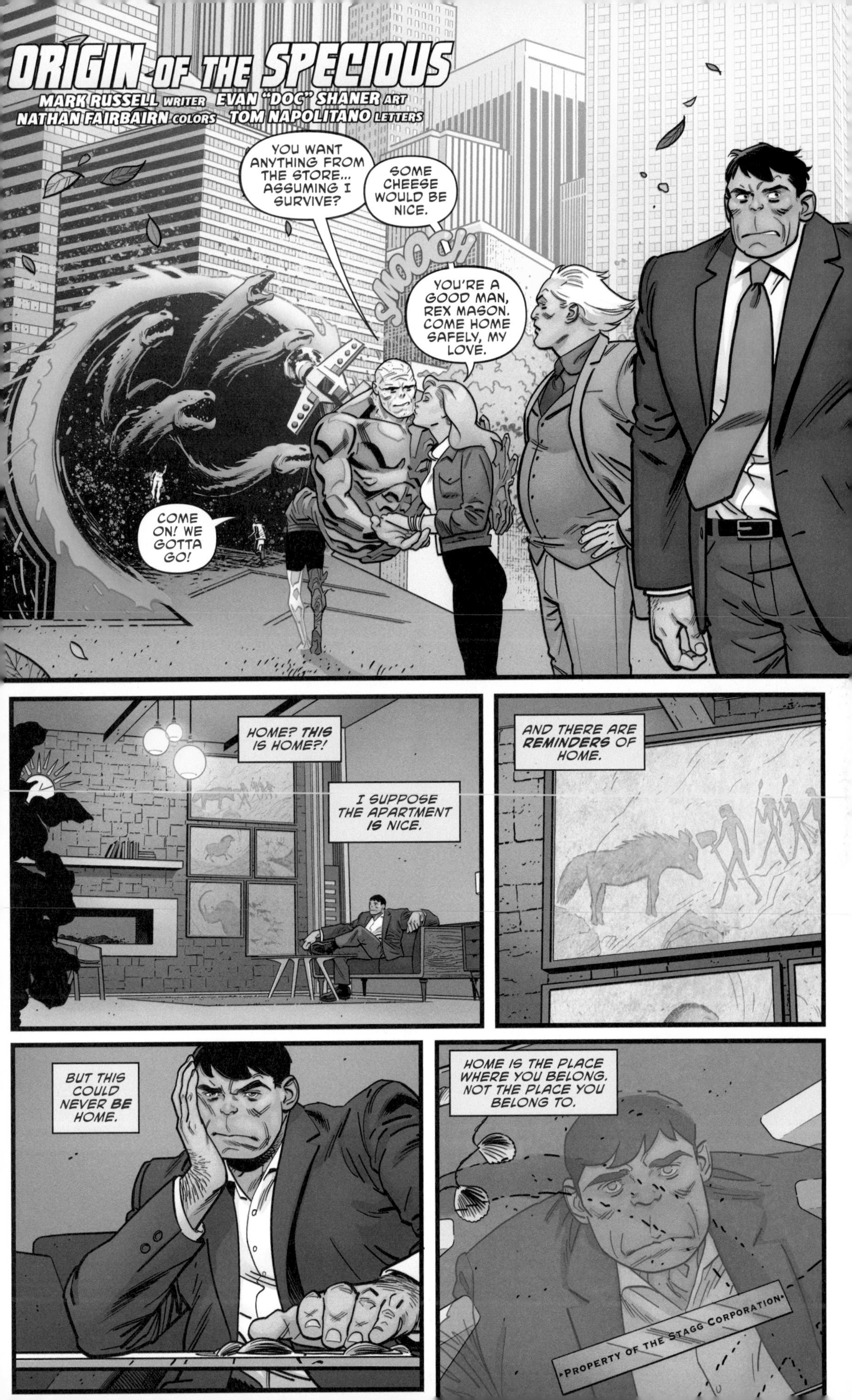
ORIGIN OF THE SPECIOUS
MARK RUSSELL WRITER EVAN "DOC" SHANER ART
NATHAN FAIRBAIRN COLORS TOM NAPOLITANO LETTERS
YOU WANT ANYTHING FROM THE STORE... ASSUMING I SURVIVE?
SOME CHEESE WOULD BE NICE.
SMOOCH
YOU'RE A GOOD MAN, REX MASON. COME HOME SAFELY, MY LOVE.
COME ON! WE GOTTA GO!
HOME? THIS IS HOME?!
I SUPPOSE THE APARTMENT IS NICE.
AND THERE ARE REMINDERS OF HOME.
BUT THIS COULD NEVER BE HOME.
HOME IS THE PLACE WHERE YOU BELONG. NOT THE PLACE YOU BELONG TO.
PROPERTY OF THE STAGG CORPORATION

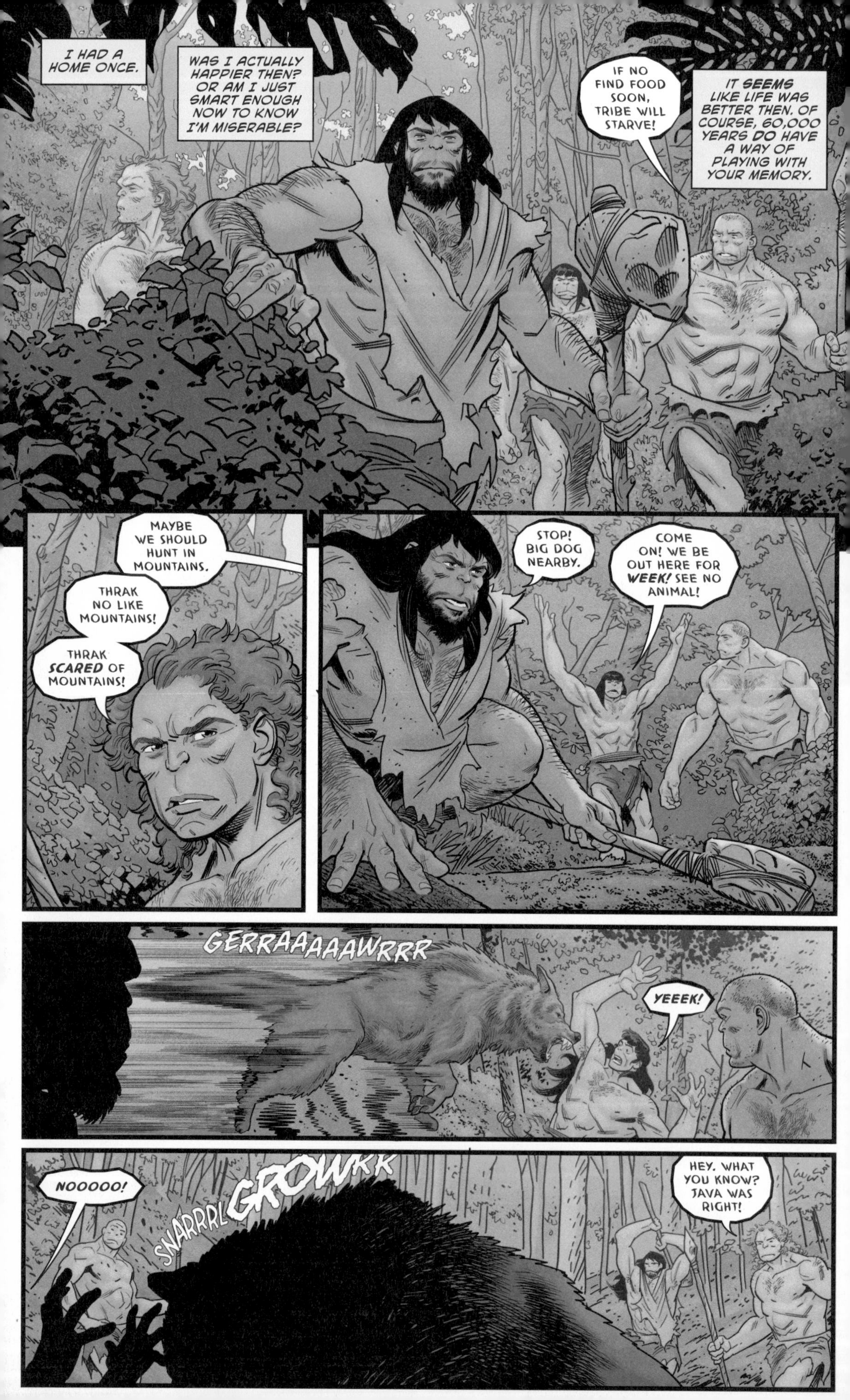
I HAD A HOME ONCE.
WAS I ACTUALLY HAPPIER THEN? OR AM I JUST SMART ENOUGH NOW TO KNOW I'M MISERABLE?
IF NO FIND FOOD SOON, TRIBE WILL STARVE!
IT SEEMS LIKE LIFE WAS BETTER THEN. OF COURSE, 60,000 YEARS DO HAVE A WAY OF PLAYING WITH YOUR MEMORY.
MAYBE WE SHOULD HUNT IN MOUNTAINS.
THRAK NO LIKE MOUNTAINS!
THRAK SCARED OF MOUNTAINS!
STOP! BIG DOG NEARBY.
COME ON! WE BE OUT HERE FOR WEEK! SEE NO ANIMAL!
GERRAAAAAAWRRR
YEEEK!
NOOOOO!
SNARRRL GROWKK
HEY. WHAT YOU KNOW? JAVA WAS RIGHT!

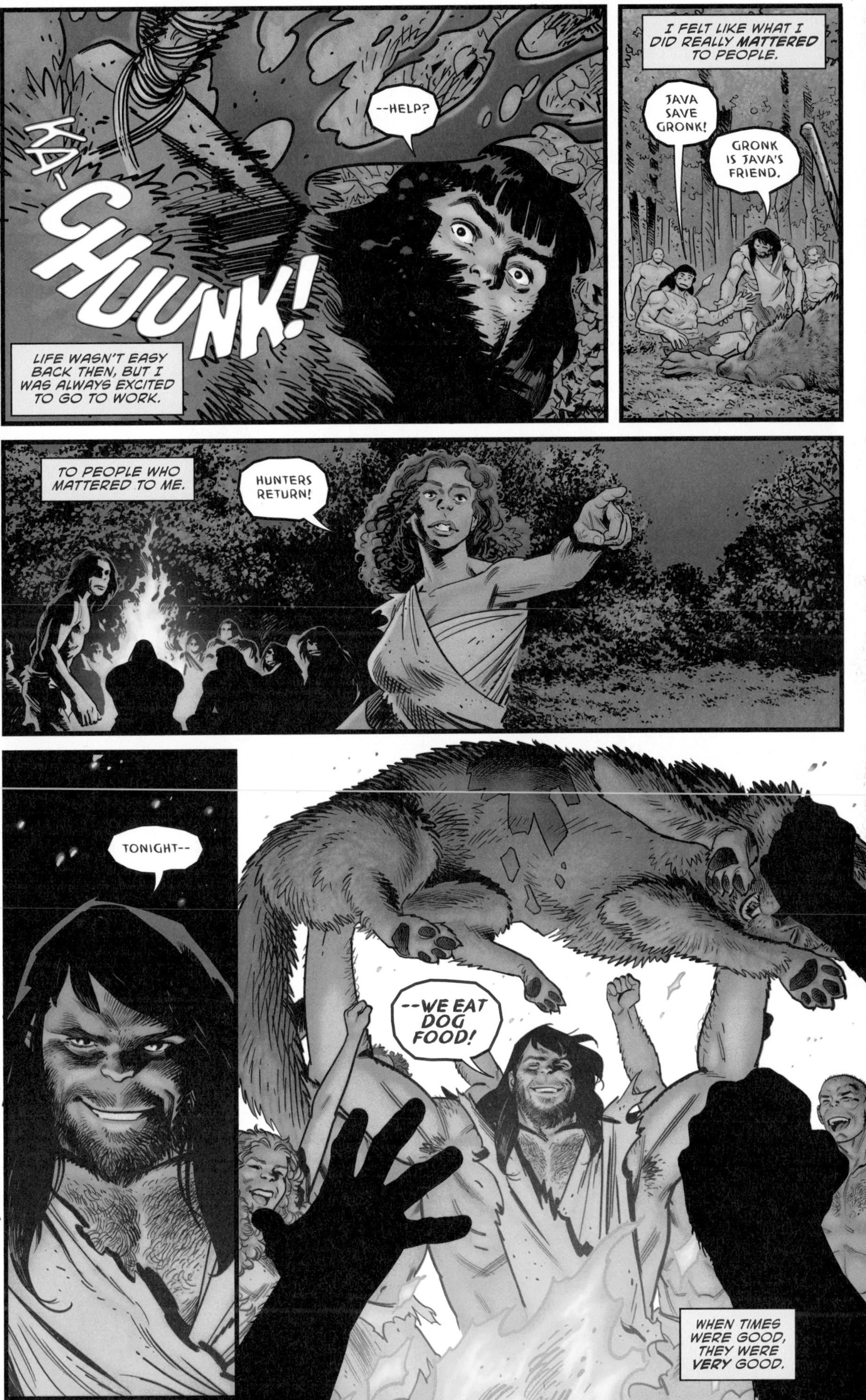

KA-CHUUNK!
--HELP?
LIFE WASN'T EASY BACK THEN, BUT I WAS ALWAYS EXCITED TO GO TO WORK.
I FELT LIKE WHAT I DID REALLY MATTERED TO PEOPLE.
JAVA SAVE GRONK!
GRONK IS JAVA'S FRIEND.
TO PEOPLE WHO MATTERED TO ME.
HUNTERS RETURN!
TONIGHT--
--WE EAT DOG FOOD!
WHEN TIMES WERE GOOD, THEY WERE VERY GOOD.

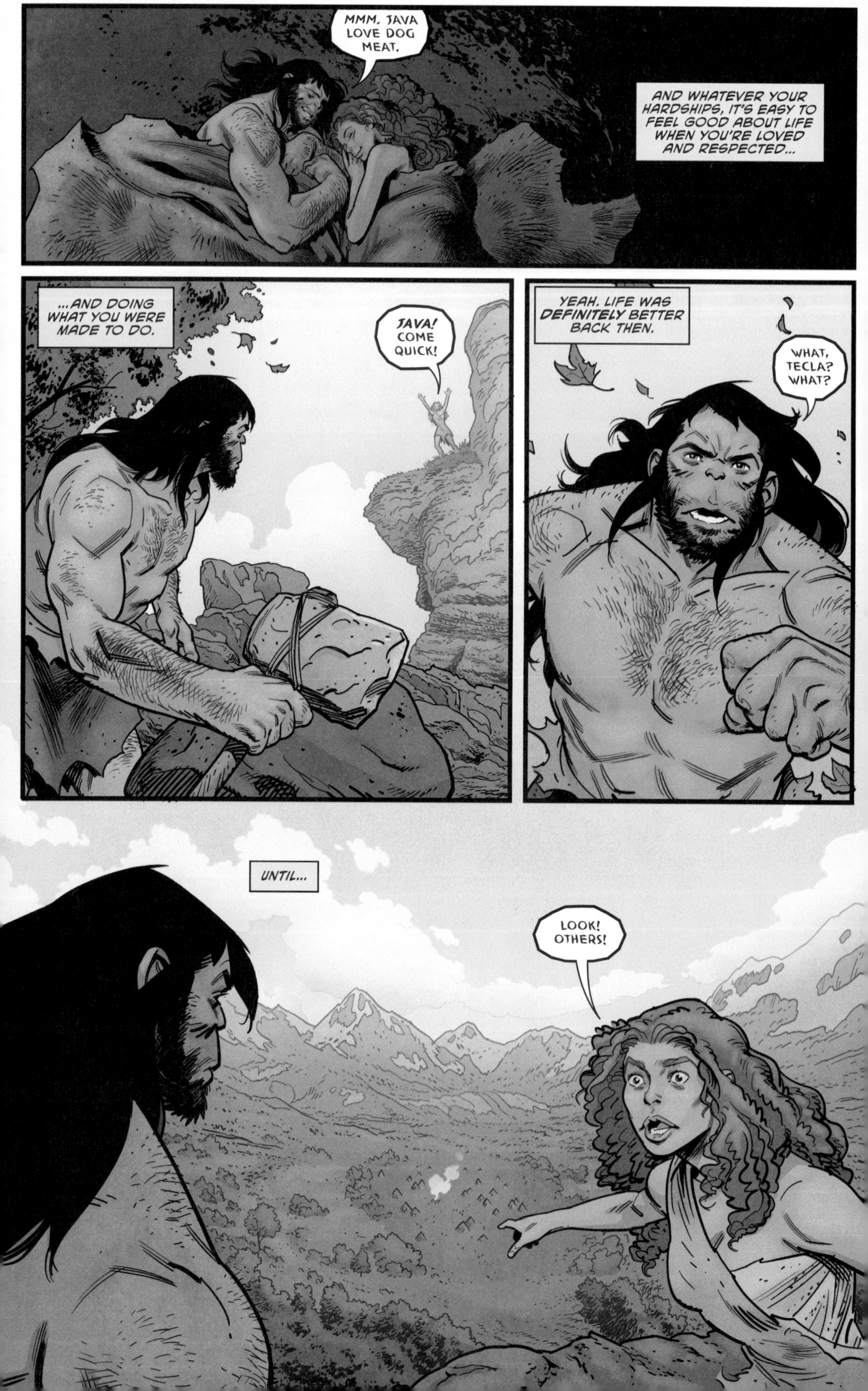
MMM. JAVA LOVE DOG MEAT.
AND WHATEVER YOUR HARDSHIPS, IT'S EASY TO FEEL GOOD ABOUT LIFE WHEN YOU'RE LOVED AND RESPECTED...
...AND DOING WHAT YOU WERE MADE TO DO.
JAVA! COME QUICK!
YEAH. LIFE WAS DEFINITELY BETTER BACK THEN.
WHAT, TECLA? WHAT?
UNTIL...
LOOK! OTHERS!

THEY SO PUNY! WHAT WRONG WITH THEM?

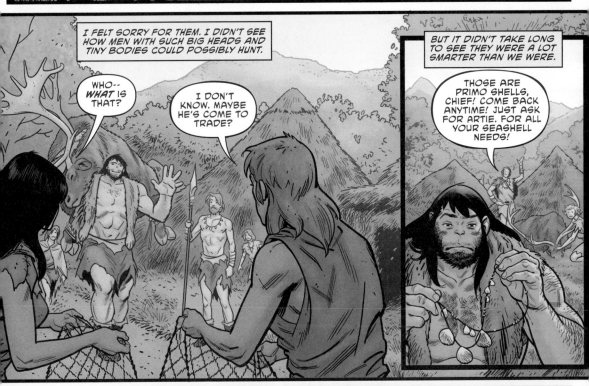

I FELT SORRY FOR THEM. I DIDN'T SEE HOW MEN WITH SUCH BIG HEADS AND TINY BODIES COULD POSSIBLY HUNT.

WHO-- WHAT IS THAT?

I DON'T KNOW. MAYBE HE'S COME TO TRADE?

BUT IT DIDN'T TAKE LONG TO SEE THEY WERE A LOT SMARTER THAN WE WERE.

THOSE ARE PRIMO SHELLS, CHIEF! COME BACK ANYTIME! JUST ASK FOR ARTIE. FOR ALL YOUR SEASHELL NEEDS!

I SUPPOSE YOU COULD ACCUSE ME OF BEING NOSTALGIC. BUT YOU'D BE WRONG.

JAVA, WHERE IS CARIBOU? TECLA WAS GOING MAKE DINNER!

IT'S NOT NOSTALGIA I FEEL, BUT ITS OPPOSITE...

...THE ECHOING PAIN OF LOST LOVE.

FOR YOU.

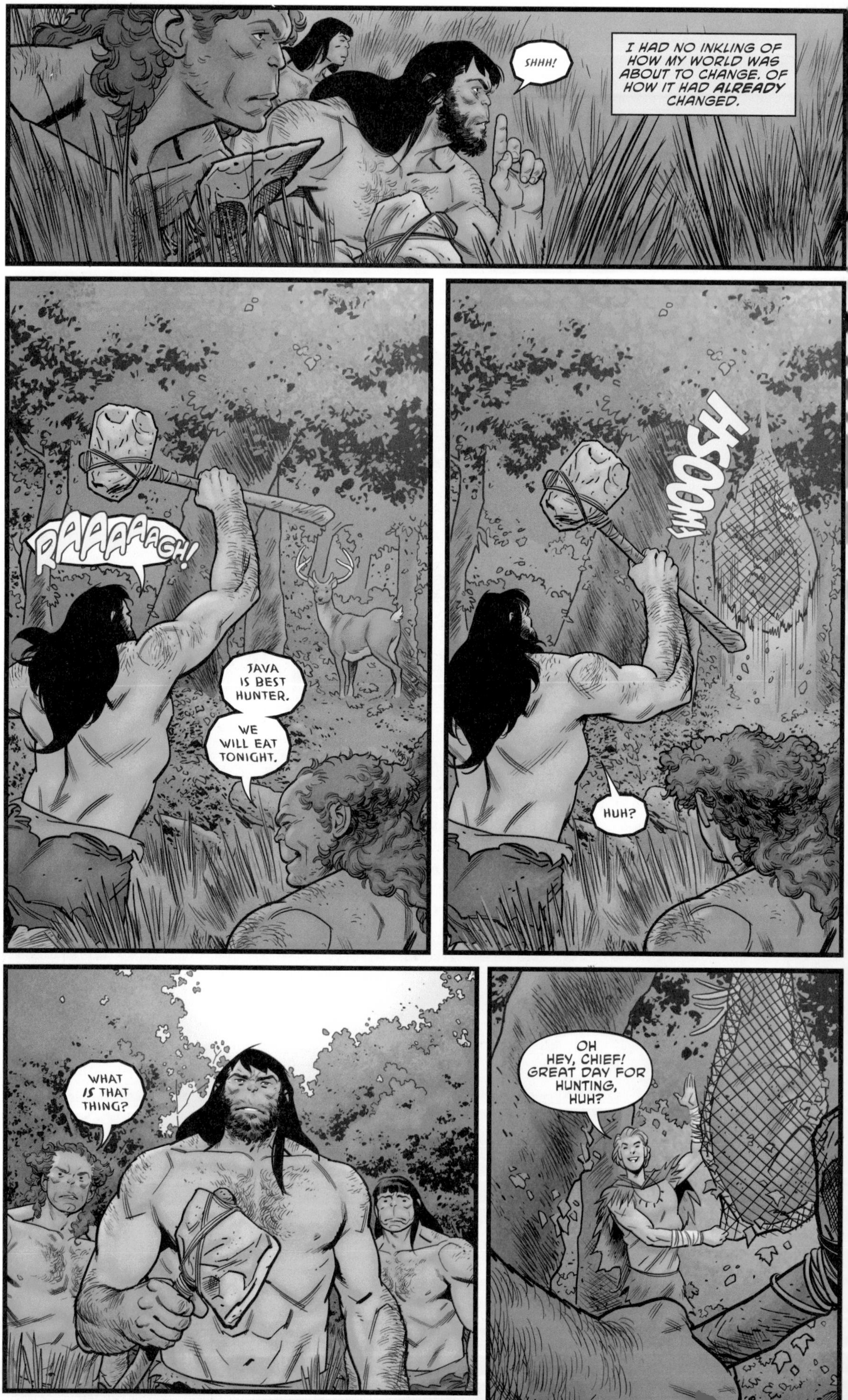
SHHH!
I HAD NO INKLING OF HOW MY WORLD WAS ABOUT TO CHANGE. OF HOW IT HAD *ALREADY* CHANGED.
RAAAAAAGH!
JAVA IS BEST HUNTER.
WE WILL EAT TONIGHT.
FWOOSH!
HUH?
WHAT *IS* THAT THING?
OH HEY, CHIEF! GREAT DAY FOR HUNTING, HUH?

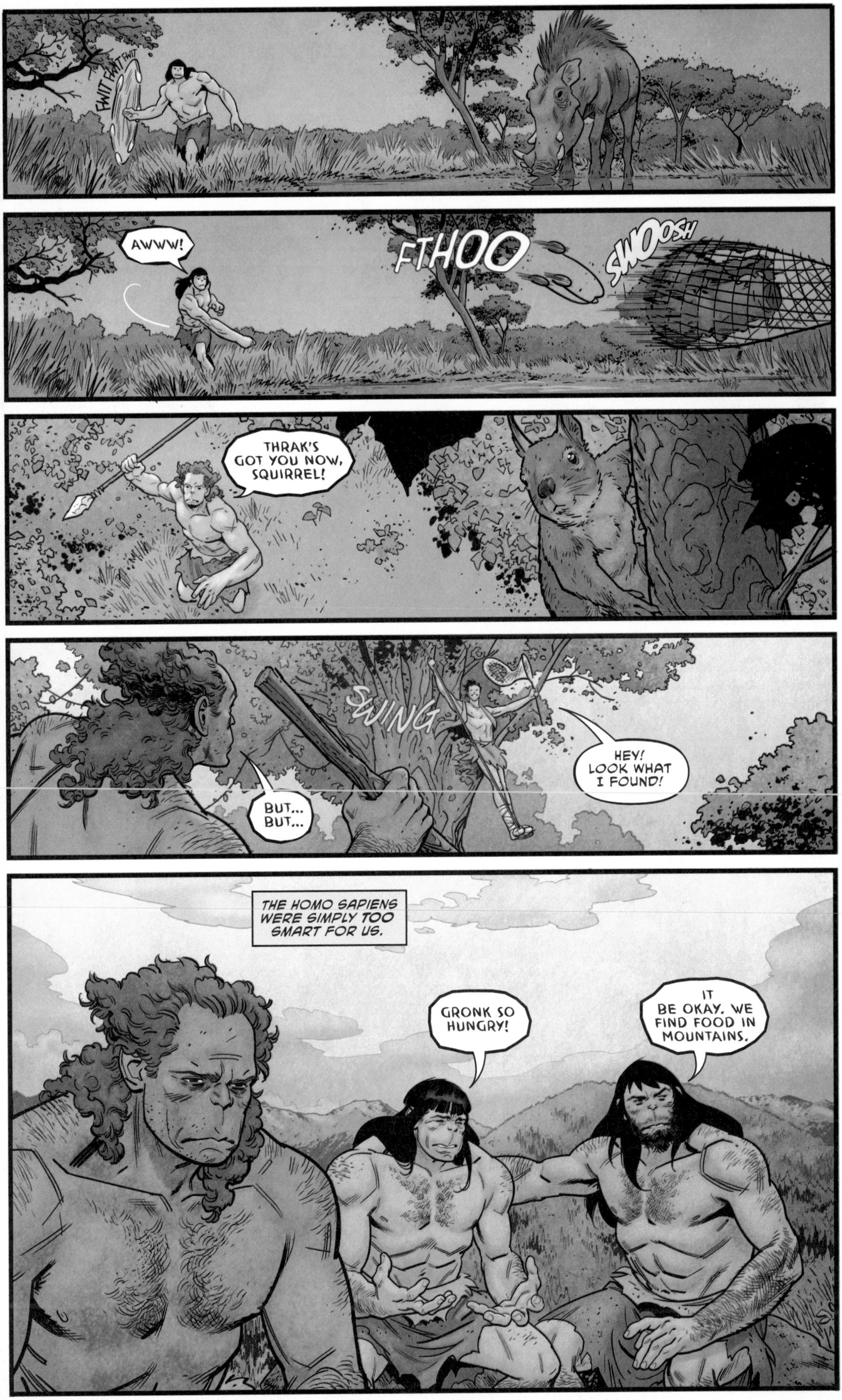
FWIT FWIT FWIT
AWWW!
FTHOO
SWOOSH
THRAK'S GOT YOU NOW, SQUIRREL!
SWING
BUT... BUT...
HEY! LOOK WHAT I FOUND!
THE HOMO SAPIENS WERE SIMPLY TOO SMART FOR US.
GRONK SO HUNGRY!
IT BE OKAY. WE FIND FOOD IN MOUNTAINS.

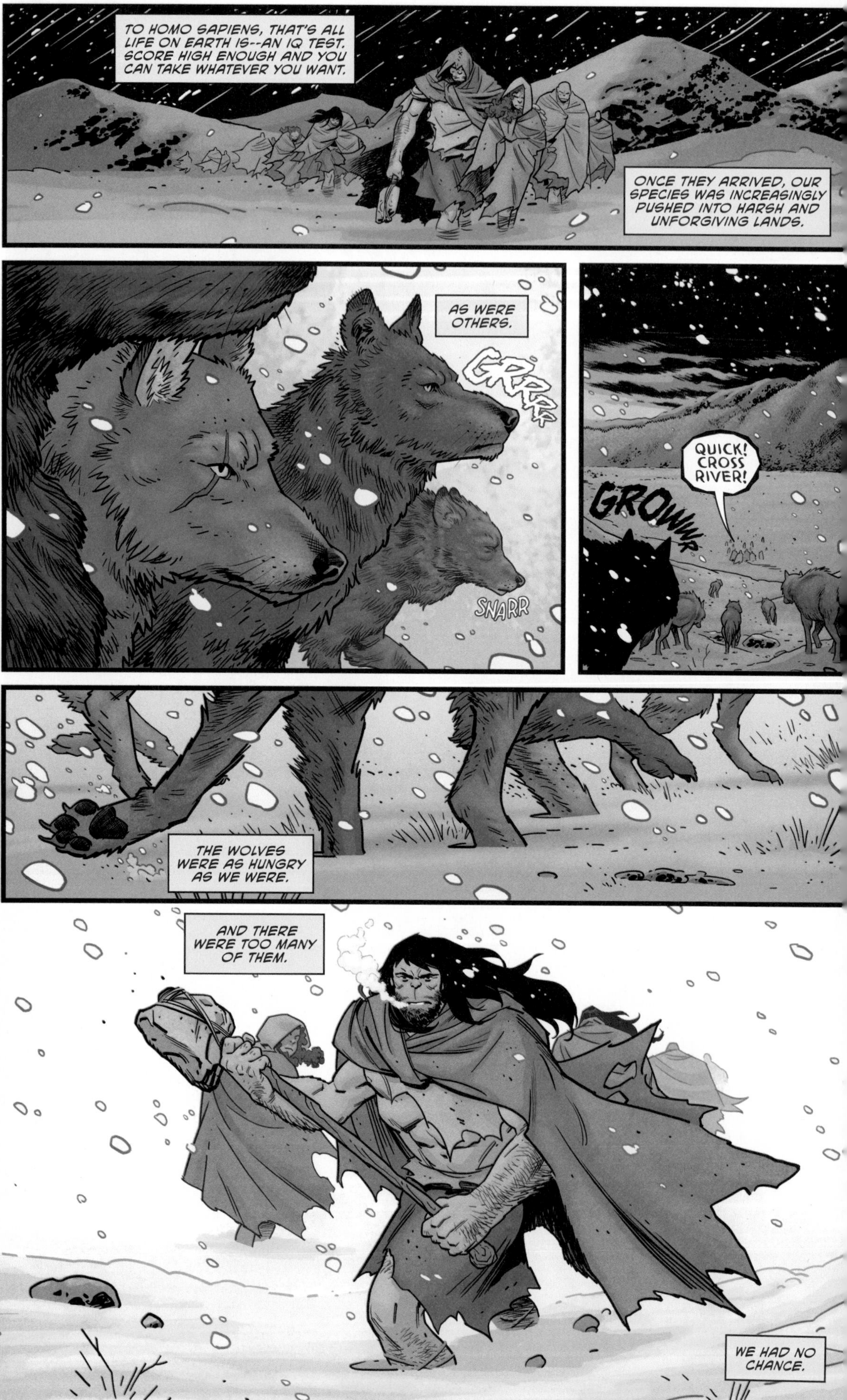
TO HOMO SAPIENS, THAT'S ALL LIFE ON EARTH IS--AN IQ TEST. SCORE HIGH ENOUGH AND YOU CAN TAKE WHATEVER YOU WANT.
ONCE THEY ARRIVED, OUR SPECIES WAS INCREASINGLY PUSHED INTO HARSH AND UNFORGIVING LANDS.
AS WERE OTHERS.
GRRRR
SNARR
QUICK! CROSS RIVER!
GROWWR
THE WOLVES WERE AS HUNGRY AS WE WERE.
AND THERE WERE TOO MANY OF THEM.
WE HAD NO CHANCE.

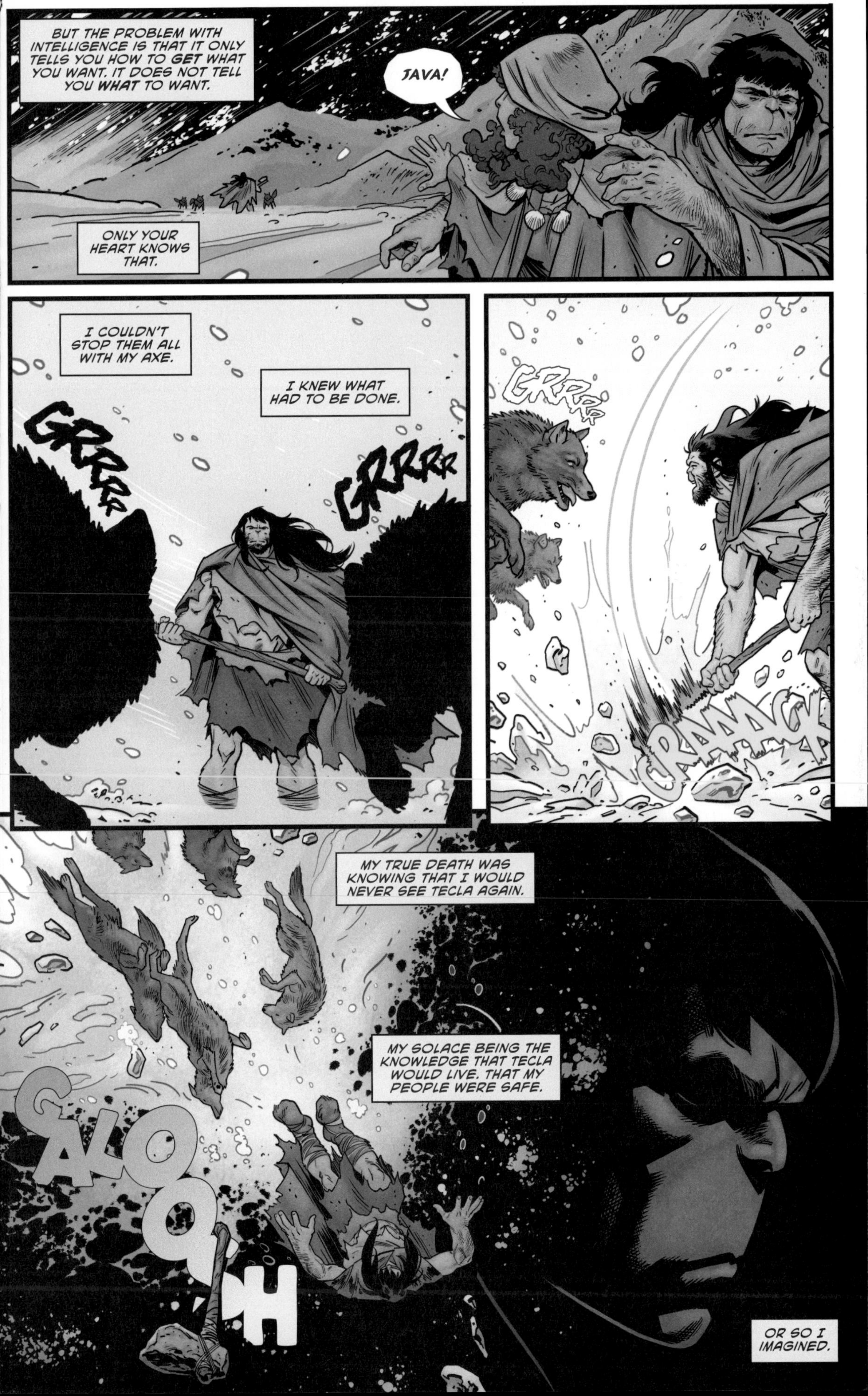
BUT THE PROBLEM WITH INTELLIGENCE IS THAT IT ONLY TELLS YOU HOW TO GET WHAT YOU WANT. IT DOES NOT TELL YOU WHAT TO WANT.
JAVA!
ONLY YOUR HEART KNOWS THAT.
I COULDN'T STOP THEM ALL WITH MY AXE.
I KNEW WHAT HAD TO BE DONE.
GRRRR
GRRRR
GRRRR
CRAAACK
MY TRUE DEATH WAS KNOWING THAT I WOULD NEVER SEE TECLA AGAIN.
MY SOLACE BEING THE KNOWLEDGE THAT TECLA WOULD LIVE. THAT MY PEOPLE WERE SAFE.
GALOOOSH
OR SO I IMAGINED.

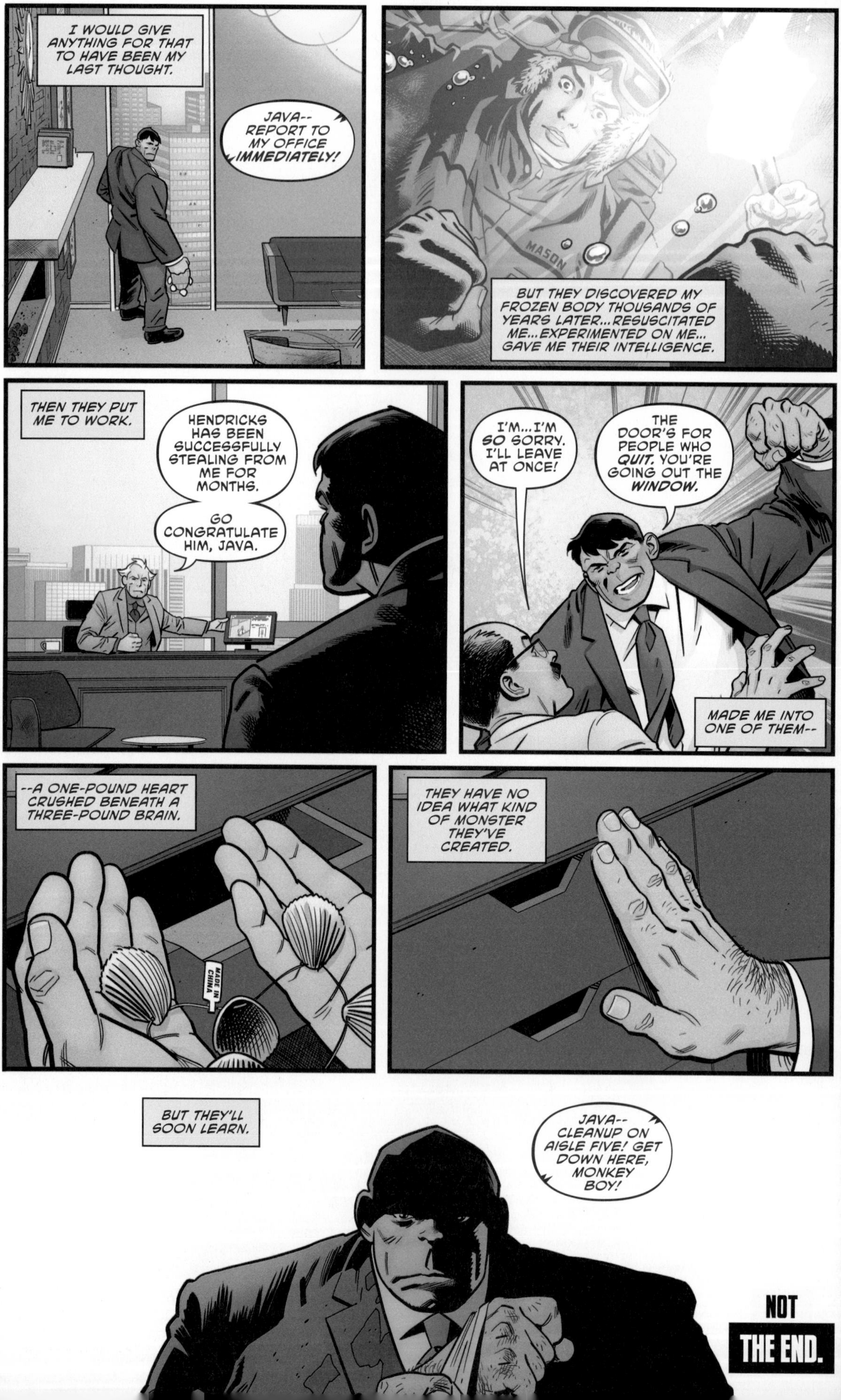
I WOULD GIVE ANYTHING FOR THAT TO HAVE BEEN MY LAST THOUGHT.
JAVA-- REPORT TO MY OFFICE IMMEDIATELY!
MASON
BUT THEY DISCOVERED MY FROZEN BODY THOUSANDS OF YEARS LATER...RESUSCITATED ME...EXPERIMENTED ON ME... GAVE ME THEIR INTELLIGENCE.
THEN THEY PUT ME TO WORK.
HENDRICKS HAS BEEN SUCCESSFULLY STEALING FROM ME FOR MONTHS.
GO CONGRATULATE HIM, JAVA.
I'M...I'M SO SORRY. I'LL LEAVE AT ONCE!
THE DOOR'S FOR PEOPLE WHO QUIT. YOU'RE GOING OUT THE WINDOW.
MADE ME INTO ONE OF THEM--
--A ONE-POUND HEART CRUSHED BENEATH A THREE-POUND BRAIN.
MADE IN CHINA
THEY HAVE NO IDEA WHAT KIND OF MONSTER THEY'VE CREATED.
BUT THEY'LL SOON LEARN.
JAVA-- CLEANUP ON AISLE FIVE! GET DOWN HERE, MONKEY BOY!
NOT
THE END.

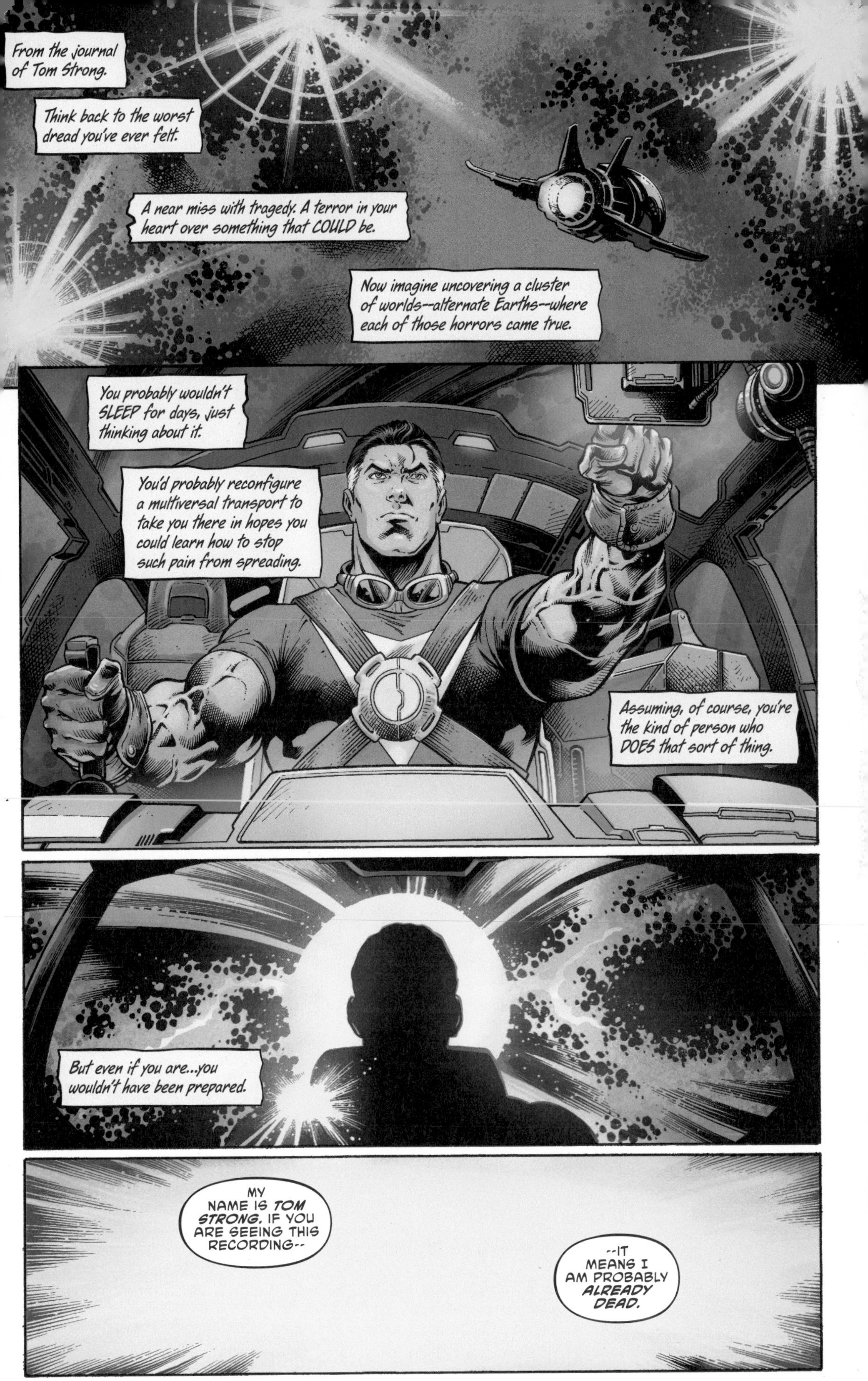
From the journal of Tom Strong.
Think back to the worst dread you've ever felt.
A near miss with tragedy. A terror in your heart over something that COULD be.
Now imagine uncovering a cluster of worlds--alternate Earths--where each of those horrors came true.
You probably wouldn't SLEEP for days, just thinking about it.
You'd probably reconfigure a multiversal transport to take you there in hopes you could learn how to stop such pain from spreading.
Assuming, of course, you're the kind of person who DOES that sort of thing.
But even if you are...you wouldn't have been prepared.
MY NAME IS TOM STRONG. IF YOU ARE SEEING THIS RECORDING--
--IT MEANS I AM PROBABLY ALREADY DEAD.

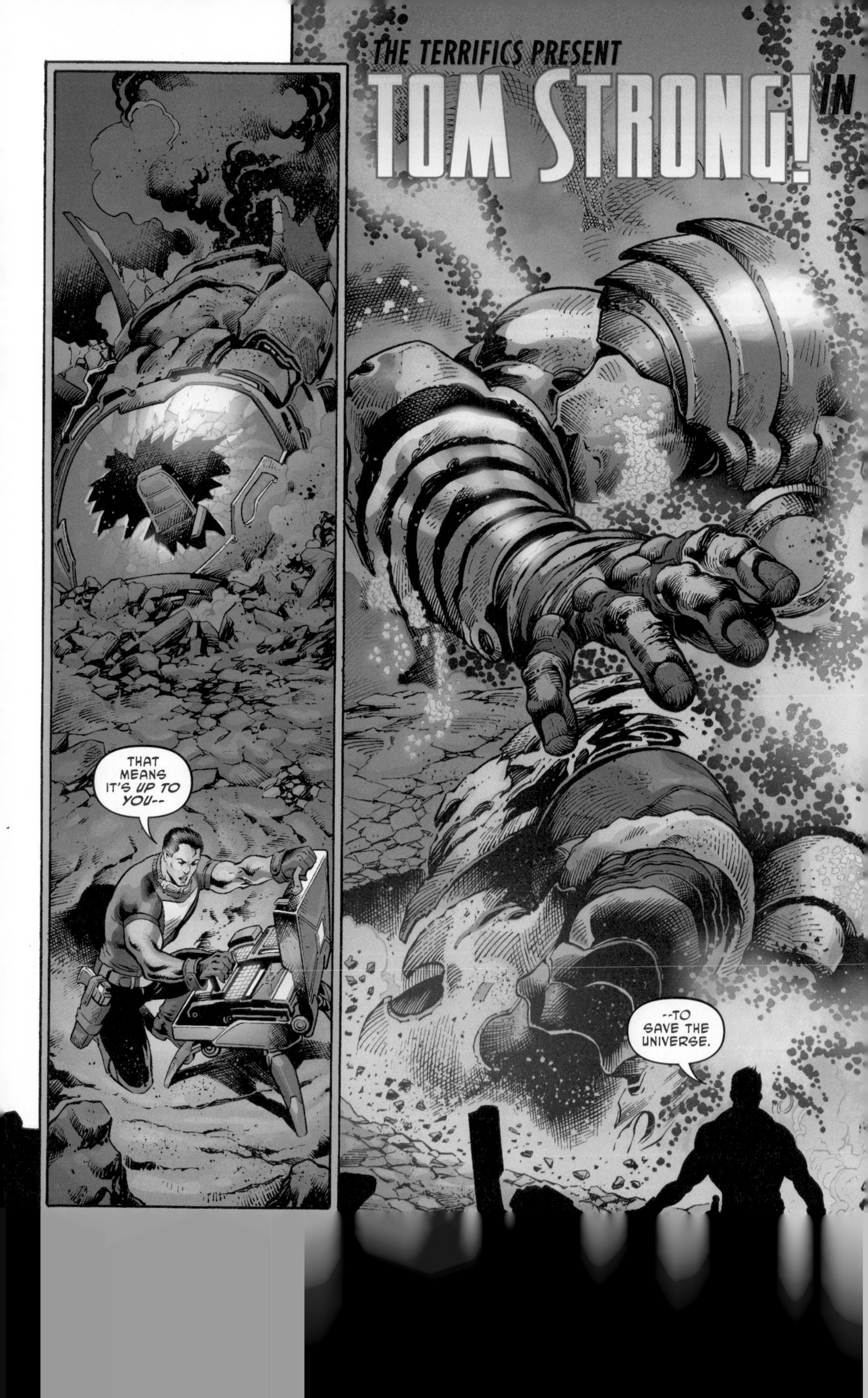
THE TERRIFICS PRESENT
TOM STRONG! IN
THAT MEANS IT'S UP TO YOU--
--TO SAVE THE UNIVERSE.

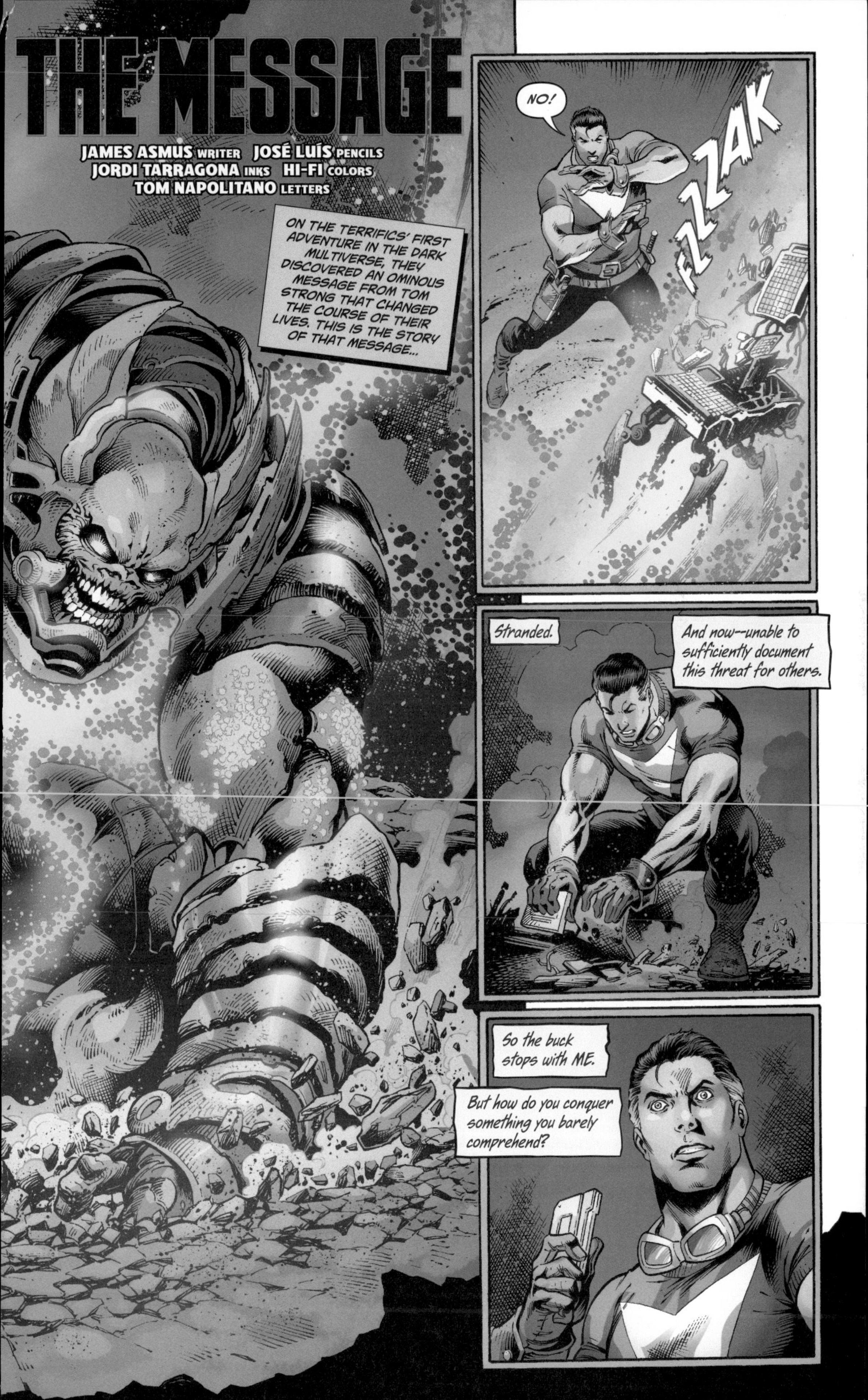
THE MESSAGE
JAMES ASMUS WRITER JOSÉ LUÍS PENCILS
JORDI TARRAGONA INKS HI-FI COLORS
TOM NAPOLITANO LETTERS
ON THE TERRIFICS' FIRST ADVENTURE IN THE DARK MULTIVERSE, THEY DISCOVERED AN OMINOUS MESSAGE FROM TOM STRONG THAT CHANGED THE COURSE OF THEIR LIVES. THIS IS THE STORY OF THAT MESSAGE...
NO!
FZZZAK
Stranded.
And now--unable to sufficiently document this threat for others.
So the buck stops with ME.
But how do you conquer something you barely comprehend?

With SCIENCE.

And the scientific method dictates you start by collecting data.

The observable aspects.

Its effect on its environment.

Vice versa.

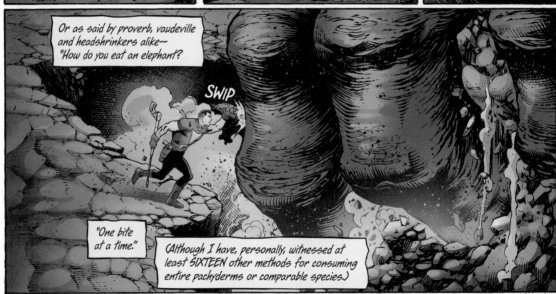

Or as said by proverb, vaudeville and headshrinkers alike-- "How do you eat an elephant?"

SWIP

"One bite at a time."

(Although I have, personally, witnessed at least SIXTEEN other methods for consuming entire pachyderms or comparable species.)

In this case, my first bite is to test for elements or energies native to only one reality--

Of course.

These ARE beings who CROSS realities...

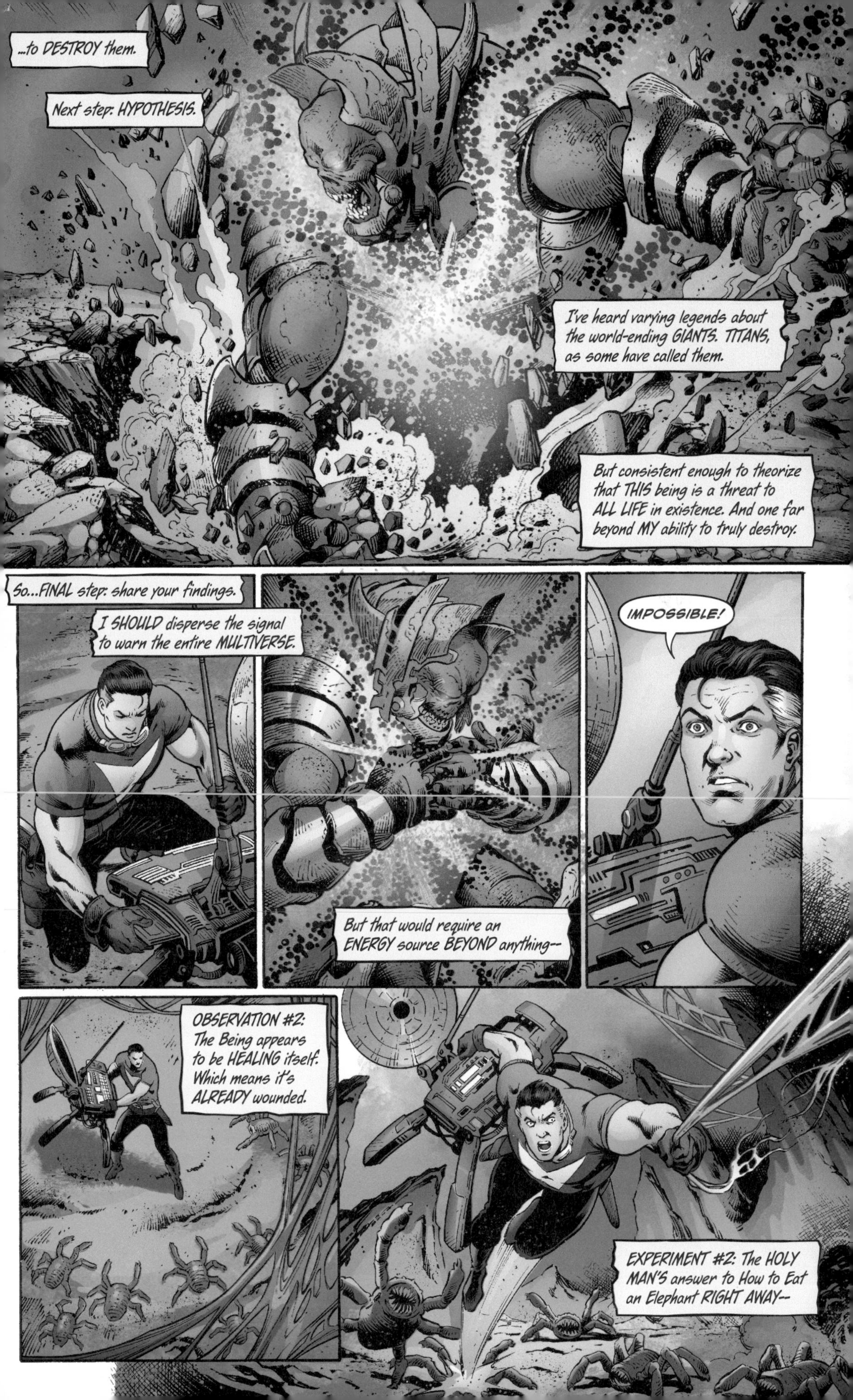

...to DESTROY them.
Next step: HYPOTHESIS.
I've heard varying legends about the world-ending GIANTS. TITANS, as some have called them.
But consistent enough to theorize that THIS being is a threat to ALL LIFE in existence. And one far beyond MY ability to truly destroy.
So...FINAL step: share your findings.
I SHOULD disperse the signal to warn the entire MULTIVERSE.
But that would require an ENERGY source BEYOND anything--
IMPOSSIBLE!
OBSERVATION #2: The Being appears to be HEALING itself. Which means it's ALREADY wounded.
EXPERIMENT #2: The HOLY MAN'S answer to How to Eat an Elephant RIGHT AWAY--

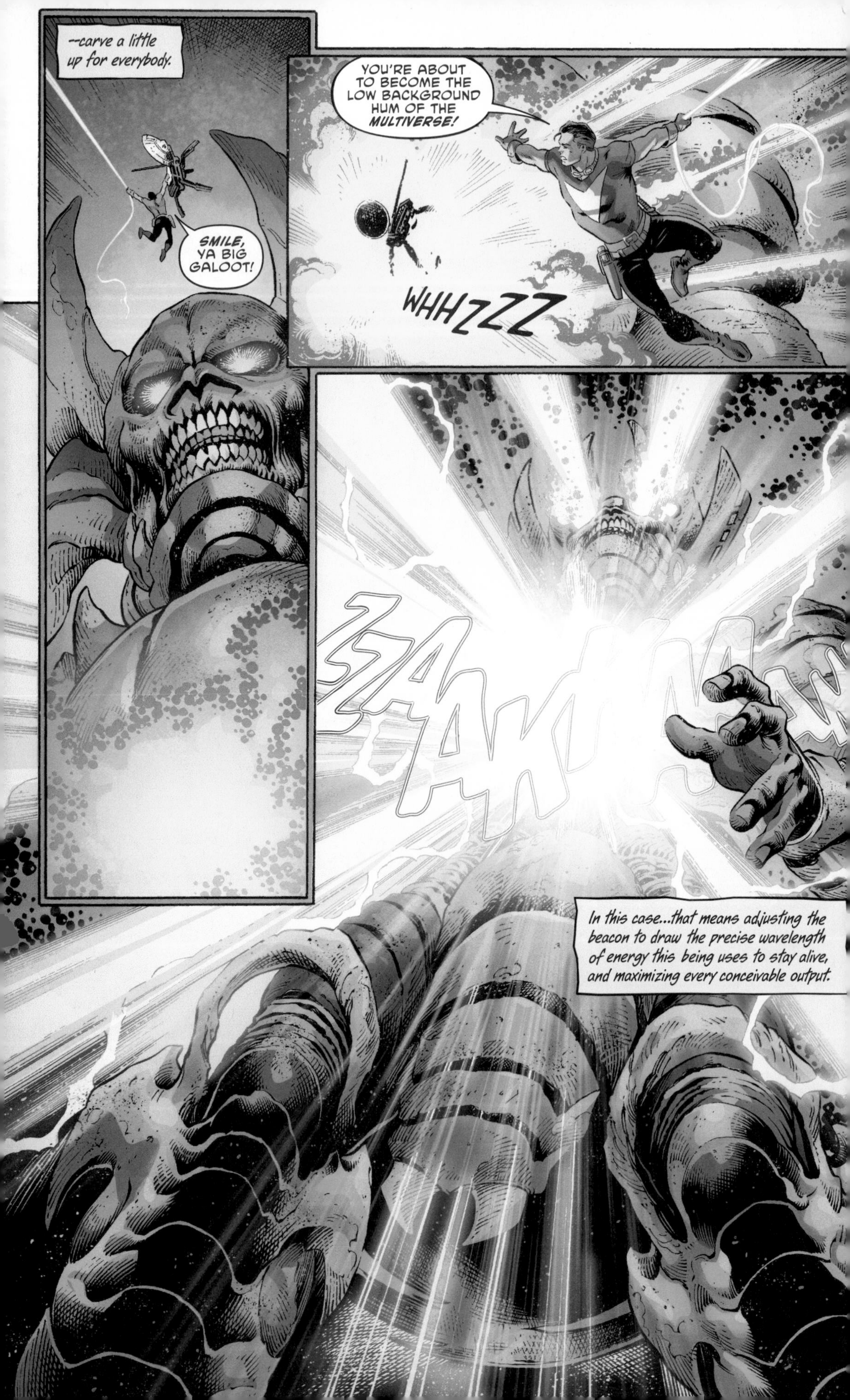

--carve a little up for everybody.
SMILE, YA BIG GALOOT!
YOU'RE ABOUT TO BECOME THE LOW BACKGROUND HUM OF THE *MULTIVERSE!*
WHHZZZ
In this case...that means adjusting the beacon to draw the precise wavelength of energy this being uses to stay alive, and maximizing every conceivable output.

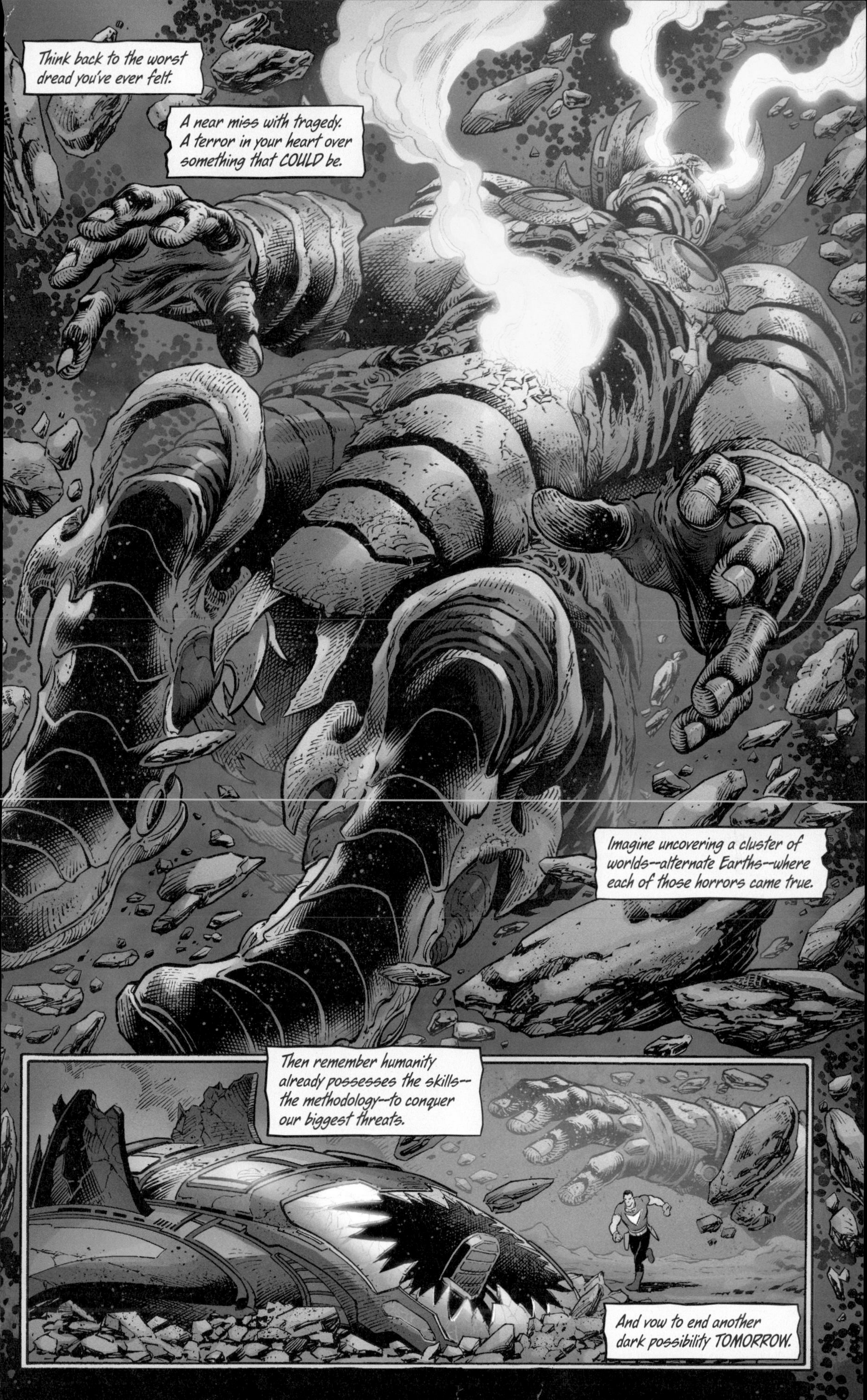
Think back to the worst dread you've ever felt.
A near miss with tragedy. A terror in your heart over something that COULD be.
Imagine uncovering a cluster of worlds--alternate Earths--where each of those horrors came true.
Then remember humanity already possesses the skills--the methodology--to conquer our biggest threats.
And vow to end another dark possibility TOMORROW.

SEVERAL TOMORROWS LATER.

Finally. Though the irregular flow of TIME in this DARK MULTIVERSE makes my tenure impossible to gauge--

--I managed to sufficiently reconstruct my multiversal transport.

Yet my TRUE struggle has been deciding whether to dismantle the beacon--

--so as not to lead anyone else to this horrid dimension.

But the beacon's very signal is what has paralyzed the beast.

So leave it, I MUST.

This isn't the end, I WILL be back one day.

And until I do, I truly hope that no other being ever finds this place--

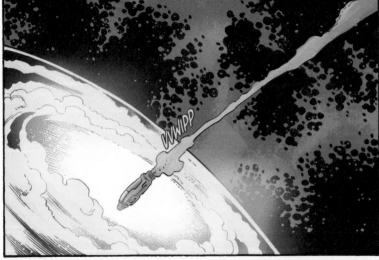

VVWIPP

--and tragedy can be averted.

THE BEGINNING...

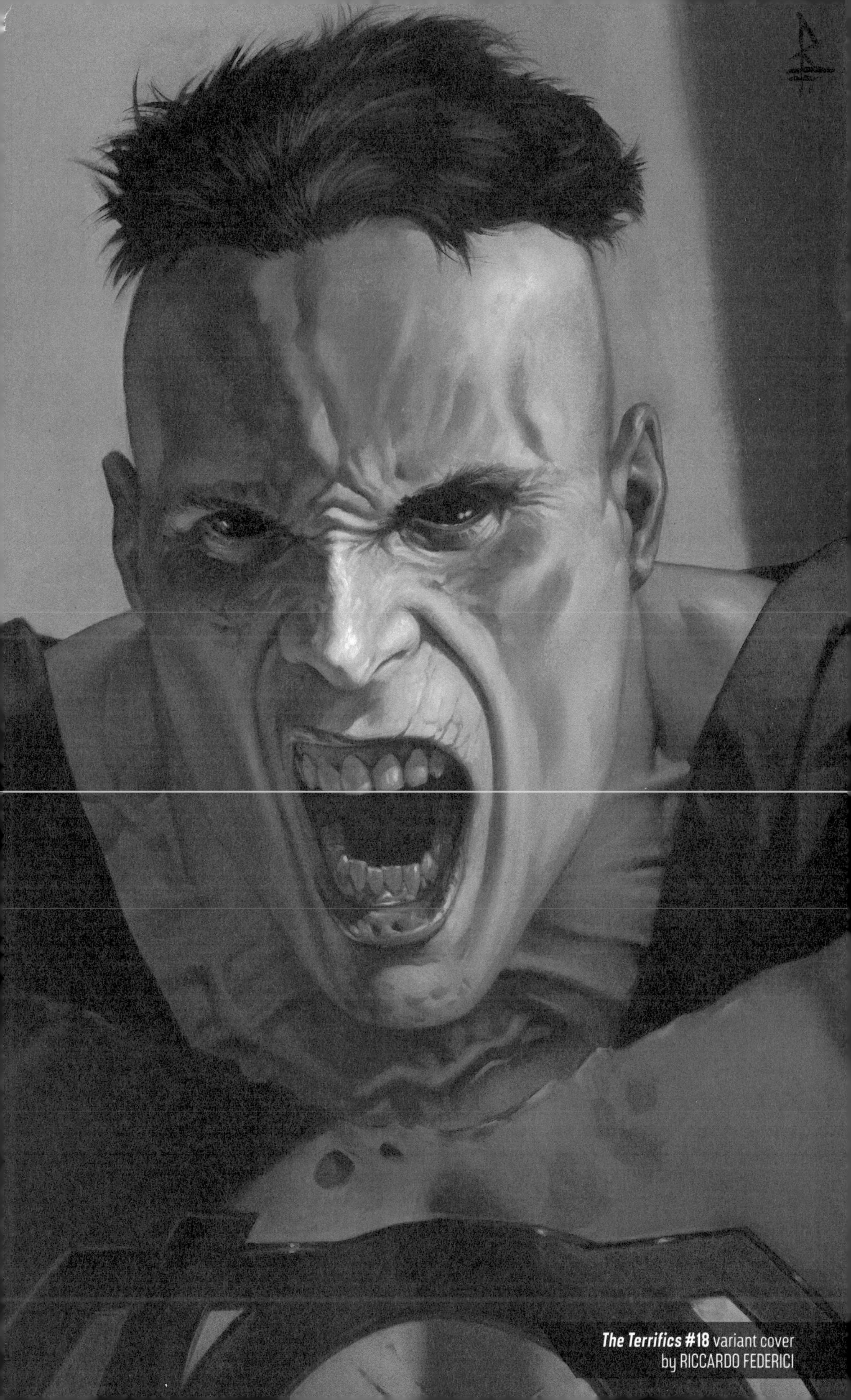

***The Terrifics* #18** variant cover
by RICCARDO FEDERICI

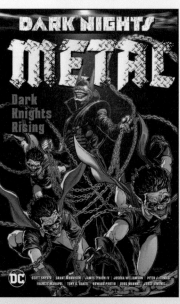